SOJOURNERS AND SETTLERS
THE MACEDONIAN COMMUNITY IN TORONTO TO 1940

Macedonian immigrants to Toronto – a group so poignantly depicted in Michael Ondaatje's *In the Skin of a Lion* – have never had until now a comprehensive history of their early years in the city. Lillian Petroff evokes their moving, sometimes tragic history, charting their living and working conditions, their social and religious life, and their deep and complex relations with their troubled homeland from the early twentieth century to the Second World War.

The first Macedonians who came to Toronto lived an almost completely isolated existence in a distinct set of neighbourhoods centred around their church, stores, and boarding-houses. They moved with little awareness of the city around them, since the needs of their families in the old country and the political events in their homeland were more important to them than developments in Toronto and Canada. A greater interest in Canada began to take root only after Macedonians began to think less like sojourners and more like settlers. This transition was often accompanied by a move from single to married life and from industrial labour to individual entre-preneurial activities.

In preparing this book, Petroff has employed her own extensive interviews, Macedonian Canadians' letters and memoirs, the records of the mutual societies and the national parish, and the observations of the Anglo-Canadian 'caretakers.' She tells the remarkable story of the women and men who laid the foundations for what today is the world's largest community of Macedonians outside the Balkans.

LILLIAN PETROFF is the Senior Coordinator, Educational Programs, Multicultural History Society of Ontario.

ETHNIC AND IMMIGRATION HISTORY SERIES
Multicultural History Society of Ontario

The Multicultural History Society of Ontario gratefully acknowledges
the support of the Province of Ontario's Ministry of Culture, Tourism
and Recreation and the University of St. Michael's College of the
University of Toronto.

LILLIAN PETROFF

Sojourners and Settlers: The Macedonian Community in Toronto to 1940

Multicultural History Society of Ontario
Toronto

University of Toronto Press
Toronto Buffalo London

© 1995 Multicultural History Society of Ontario
Toronto
University of Toronto Press
Toronto Buffalo London

ISBN 0-8020-0452-0 (cloth)
ISBN 0-8020-7240-2 (paper)

∞

Printed on acid-free paper

Canadian Cataloguing in Publication Data

Petroff, Lillian.
  Sojourners and settlers

  Co-published by the Multicultural History Society
  of Ontario.
  Includes bibliographical references and index.
  ISBN 0-8020-0452-0 (bound). ISBN 0-8020-7240-2 (pbk.)

  1. Macedonians – Ontario – Toronto – History – 20th
  century. I. Multicultural History Society of Ontario.
  II. Title.

  PC3097.9.M3P47 1994   305.891'8190713541   C94-932118-4
  P1059.5.T689M364 1994

University of Toronto Press acknowledges the financial assistance to its publishing program of the Canada Council and the
Ontario Arts Council.

Sojourners and Settlers **is available from:**
    Order Fulfilment Department
    University of Toronto Press
    5201 Dufferin Street
    North York, Ontario, Canada M3H 5T8
    Phone toll-free: 1-800-565-9523

For Foto Spiro Tomev

and in memory of Gina and Noe Petroff,
Dana and Lambro Spero Nicoloff,
Dimka Tomev, and Robert Forest Harney

Better a Gypsy wife or a boat at sea than a home in Macedonia

Balkan folk saying

Contents

FOREWORD xi
PREFACE xv
ACKNOWLEDGMENTS xvii

1 Village Life 3

2 A Temporary Stay 13

3 Seasoned Artisans 31

4 Village Societies, National Church 47

5 Preachers, Teachers, Soldiers, War 59

6 Settler Households 75

7 Cooperation and Competition 95

8 Community Life 111

9 The Church and Ethnicity 129

10 The MPO: Balkan Dreams, Canadian Reality 147

11 Evolving Definitions 167

CHRONOLOGY 1885–1993 177
NOTES 185
NOTE ON SOURCES 207
INDEX 209

Foreword

As I read Lillian Petroff's *Sojourners and Settlers: The Macedonian Community in Toronto to 1940*, I recalled a visit some years ago to a park in the state of Washington. At the entrance to a hiking trail, authorities had placed a sign: 'Take only pictures and leave only footprints.' Look and appreciate the natural beauty of the area, but do not disturb, distort, or otherwise alter the surrounding environment. Leave it as you found it.

I have a sense that this same sentiment underlies the research and writing of *Sojourners and Settlers*. Always careful never to distort, never to step further than her sources permit, Lillian Petroff guides her readers across the craggy landscape of Toronto's Macedonian community during its formative years. She gives us a sense of the life led by Macedonian village men who were forced to look beyond their home villages in search of work and who, when pressed by economic necessity, gradually expanded the circle of Macedonian labour outposts far enough westwards to include Toronto, in distant 'Upper America.' She probes the factors that brought these village folk in search of work to Toronto and the growth of social and economic institutions – boarding-houses, churches, fraternal and self-help organizations, and community-based business – that gave structure to the emerging Macedonian community in Toronto. She also examines the powerful bonds to kin and village that tied migrants in Toronto to those left behind in the village. And she does this without sacrificing the human dimension. Rather than let the uniqueness of the individual fall between the historical cracks, Petroff builds on the actual life experiences of community members. In so doing, she reflects a deep respect for the internal history of the Macedonian community in Toronto as its members lived it and as her research revealed it.

In writing this kind of history, social historians such as Petroff have come to regard the past not as a patchwork of dates and events but as the intricate 'tapestry' of ideas and experiences that tie all human experience together. Historians unravel the treads of that history so as to understand social interaction – the process by which our own society took shape. And, as Petroff demonstrates in this most human of studies, this process must be inclusive. It should not be reserved for the achievements of the captains of society, the giants, good and bad, who wield political and economic power. Certainly the powerful still dominate much of our received history, the stuff of most history texts. But just as individual experience, the stuff of our personal histories, is shaped by our personal encounters, so too the history of our society is to be found in the life experiences of ordinary people, as each attempts to make the most of life's chances. Some succeed far better than others. But all are part of our shared historical legacy.

The attempt to give voice to those previously relegated to the margins of the historical narrative – the poor, women, children, labourers, the elderly, immigrants – is not new. But surprisingly, less research has been conducted on the history of Canadian immigration than one might imagine. Before the early 1980s, what little was done focused largely on government immigration policy. But the situation has gradually changed. As exemplified by Petroff, a new generation of immigration historians is broadening its horizons so as to include the actual life experience of immigrants, their hopes and fears, their achievements and failures.

To research and write this kind of history often demands special research skills – not least, command of the languages or dialects of those being studied. Such knowledge makes accessible letters from home, diaries, immigrant publications and organizational records that shed light on the immigrant experience. Such documentary materials, however, can be scarce. The lives of many unschooled immigrants concentrated on labour, not paper. Immigration historians therefore have to look for alternative sources in order to reconstruct the lives of immigrant men and women who might otherwise remain voiceless and in the shadows of our history.

Collecting material on the Macedonian community in Toronto presented Lillian Petroff with special challenges. Macedonian immigrants did not arrange their affairs to make it convenient for a later generation of historians to do research. And, compared to some other immigrant groups that came to Toronto during the first decades of this century, the Macedonians did not leave behind nearly the volume of written manuscript materials – in English or Macedonian – that the historian would have wanted. Surviving records of government and other officials are often very impressionistic. Even the most sympathetic of 'gatekeepers' or onlookers was still standing on the outside looking in; the Macedonian community was for them a curiosity or a paid responsibility. Their observations do not have the intimacy and immediacy of those of the people who lived their lives in that community.

Petroff's task was to uncover and reconstruct the history as people lived it, to understand their immediate lives, their proximate history. Recognizing that fragments of the past are scattered in the memories of the immigrant generation, she reached out to those she studied and initiated an oral history collection. She systematically recorded the testimony of those for whom immigrant history is their life's story. And in tapping into the deep reservoir of 'memory history' that opened up to her, she was able to secure that which might otherwise have been lost for ever – an unwritten record of the experiences and concerns of immigrants who might have previously valued the events of their own lives as the stuff of history.

Harold M. Troper
Department of History
Ontario Institute for Studies in Education
Toronto

Preface

What began as a study of Macedonian migration became during my research an ethnohistory of villagers-turned-Macedonians in Toronto. The larger, Macedonian identity in Toronto emerged as the villagers moved along a continuum from Old World seasonal and overseas migration to permanent settlement abroad. Work and enterprise, living arrangements, village loyalties, evolving religious practice, and political participation shaped the new ethnic identity and ethnoculture that emerged in Toronto in Cabbagetown and, slightly later, around Niagara Street and the Junction. Macedonians in Toronto were, as I seek to show, experienced, thoughtful, resourceful and made good choices. They built a new community in an urban industrial context different from, but perhaps less complex than, the rural villages where their ancestors, over many centuries, had built a vibrant culture.

In my attempt to understand how villagers became Macedonian Canadians, I have examined migration, sojourning and settlement, and the formal and informal institutions – boarding-houses, cafés, village mutual aid societies, steamship agencies, language classes, a national church – launched within the immigrant community. My research has allowed, even forced me to recognize the sojourner and settler states as important and distinct conditions. Robert F. Harney and Harold M. Troper first applied this framework in their study of Toronto, *Immigrants: A Portrait of the Urban Experience, 1890–1930*.[1] For Macedonians, the sojourner period in Toronto was approximately 1903–12; the settler era, the 1920s and 1930s. The 1910s virtually froze the community in its tracks: the partition of Macedonia by the Treaty of Bucharest after the Balkan Wars of 1912–13 shattered their dreams of return, and the First

World War blocked the exodus of family members from the homeland.

Individual and collective memories of the Macedonian experience in Toronto have already inspired writers of fiction; Macedonians figure prominently in Hugh Garner's *Cabbagetown* (1950) and in Michael Ondaatje's prize-winning *In the Skin of a Lion* (1987), where Nick Temelcoff is a central character. Temelcoff appears in this book as well.[2]

I have attempted to write an interior history of Macedonians in Toronto to 1940. As a result, this book is largely the product of oral testimony collected through hundreds of hours of interviewing. The Macedonian community was often unnoticed or imperfectly perceived in Canadian records. Used to avoiding Ottoman authorities, Macedonians tried at first to evade Canadian officialdom as well. Macedonians disappeared within official listings, obliterated by Canadian use of inadequate passport definitions of their nationality – as Bulgarian, Greek, Serb, or Turk – in government indices of population. Compilers of city directories in Toronto were apt to list Slavic boarding-house denizens simply as foreigners. Tax assessment rolls held little information about unpropertied and transient sojourners. As in the old country, many Macedonians in North America sought official non-existence. Consequently, only individuals' memories, letters, photos, and possessions, and the records of the institutions that they created, can help us recapture the history and magnitude of the community.

Scores of Macedonians in Toronto have graciously permitted me to listen to their recollections of life in Macedonia and in Toronto. I hope that they will recognize here the materials – the threads, the textures, and the colours – of their lives and experiences and those of their forebears. I hope, too, that they will see something of themselves in the tapestry that they have helped to weave.

Lillian Petroff
June 1994

Acknowledgments

Robert F. Harney was always a student of neighbourhoods. One day, he came to my house, picked up my grandmother and me, and took us to West Toronto Junction, my grandmother's former stomping grounds, the place where she spent the first thirty years of her life in Canada. As we drove up and down the side streets, past the old homestead and slaughterhouses, Bob gently and patiently quizzed Granny about home and neighbourhoods. That afternoon, he in effect introduced me to my grandmother. I began to learn that the immigrant experience was both ordinary and extraordinary. My grandmother, in turn, discovered her own voice. Thus began what may prove to be the most interesting scholarly and literary venture of my life.

I wish to thank the many men and women of the Macedonian community who gave unselfishly of their time and knowledge. The support, advice, and honest criticism provided by my grandmother, Gina Petroff, and artist Foto Spiro Tomev are especially worthy of note. The door was always open and the tea was always on at the Tomev household. Tomev's artistic contributions speak for themselves in this book. His oil paintings *The Balkan Cafe* (1981), *Slaughterhouse* (1981), and *Boardinghouse* (1982), as well as Alex K. Gigeroff's *Stringing Peppers on Niagara Street, Toronto, 1936*, a masterful multi-media (watercolour, pen and ink) illustration, help us to understand better the sojourner and settler experience in Toronto.

The late Professor Robert F. Harney of the Department of History, University of Toronto, and Professor Harold M. Troper of the Department of History and Philosophy of Education, Ontario Institute for Studies in Education (OISE), directed my work in ethnic and immigration studies. They did so with patience and grace. My debt to them is immense.

I am particularly grateful to the Multicultural History Society of Ontario (MHSO) – to Professor Paul Robert Magocsi, director and chief executive officer; to Carl Thorpe, associate director; and to all the staff – for making it possible for me to finish the manuscript. Publication of this book was funded in part by the Department of Canadian Heritage, Multicultural Programs.

I am indebted to several people at the City of Toronto Archives – R. Scott James, at the time director of records and city archivist; archivist Linda Price; and Tony Rees, then supervisor of the archives – who gave of their time and energy to ensure my access to the collections of city directories and tax assessment rolls for the period up to 1940.

For the production of the book I gratefully acknowledge the work of Catherine Waite, publications co-ordinator at the MHSO. I am also grateful for the support and assistance provided by the staff of University of Toronto Press, led by Gerry Hallowell, history editor. Particularly helpful were Rob Ferguson and Karen Boersma, assistant editors, and Barb Porter, production planner. Stuart Daniel redrew the maps.

With his unmatched editing skills and good cheer, my editor, John Parry, has been a mainstay throughout, for which I am extremely grateful.

Finally, I wish to thank my parents, Anne and George Petroff, for their tireless support and endless words of encouragement.

A Macedonian wedding group in West Toronto Junction, 1921. George Petroff Family Collection; on deposit, Multicultural History Society of Ontario (MHSO)

SS Cyril and Methody Church picnic, 24 August 1924. SS Cyril and Methody Church *50th Anniversary Almanac, 1910–1960* 52

Slaughterhouse, by Foto S. Tomev, 1981. George Petroff Family Collection; on deposit, MHSO

Church school children celebrate SS Cyril and Methody Day, 24 May 1931.
50th Anniversary Almanac 70

Volunteer painters spruce up the exterior of SS Cyril and Methody Church,
n.d. *50th Anniversary Almanac 76*

Mixed Choir, SS Cyril and Methody Church, 1927. *50th Anniversary Almanac* 65

The Balkan Cafe by Foto S. Tomev, 1981. George Petroff Family Collection; on deposit, MHSO

Boarding-house by Foto S. Tomev, 1982. George Petroff Family Collection; on deposit, MHSO

Money collector with donations box, SS Cyril and Methody Church, 1909.
Floroff Family Collection; on deposit, MHSO

Stringing Peppers on Niagara Street, Toronto, 1936 by Alex K. Gigeroff, 1989.
George Petroff Family Collection; on deposit, MHSO

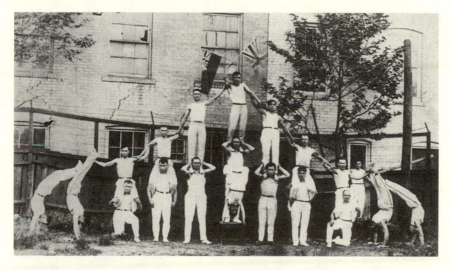

Members of the Balkanski Unak perform a gymnastic routine, Toronto, n.d.
50th Anniversary Almanac 35

Consecration of SS Cyril and Methody Church, Toronto, 24 May 1911.
50th Anniversary Almanac 29

Macedonian girl (right) posing with her fiancé's family before leaving for
Canada, 1921. George Petroff Family Collection; on deposit, MHSO

Macedonia

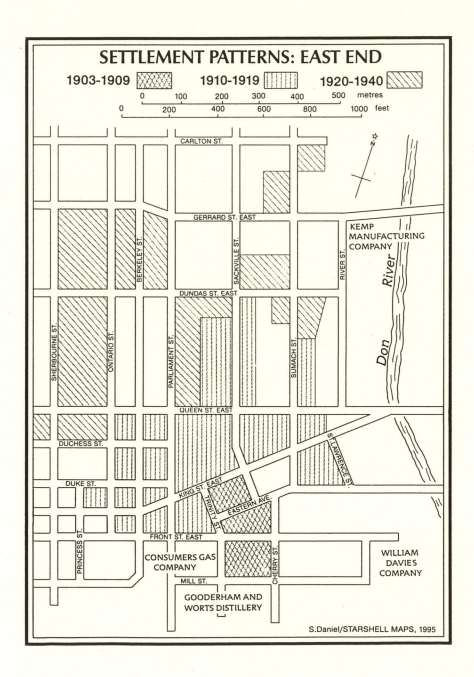

SETTLEMENT PATTERNS: EAST END

1903-1909   1910-1919   1920-1940

0   100   200   300   400   500   metres
0   200   400   600   800   1000   feet

CARLTON ST.

GERRARD ST. EAST

BERKELEY ST.

SACKVILLE ST.

RIVER ST.

KEMP
MANUFACTURING
COMPANY

Don River

DUNDAS ST. EAST

SHERBOURNE ST.

ONTARIO ST.

PARLIAMENT ST.

SUMACH ST.

QUEEN ST. EAST

DUCHESS ST.

ST. LAWRENCE ST.

DUKE ST.

KING ST. EAST

TRINITY ST.

EASTERN AVE.

PRINCESS ST.

FRONT ST. EAST

CONSUMERS GAS
COMPANY

CHERRY ST.

WILLIAM
DAVIES
COMPANY

MILL ST.

GOODERHAM AND
WORTS DISTILLERY

S.Daniel/STARSHELL MAPS, 1995

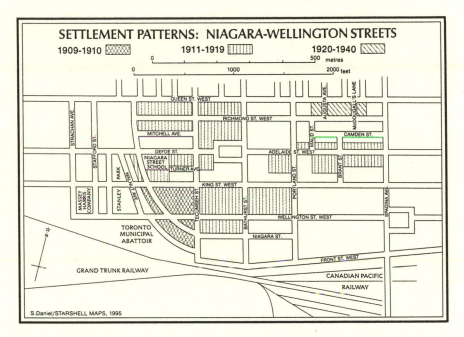

Macedonian settlement in Toronto's Niagara-Wellington district, 1909–40

Opposite: Macedonian settlement in Toronto's East End (Cabbagetown), 1903–40

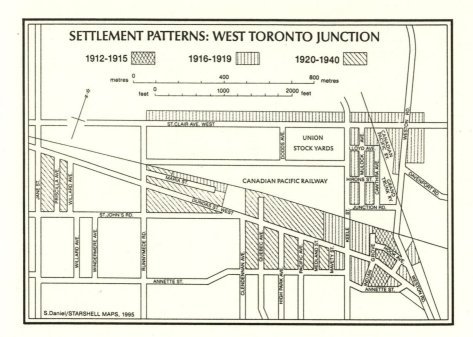

Macedonian settlement in Toronto's Junction district, 1912–40

SOJOURNERS AND SETTLERS

1

Village Life

A TRADITION OF MIGRATION

'In the mountain villages where Greece, Bulgaria, Serbia and Albania meet,' a people struggled for its national identity at the same time as it struggled to eke out a living from the soil. Until the Balkan Wars of 1912 and 1913, most Macedonians lived as Christian peasants in a Muslim land under Ottoman rule. Both their religious and linguistic folkways made them turn to independent Bulgaria and its Orthodox church for leadership. In the nineteenth century, priests, intellectuals, and comitadjiis (national guerrillas) drew these villagers into a larger national identity. Macedonians – in such villages as Besvina, Bobista, Gabresh, Oshchima, Smerdesh, and Zagoricheni, in the district of Kostur (Kastoria), and in Armensko, Banitsa, Buf, Nevoleni, and Tersie, in the district of Lerin (Florina) – remained first and foremost village people. The new, larger national identity had not displaced their more local and fractured loyalties as the age of mass emigration began. Some of the parameters of identity were set, though; these people were neither Turk nor Muslim, and most chose not to be Greek Orthodox or grecophone.

While the nationalist ferment and the ongoing 'war of liberation' around them brought questions of identity to the forefront, a much older tradition helped Macedonians measure themselves against those beyond the mountain village. Men from the mountainous region had worked elsewhere in the Balkans or in Istanbul (Constantinople) 'since time immemorial,' according to an almanac of Toronto's SS Cyril and Methody Church. At the turn of the century, local migration targets were replaced by the possibility of working in 'Upper and Lower

America' – Canada and the United States. For Macedonians, living in a remote, almost landlocked region of the Balkans, Toronto was to help shape their economy and their development of nationality, first as a migratory stop and later as a centre for settlement. 'Toronto and its hinterland became a source of the cash necessary to buy arms and carry on the war against oppressors or the prepaid tickets that delivered people from the dangers of staying in the strife-torn mountains.'[1]

At first, in the late nineteenth century, men worked in neighbouring villages and districts. They also travelled within the Ottoman Empire, selling milk and yoghurt in Istanbul. Some went to Greece, Romania, Serbia, and Bulgaria – as artisans, apprentices, and labourers. Men sojourned for a season or for several seasons. They spent their winters working in the building trades of Athens or cutting timber in the surrounding areas of Salonica. They acquired special skills on those migrations. Apprentice housebuilders from Zhelevo and other villages learned their craft in nearby villages; when they grew older, they took those skills to the more distant areas of Asia Minor.[2]

Ventures to Bulgaria and Istanbul lasted longer than a season. In Romania, Macedonians served as hired hands and in the restaurants and coffee-houses of Bucharest. They also worked as market gardeners and dairymen in Istanbul, usually returning at the end of migratory cycles of one, two, or three years. Embore, for example, was proud of its kaimak or sweet-milk (junket) vendors who ran businesses in the metropolis's teeming streets. Other villages, such as Tersie, had alternative, more modest migrant traditions. One respondent said: 'Our people [were] not ambitious to go far and so they were content to work as sawyers in the lumber yards around Salonica.' While men were away, their immediate and extended families watched over their interests at home.

The length of the men's ventures was determined by an interplay of village customs and beliefs and family needs and resources. Most lasted only a season – usually during winter, when the family fields lay fallow – while others evolved into lengthy or 'permanent' migration. Some milkmen from Bobista stayed in Istanbul for twenty years. In *Macedonia: Its Races and Their Future* (1906), the British relief worker and journalist H.M. Brailsford told of Smerdesh, whose enterprising young men spent 'as much as seven continuous years abroad.' Market gardeners and vegetable hawkers also had lengthy stays abroad, especially in Istanbul. With a mixture of pride and pain, SS Cyril and Methody's calendar stated: 'Our people were raising their voices selling their vegetables, carrying them on their shoulders in a large basket [then there were no push-carts] and bending down by the heavy weight of the large basket the men slowly made their way down the city's narrow streets.' A young market gardener from Embore remained in Istanbul indefinitely while his father stayed in charge of the village field and family farm. Even after his father's death, he stayed in the Turkish city, and then so did his grown sons, by renting out his fields and farm animals back home to Turks.[3]

Migration was more than a family concern in districts such as Kostur and Lerin. It became a village strategy, and migrants were subject to community standards. Villages specialized in certain trades and migration targets. One acquired a reputation for its carpenters, another for its stonemasons and plasterers; one dispatched housebuilders to the Levant, while others set up chain migration to Bulgaria and Romania. Young migrants travelled through family networks. In the company of fathers, brothers, or uncles, they moved to work possibilities far from home. Alternatively, they found employment through labour agents or village chums. Mobile bands of novice labourers and apprentice tradesmen emerged. This strategy for bringing cash to the village and regulating creation of new households merely awaited opening of transatlantic network and intelligence systems.

Despite chronic shortage of good and arable land, rising expectations – the desire not only to subsist and survive but to improve and make better – affected the villages. The state of the economy and social decisions, as well as the political background – first of Turkish, and then of Greek, oppression, and the constant warfare – made leaving even more attractive. H.M. Brailsford gave a rather poetic description of Macedonia in 1906: 'The typical village, isolated without teacher or priest in some narrow and lofty glen, leads its own imperturbable life, guided by the piety of traditions which date from pagan times. It hears strange rumours of a railway which has invaded the legendary plain beyond its mountains. But the world of innovation lies outside its experience.'[4]

Nonetheless the villages of Macedonia – indeed, most of Europe's peasants – were neither primitive nor isolated from the larger economy and the world flow of labour to capital. The intrusion and impact of capital were deep and profound. The presence of cash – Turkish lira or Greek paper – was readily visible at all levels of the village economic structure. Armed with cash, peasants from the village of Oshchima could go to the city of Lerin to supplement their household supply of such items as salt, sugar, coffee, rice, and lamp oil – items that they could not produce for themselves but which became essential to even a subsistence household.

The bartering system and payment in goods for services rendered were giving way to currency. The pedlars who sold a variety of cloth materials, threads, and notions to the residents of Tersie increasingly expected payment in cash. Gypsy traders who sold and polished pots and kettles – 'they get inside the big pots and polish them with their feet' – told the people of Verbnik village of their preference for cash. Even the proprietors of general stores and coffee-houses began to expect cash, and men were increasingly expected to fulfil their bride price obligations with money. One future father-in-law required a peasant to pay no less than seventeen Turkish lira to acquire his bride. A Nevolani father demanded cash from his daughter's suitor for the purchase of property: 'If you send me some money to buy you property, I'll give you my daughter. If you don't, you will never see [my daughter].' Five hundred lira was subsequently dispatched to the village and used by the father to buy a ten-acre plot for the couple. With money, men could also tackle such difficulties of village life as Ottoman head taxes, tithes on produce, and the shortage and acute overdivision of land.

The villages that experienced heavy migration were frequently situated along mountainous areas of exceptional beauty, but safety, not fertility of the soil, had inspired settlement. Turks and converts to Islam owned the rich bottom lands. A respondent described Gabresh as being comprised of 'over a hundred houses, mountains, rocks [and] different kinds of trees. The spring was five or ten minutes from the village.' Verbnik was also located in a mountainous area, amid marble and cobblestones. 'Three-quarters of the territory of Zhelevo is mountainous and the remainder [is] a plain.' An unsuccessful uprising against the Turks had forced residents of 'Old Zhelevo' to abandon their first settlement and move higher up to a new area, made inaccessible by mountains and 'dense and impenetrable forest.' Fertile plains or good patches of land were at a premium. Most villagers tended small orchards, grain, and vegetable plots. Only transhumance – some stock-breeding and raising of sheep and goats – was possible on the slopes and high pastures. Yet, whatever the emphasis or effort, most families could eke out only a meagre yield and so sustain life at a subsistence level.

Diminished land holdings were also a problem because of the system of inheritance. As all sons were entitled to a share of the family holdings, each generation saw smaller individual holdings. Men went on the move to help, through cash income, to overcome the dire consequences of this overdivision of land – or because it was already too late. One respondent from Gabresh summed up an all-too-familiar situation:

'Father was in a family with three brothers and one sister. [They] divided the land [and] then started coming to Canada.'[5]

Individuals – indeed, villages as a whole – tried to stem the growing shortage of land for the next generation through purchasing additional land. By 1900 the Zhelevtsi had jointly bought a tract of land, just north of the village, from a Turkish bey, Husain Efendi. Residents of Psoderi had also made an unsuccessful offer to the bey for that land. Villages and their residents needed enough cash to make purchases and survive the bidding wars. Migration soon became an efficient means to acquire the cash. The miller of the village of Bobista, who was also a farmer and property owner, eventually went to North America to make money for a new and larger house. A Gabresh landowner who had 'everything: horses, sheep, goats, around 150 altogether' became a migrant to supplement his farm income.[6]

Migration became prerequisite for the simple working and survival of family life and the village order. By 1911, Konomladi had more men abroad than at home. The majority of households could thus lay claim to the support of a sojourning son, brother, or father, and so young boys waited and conditioned themselves for their eventual entry into the migratory scheme of things. Meisters – the German word for 'master artisan' was used in Macedonia – and carpenters from Besvina, Gabresh, and Zhelevo, for example, actively plied their trade far from home – in neighbouring settlements, the Bitola district and other areas of western Macedonia, Turkey, Serbia, Athens, and the Greek islands. Indeed, H.M. Brailsford applauded the great success of some of the builders, who eventually bought property in their home villages and built homes to rent out.[7]

THE FLOW OF IDEAS

Ideas often travelled with migrants and with the flow of goods. Russian traders and pedlars travelled to the villages of Macedonia selling scythes and other farm implements and icons, so the folk memory recalls. These men began 'to agitate the Christians to awake and fight for their liberation from the Turks.' It is unclear whether such pedlars were simply Pan-Slav in sentiment, or were Russian or Bulgarian agents.

New ideas came to the villages, but, even more, seasonal migration in the Balkans placed the villagers in contact with new ideas, as well as with Macedonians from other villages. Seasonal migration put the Greek patriarchate and the Ottoman authorities in perspective. Men who ventured to Bulgaria as master builders, labourers, and lumber-jacks 'now sampled freedom; they heard church services in their own tongue; they got acquainted with their own literary language and realized that they were not Greeks.'

The desire for change came to be expressed in many ways. The villagers of Zhelevo remember that local activists such as Hadji Pavel and Nickolov Tashov led the battle for establishment of schools and churches under the auspices of the Bulgarian exarchate. They also devised popular forms of protest against the Greek church. Zhelevo community historian F.S. Tomev recalls: 'Girls from our neighbourhood and from farther away used to gather in our courtyard and on our porch to dance or compose songs against the pro-Greek priests and their andarti.'

By the turn of the century, the majority of villages and their residents had recognized the exarch and set up Bulgarian-language Christian schools. The Patriarchists, or Gurcomans (Greek sympathizers), attempted to halt the enthusiastic exarchist effort, usually by playing on Turkish fears of sedition. Their efforts failed, and so by the time of mass migration, most villagers owed allegiance to the Bulgarian exarchate and felt some fraternal relationship to Bulgarians.

Most villagers approved of the nationalist resistance to the Turks as reflected in the Internal Macedonian Revolutionary Organization (IMRO). How many actively joined the effort is more difficult to establish.[8] IMRO began as an underground liberation movement, founded in 1893 by school teachers and other intellectuals. Damien Grueff, for example, a native of Smilevo and long considered the father of IMRO, had once studied at the State University of Sofia, 'but like ever so many of his followers, he quit the student's bench to carry the pistol and the dagger.' In their own literature, the nationalists claimed to have enlisted the whole Macedonian people. Teachers and students, tradesmen and entrepreneurs, priests and their urban and rural congregations of humble men and women all 'swore upon the open Bible whereon lay crossed the pistol and the dagger' that they would work tirelessly, even at the cost of their lives, to see Macedonia both united and liberated from its oppressors.

IMRO itself established a very high profile as the party of Macedonian liberation, becoming almost synonymous with the desire for a nation. Revolutionary cells throughout Aegean Macedonia (now in Greece) and the Vardar region (in the Macedonian republic, formerly part of Yugoslavia) were linked together by a system of local county and district committees. While the bands of nationalist guerrillas or freedom fighters – comitadjiis or tchetniks – fell under the immediate command of their leaders or voyvods, all power rested with the central committee. The committee was the supreme governing body of the organization and had three members, each duly elected for a three-year period by the triennial revolutionary congress.

The memory culture of the villagers who settled in Toronto included much real information and much romanticization about IMRO and the freedom fighters. For example, many people know the story of Boris Saraffoff, the IMRO fundraiser and organizer, who offered the United States the services of an entire Macedonian legion during the Spanish-American War, in exchange for a supply of arms. They recall the flamboyant gestures of the nationalist movement more than its steady work of raising consciousness. They recollect that the 1901 kidnapping of an American Protestant missionary, Miss Helen Stone of Boston, just outside the village of Bansko on the road to Gorna-Djumaya, netted the organization a particularly lucrative ransom of 14,000 Turkish gold pounds. This money, which was paid by the Turkish government, amounted to approximately US$70,000 and received the special and notorious name 'Miss Stonki.'[9]

Through its revolutionary bands, IMRO subsequently went on to establish its name and mark against the Turks. The freedom fighters engaged frequently in open battle against the beys, aghas, and bashibozuks. The comitadjiis, some of them fellow villagers, took on the characteristics of such primitive rebels and popular champions as Robin Hood. They are seen, at least through the memory culture, as righting villagers wronged as much as concerning themselves with the larger question of national self-determination. In *The Eagle and the Stork: An American Memoir* (1976), the great Macedonian-American author Stoyan Christowe describes the relationship between the people and the nationalist movement – IMRO, 'like a jealous parent,' 'kept close vigil over our health, our well-being, our morals.'

The result of IMRO's activities and the growth of Macedonian national feeling in the villages was the 1903 Ilinden Uprising. Armed with revolvers, flintlock rifles, and pitchforks, acting with and under the direction of IMRO's local and district committees, Macedonians began an illtimed and short-lived armed struggle against the Ottoman Empire. For many, even those on the margins, the event changed the future irrevocably. Many participants had to abandon their farms and villages in fear of reprisals. Many, only marginally involved, grew tired of violence and uncertainty and emigrated. Others already in the New World lost the urge to return to Macedonia. The insurrection was a watershed –

the burned and devastated homes and crops stood as confirmation that there was no turning back. It was significant for the history of both Macedonian migration and national identity.[10]

OPPORTUNITY IN 'AMERICA'

The turn of the century saw many experienced sojourners leave their families and homesteads yet again, as they quickly joined the growing number of southeastern Europeans who went to 'America' in search of opportunity. The New World had finally been discovered as a lucrative migratory stop. Pay packets sent or brought back by pioneer migrant returnees created and spread the news 'throughout Macedonia that in Canada one could earn more than in any other country.' For example, bricklayers from Konomladi, who received the equivalent of twenty cents a day for ten hours per day of labour in the village and surrounding areas, could make abroad between fifty cents and a dollar a day in coveted Yankee dollars. Early returnees also dispelled some initial fears and superstitions – 'they think if they come over here, they disappear' – about North America.[11]

For one small group of migrants, immediate settlement, not sojourning, was necessary. Imprisonment, torture, or death threatened acknowledged political activists and comitadjiis, and some sought freedom in Bulgaria and Romania. Most, however, went to the New World. Toronto received its share of these early residents, some of whom quickly brought out their families. For example, a fiercely proud veteran of the Ilinden Uprising of 1903 (an Ilindenetz) and revolutionary courier made his way rapidly and quietly to Toronto after fleeing a Lerin jail. The community/church census in Toronto recorded 'eight with families' by 1910. By 1915, there were 43 families, with 49 children (the majority under five years of age). These settled families, obliged to stay in North America but fiercely Macedonian, marked the beginning of a permanent and stable Macedonian community.[12]

The sojourners and activists who moved to North America hailed primarily from the provinces of Kostur and Lerin, once important vilayets of the Ottoman Empire but today portions of northern Greece. Few came from western Macedonia or from towns and cities. 'Hardly anybody emigrated' to Toronto from the districts of Bitola and Skopje, 'because there is more agricultural land and most of our people cultivated the land owned by the beys.'[13]

Nationalist spirit and the assertion of identity became perhaps even more of a preoccupation in the New World, where Macedonian-ness and the programs required to free a people could be discussed openly. Boarding-houses, cafés, and worksites in Toronto brought men from various villages and districts of Macedonia, as well as Bulgarians, into contact with one another. The host society's ignorance of Balkan history and suspicion of southern and eastern Europeans prompted these men to band together in a spirit of fellow-feeling. It led as well to encounters where village of origin was irrelevant, and identification as an Ottoman subject demeaning. 'Macedonian' was the proper description to offer other Torontonians, whether immigrant or native-born. From about 1910, creation of a single Macedonian parish, not of separate village parishes, also contributed to the Macedonian sense of ethnic nationalism in Canada. This last provided a new lens through which to redefine identity back in the villages.[14]

As Macedonians, the immigrants had one early and overriding ambition: to see their homeland become more than a dream or a geographical expression.

2

A Temporary Stay

After the 1903 Ilinden Uprising against the Turks, a thirteen-year-old Macedonian boy found work at a dairy in Varna, Bulgaria, beyond the borders of the Ottoman Empire. By 1910, he had moved on towards North America, bound for California and possible railway work. Although he intended Toronto to be only a temporary stop, he decided to stay and he lived in a series boarding-houses in the East End and the West End. By 1940, he had become a barber, a grocery store operator, and an established resident and homeowner in 'The Junction.' Having done some of the most dangerous and dirtiest work in the city's slaughterhouses and factories, he took satisfaction in having become a shopowner and skilled artisan. His interest in Macedonia was purely nostalgic, he was content to tell his wife and son stories of his bachelor days in Macedonia and Bulgaria.

How and why did such migrants decide to sojourn in Toronto? How did they see the city? How did they cope? Where did they live, work, worship, relax? What were their relations with people back in Macedonia? Such simple questions can help us explore Macedonians' migration history, changing ethnicity, and adjustment in Canada. This chapter and the following ones examine the sojourners' experience – in Toronto's boarding-houses and cafés (chapter 2), at work (chapter 3), in creating village-based mutual aid organizations and a national church (chapter 4), and in dealing with Anglo-Protestant 'caretakers' (chapter 5).

The number of Macedonians in Toronto before 1903 was 'so small that it could be counted on your ten fingers.' Macedonians arriving in the city went to Cabbagetown in the East End or, from about 1909, to the

Niagara Street and Junction areas in the West End. An internal census in 1910 found about 1,090 Macedonians in Toronto – mostly sojourners – bachelors or unaccompanied married men, principally from the Ottoman-ruled provinces of Kostur (Castoria) and Lerin (Florina), now in northern Greece. The Balkan Wars (1912–13) halted emigration, and in 1913, Bulgaria, Greece, and Serbia partitioned Macedonia into Pirin, Aegean, and Vardar regions, respectively. Migration of families and brides-to-be resumed about 1920. By 1940, many of Toronto's roughly 1,200 Macedonian families – the largest Macedonian community in Canada and probably in North America – lived outside the three original settlement areas. The group and its ethnoculture, once nurtured by only a handful of poorly educated sojourners, had become a permanent and visible presence.[1]

If it is easy to see, as in chapter 1, how widely Macedonians dispersed in search of work and why they sojourned in 'America,' it is harder to understand why Toronto became a pivotal point for them. We know little about the first Macedonians in Toronto, and few historical source materials are available. In his *Short History of Zhelevo Village, Macedonia* (1971), F.S. Tomev told us of the first Zhelevtsi to set foot in Canada. Accompanied by men from the village of Buf, Lambro Nikolovsky and Andrea Nikolovsky arrived in Toronto in 1902. Tomev, however, was unable to tell us *why* they chose Toronto and if it had been their first or intended choice of destination. We know that the majority of Macedonians who migrated to Toronto arrived in the aftermath of the 1903 Ilinden Uprising. The base of pioneer migrants from Zhelevo, for example, quickly expanded at that point. In 1904, George Atanas Markovsky arrived with 36 men and settled on Front Street East; 30 more men followed in 1905. Sources in the ethnic group estimated 1,050 members in the city by 1910; most were bachelors or married men with families remaining at home.[2]

WHY TORONTO?

Why did Toronto become first a migratory way station and then a more lasting home? Travel realities or mishaps – interruptions in the movement to American destinations, followed by a secondary or later decision to stay in Toronto – may have played a role. Steamship routes and schedules coupled with the informal efforts of dockside sages, who counselled men not to be bound by their tickets and departure times but to take the first available ship, may account for the early arrivals. In the period after 1920 the explanation is simple: US immigration restrictions diverted movement to Canada and Australia.

The human demands of Toronto's industries and the availability of cheap accommodation answered the needs of the early sojourners and so set the stage for growth of the migrant community. Correspondence, money orders, and returnees with gold coins and urban, tailor-made clothes obviously enhanced the myth of opportunity. In Zhelevo, family members were expected to serve raisins and chickpeas to the steady stream of visitors that appeared at the door once a migrant returned.

Returnees proudly counted their earnings – a three-year stay in Toronto usually netted about four hundred dollars – in the presence of their wives, who then reported the earnings to early-morning gatherings at the village's water fountain. These gatherings were often a catalyst in migration: they measured, monitored, and exchanged vital information and reflected the effects of this human movement. Competition arose. At one such gathering, a Zhelevo woman 'heard that [her friend's] husband [had] brought more money than her [own] husband for the same period of [migration] time ... As soon as she returned home she began to fight with her husband: "Aren't you ashamed of yourself!"'

Standards of achievement – rising expectations fast became village norms – could be measured and compared. Dialogues at the fountain, the need for and dependence on the influx of cash, and the blurred relationship between expectations and norms all underscored the familial and village basis of the migratory process. One Zhelevo mother told her son to cast aside a rare opportunity to attend school in Lerin on scholarship because his duty was to join his migrant father in Canada when called on. The level of this village commitment to migration could be demonstrated by the example of Bobista. Fifteen of the village's thirty houses sent men abroad. This became an expected and natural process – one respondent recalled: 'My chums left [Zhelevo] one by one and came here to Canada. I had to come too as I was left alone.' – 'My brother came before me. Our Uncle [was already] in Canada. My brother wrote [to] him: "Any chance [that] I can come to Canada?" [My uncle replied] "Come on over and we'll get you a job." My mother passed away in 1911. My father remained [after one or two years]. My brother decided to bring me in [to] Canada. Brother send me the money [to come]. [I] joined [my] brother and uncle on Trefann [Street].'[3]

As such oral testimony demonstrates, growth of the Macedonian migrant community was accelerated by creation and use of village and family migration chains – 'that movement in which prospective migrants learn of opportunities, are provided with transportation, and

have initial accommodation and employment arranged by means of
primary social relations with previous migrants.'

Rapid peopling of the Toronto community depended also on migrants' willingness to make or break these chains as demanded by
occasion, or by altered, New World perceptions of opportunity, success,
and ambition. Noe Petroff broke free and probably severed a chain that
ran from Bulgaria to California. He eventually went on to set up his
own business when he decided to take a wife. Blazo Markoff turned
down the initial and immediate employment presented in Toronto by
his restaurateur father. He chose to strike out on his own: 'Look, father,'
he said, 'this country is different altogether. You brought me here. You
live for yourself. I live for myself.' Markoff then secured his first local
job at a manufacturer of headstones and monuments on Kingston Road.
He subsequently got hired as a factory hand at the Barrymore Cloth Co.
He lived, however, with his father at his East End restaurant at King
and Power streets and dutifully ate his meals 'at father's place.' With
independence came a measure of difficulty. Barrymore Cloth was located in the West End (at King and Dufferin streets), and the trip to work
took valuable time and money, whether he walked or rode the streetcar.
The future artist Foto S. Tomev came unwittingly on a chain that his
father did not create or want. Tomev had arrived in Toronto in the
mistaken belief that his father had asked him to do so. The request in
a letter – 'Do whatever you must, but come' – was invented by a
boarding-house scribe when he wrote on behalf of Tomev's illiterate
father.[4]

COOPERATIVE BOARDING-HOUSES

Photographs taken by Toronto's Department of Health also revealed –
although officialdom failed to understand it – that these men in layered
and ill-fitting clothing were preoccupied with their Old World commitments and responsibilities. They needed to save for purchase of a piece
of land on return to Macedonia or to remit money home for a sister's
dowry. Such commitment precluded major expenditures on housing.
Sojourners' sense of order and organization in the New World was
functional; it anticipated temporary deprivation. The devotion to frugal-
ity was total, even if the men understood all too well how substandard
living conditions were in their cooperatively run boarding-houses.

A complex order emerged in most establishments, with house rules
and codes about residents' responsibilities. In many boarding-houses,
tenants often cooked and did other household chores on a rotating

basis. The more than 15 men who occupied a boarding-house on Wellington Street West clearly understood and performed their duties in that way: 'Early in the morning, the person that was on duty for the day got up before the others, lit the stove, fried the meat in the big stew pan. After work, he prepared supper and saw to it that all the men had their fair share. He then washed the dishes after all had eaten and swept the floor. The household chores were now done for the day.'

In other households, responsibilities were assigned according to age and were not egalitarian. Remembering his additional duties in a Macedonian establishment on Front Street East, one immigrant recalled that 'the young fellows in the house [fourteen or fifteen years of age] were responsible for washing the older fellows' clothes.' In his unpublished 'Memoirs' (1979), F.S. Tomev recalls that major household tasks were performed once a week by the residents as a group. In his West End boarding-house, 'the floor was usually washed on Saturday afternoon or on Sunday. We used the garden hose and a brush like those used by the street cleaners to wash the floor. We then burrowed a hole in the floor in order to let the water run down to the basement [with a dirt floor] when the washing was completed.' Most men honoured such obligations. The few who did not were, more often than not, asked or forced to move out. Unclean and untidy men were also requested to leave. Conversely, one man who 'was very much in favour of cleanliness' came to be despised for his fastidious nature; he acquired 'a bad name' among boarding-house residents and so was 'chased from house to house.'[5]

The group's letter-writing manuals and dictionaries provide some insight into the problems of boarding-house management. For example, readers could find out how to summon company representatives and repairmen or could read a sample request to delay payment of rent in A.C. Yovcheff's *Various Bulgarian-American Letters* (n.p., 1917). (During this period, Bulgarian was the language of literature and liturgy for most Macedonians; their own language was not codified until 1944.) C. Nedelkoff's *English-Bulgarian and Bulgarian-English Letters* (Granite City, Ill., 1911) offered samples of a lease agreement and a tenant's letter of complaint to the landlord. Food was one subject covered by the *First Bulgarian-English Pocket Dictionary* (Toronto 1913), written by D.G. Malincheff (= J. Theophilact, priest of Toronto's SS Cyril and Methody Church, who later became Dr Demitrius Mallin). The last-mentioned volume acquainted readers with the system of weights and measures and it also offered lists of meat, vegetable, fruit, and bread items in translation:

White bread
Brown bread
Rye bread
Stale bread
New bread

Bread was the staple. One Niagara Street boarding-house with only male residents ordered twenty loaves a day. The breadman who delivered to the area soon was promoted to supervisor because management mistook Macedonian need for the man's sales prowess.[6]

There was also fellow-feeling. The shabby physical surroundings were tempered by the warmth of human relationships, which were strengthened by ties of language, custom, and hard work. Men from the same village often shared friendships, memories, and moments of lightheartedness. Residents of a Niagara Street district boarding-house 'celebrated all the church holidays ... They celebrated namedays [the day of the saint after whom a person is named]. They sang patriotic and folk songs. They danced "horos." They talked about their places of birth, about their families and relatives, about the heroic "chetnicks" [freedom fighters] and their leaders, and the struggles of their people.' The men of this house also contributed money towards improving facilities back home in the building of a new bridge. Some of them, believing that their village should be placed under the spiritual jurisdiction of the Bulgarian exarchate, used their new status and income to influence those who stayed behind in Zhelevo to make that decision.

In many boarding-houses, there was also talk about survival and success in the New World and much planning of job or worksite strategies. Workers discussed, for example, how and when to ask for raises. In such moments, men who possessed a degree of literacy and an understanding of English were very much appreciated. One such individual was frequently called on to pen 'Please, Boss' notes – requests for a raise. Success at work was earnestly sought and celebrated. A former tin-metal worker recalled: 'I was talking to the boys at the house rented among ourselves. Somebody ask me, "Why don't you ask for a raise?" I got a fifty-cents raise. I comes home to the house with all the boys. I told them I got the raise. [They] all laughing, so happy.' The availability of informal loans in boarding-houses suggests high levels of mutual trust. Men from Gabresh who were residents of an East End house had such faith in each other. One respondent remembered that no receipts were ever demanded on loans, even on those as high as $300.

Fellow-feeling did not always prevail, however; the business of living together often created tension and anger. F.S. Tomev writes of the scolding that he received from another boarder for burning onions while preparing the daily stew. Tomev's father came to his defence and was soon arguing with the other residents. The Tomevs felt bound to move out, despite subsequent apologies. Another father and son dealt with their mutual disagreements and anger by placing a wooden board between them – a sort of temporary partition – in the double bed that they shared in a house in the West End.[7]

Toronto was not a city of tenements, so early Macedonian sojourners lived in two- and three-storey roughcast or frame houses. Some later occupied the top floors and rear rooms of Macedonians' stores and businesses. Junction confectioner John Christo housed at least nine boarders – six of whom worked at Gunn's slaughterhouse – at his shop on St Clair Avenue West during the Great War. The 1915 Tax Assessment Rolls record a King Street East restaurateur, thirty-three-year-old George Uzunoff. He also, however, operated a rooming-house between Parliament and Power streets that served ten men in 1915.[8]

The three areas of the city in which Macedonians did settle were similar to one another by most urban indices. The average value of land and buildings was about the same in each area, with the East End having the lowest values and the Niagara district, in the West End, the highest. In 1910, the land and buildings at 18–20 Eastern Avenue (at Gilead Place) – site of grocer and steamship agent H.D. Peroff's store and twelve-man boarding-house – were valued at $489 and $500, respectively. That same year, a house at 35 Eastern Avenue (at Cherry Street), owned by the Canadian Northern Ontario Railway and occupied by twelve Macedonians, had land valued at $168 and a building worth $350. In 1915, the house and land at 6 Trefann Street – site of another Macedonian boarding-house – were of comparable value, $400 and $410, respectively.

In the Niagara Street district, a house on Tecumseth Street had land valued in 1919 at $857, while the building was assessed at $1,450. That year, houses at 131 and 151 Niagara Street, between Tecumseth and Wellington, had land valued at $829 and $821, respectively, and buildings at $800 apiece. In the Junction, 51 Dods Avenue (between West Toronto and St Clair West) a house was valued at $1,000; its property at $306 in 1915.

In all these neighbourhoods, buildings were generally worth more than the land on which they sat. That was in sharp contrast to Toronto's most celebrated ethnic quarter, St John's Ward ('The Ward'), in the centre of town – north of City Hall, at Queen Street West and Bay. The Macedonian areas were not slums; landlords were not speculators in search of a quick turnover; buildings were not allowed to deteriorate as their owners waited to sell out. Since they found accommodation in areas not as valuable or central as the Ward, Macedonians probably enjoyed greater stability and better living conditions than the Jews, Italians, and Chinese of the city's core. City officials, however, did not see it that way, equating crowding, which obviously did exist in the boarding-houses, with the social disintegration characteristic of slums.

Macedonian migrants went to the three areas that best fulfilled their needs as sojourners for cheap housing and proximity to worksites. That other Macedonians lived nearby, or that members of the group continued to move in and about these areas, was only another attractive feature, never the central reason for residing in either the East or West End settlement areas.[9]

Despite the presence of some settler families, early Macedonian migration to Toronto was the preserve of young men, bachelors, or the recently married and childless. Youth eventually even came to be reflected in the leadership ranks. Most of the men who guided the fortunes of the church and religious life in Toronto in the 1910s were only in their early to mid- twenties. The first executive committee of SS Cyril and Methody was composed of men such as Nikola Elieff, aged twenty-one, and Stavro Zolumoff, an energetic and opinionated twenty-four-year-old.

Thirteen- and fourteen-year-olds were welcomed into the early sojourner fold, commended for their vitality and enthusiasm, and yet the subject of worry. An older and experienced West Ender wondered seriously about a young migrant's survival – a fellow boarder who needed to stand on a chair to make good use of the sink – and success in the New World. A fifteen-year-old migrant from Gabresh was quickly introduced to life in a sheet-metal factory and Front Street East boarding-house by a concerned labourer brother. Unemployment, even temporary, threatened the delicate economy of the sojourners. In *The Eagle and the Stork*, Stoyan Christowe recalls the initial clucking of his compatriots and fellow-boarders in St. Louis, Missouri, shortly after his arrival from the old country: 'He's too young, brei, too young. It will be hard for him to get a job. In another year or two, maybe, he should have come.'

In Toronto, both industries and experienced migrants satisfied their labour needs through creation of such positions as water boys and workers' helpers. These jobs were designed to minimize injury, escape possible suspicion and charges of abuse of child labour laws, familiarize migrants, and set the stage for regular positions when these arose. For example, a future master butcher, foreman, and union steward, Anastas Petroff, entered the world of the slaughterhouse as a water boy at Harris Abattoir.[10]

Each resident in a household of twelve or fifteen men paid only a little more than a dollar a month towards rent and expenses. Rent money was never trusted to the mails. Macedonians took turns taking it down to the offices of various corporate landlords, including the Canadian Northern Ontario Railway, the Swift Canadian Co., and the Union Stock Yards, or to the offices of various trust and land development companies. The Toronto Dwellings Co., for example, was a landlord on Eastern Avenue; some Macedonian entrepreneurs paid rent to the York Farmers' Colonization Co. for use of its buildings and properties on King Street East. Toronto General Hospital was also a landlord to Macedonians on King Street and Queen Street East through its property and endowment office and the Hospital Trust. If a number of residences on a street were owned by a common landlord, the groups of Macedonian tenants appointed one individual to deliver the rent monies.

Of course, private individuals were also landlords. Some among them actually lived in 'The Ward' or in the Macedonian neighbourhoods. Two residents of Chestnut Street, Moses Berinkrantz and Chaim Wilder, were landlords to East End Macedonians in 1915 at 357 Gilead Place and 1 Danvers Avenue, respectively. East End landlord Max Beber, a junk dealer and resident of 48 Berkeley Street, owned neighbouring houses (38–46 and 50 Berkeley), all rented to Macedonians by 1915. Judah Levi, an Argyle Street resident and manager of the Star Coal Co. on Queen West, owned property on King East. He also owned the fourteen houses that made up Percy Street, which ran south of King; there, he rented to Macedonians. In 1918, Macedonians occupied thirteen of his buildings. This 'sharp, wide awake' man had one of his tenants, Elia Butseff, a Macedonian barber, act as his agent and representative, collecting rents and attracting new tenants. The landowner, in turn, was a frequent visitor to the barber shop and to all his property and holdings.

In some boarding-houses, leadership was provided by a dominant male, usually an older, more experienced sojourner or a man of good standing in the village who presided over the house 'with seigniorial authority ... who had to be consulted about everything.' In others, the equality of migrant conditions led to democracy; the consensus of the group that created each household usually sustained it. Differences in jobs and incomes did cause a natural hierarchy to emerge sometimes. For example, slaughterhouse labourers and butchers who shared a house in the Junction at 50 Cloverdale Road (at St Clair West) in 1919 showed annual taxable incomes from work at Gunn's ranging from a low of $336 to a high of $450 – a butcher was collecting the lowest pay, and a labourer the highest. Only further oral testimony can reveal whether boarding-house status depended on income, on job skills, or on ethnic ascriptive values that had nothing to do with work.[11]

In the first decades of the century, foreign receiving and settlement areas in Toronto came under careful scrutiny and study by some of the city's 'caretakers' – the local Department of Health and its documentary photographers. What the camera saw was explicated by the city's chief medical officer of health (MOH), Dr Charles Hastings, in his 1911 report on slum conditions. He found the Eastern Avenue and Niagara Street districts, among others, to be the sites of many violations of Toronto's health and housing standards. (Hastings was silent about the Junction, although the area had been annexed by the city in 1909.) Rooms in many houses were found to be insufficiently lighted and badly ventilated. In cellars and basements where men might bed down at night, dampness was also a serious problem. Indeed, one home near Niagara Street was found to have four inches of water in the cellar.

The MOH went on to cite problems arising from the lack of adequate water and sanitary facilities. Many residents, for example, had no running water in their homes and so were forced to use outside taps. Other residences lacked drainage systems or baths. A sample of 851 housing units in the Eastern Avenue area revealed the presence of only 193 baths. Dr Hastings also examined the state of things outside buildings: 'Some of the yards ... were found filled as high as the roof of the house. Both the back yard and the front have bottles by the thousands: beds, mattresses, old furniture, junk ... [are] piled out to the edge of the sidewalk. Garbage in the lane and yards is very carelessly dealt with.'

Concerned with the plight of individuals and local residents, Hastings also considered overcrowding. One four-room boarding-house on Eastern Avenue, for example, housed twelve to fifteen men. Each room except the kitchen had been converted into men's sleeping quarters with three or four beds. Older respondents still vividly remember overcrowding and acknowledge the medical reports' accuracy. Four- and five-room houses on Niagara Street, for example, were known to have held as many as twenty Zhelevtsi at a time.[12]

CATERING TO THE SOJOURNER

The boarding-house allowed sojourners to live a frugal life and save money and helped shape the men's larger identity, that of being Macedonians in Canada. They offered a model and training for such future settler-group endeavours as creating a community parish and nationalist political organizations. As the initial settlement area, the East End was the site of the earliest Macedonian enterprise. Businesses that catered to sojourners' needs, such as cafés, steamship agents, grocers, and bankers, appeared first on Eastern Avenue, Trinity Street, and King Street, before the First World War. Eastern Avenue was early a centre of the grocer merchants. Men such as George Dimitry and Dimitry Peroff ran shops on the north side (at Gilead Place); George and Samuel T. Stoyanoff had a store on the south side (at Eastern Place). The east side of Trinity Street (at Eastern Avenue) was the site of two restaurants, including Jordan Belcheff's International Restaurant, which quickly became a popular gathering place and a favourite for those sojourners who bought weekly meal tickets. The north side of King East (between Parliament Street and Wilkins Avenue) was the site of a variety of establishments and services, including restaurants, grocery stores, butcher shops, and haberdasheries, such as the men's furnishings store of proprietor and railroad labour agent Andrew D. Georgieff at number 364.[13]

Malincheff/Theophilact's *First Bulgarian-English Pocket Dictionary* (Toronto 1913) reflected and even encouraged this rapid commercial development of the ethnic group in Toronto in its back-page advertisements. Hadji D. Peroff informed readers of the many services that his company, at 18 Eastern Avenue, could provide: 'Our firm's business is selling large and small old country foodstuffs and products, issuing ship cards with the best steamships, sending money to Bulgaria and Macedonia through express and exchanging Napoleons.' Promising to serve customers 'quickly, honestly and accurately,' the steamship agency Slave Petroff and Co., of 457 King East, offered the services of a labour bureau, post office, and address bureau. It also sold insurance and first-aid preparations. Compiler Theophilact directed readers to the East End colony and encouraged patronage of those who advertised in his book.

These early enterprises were the beginnings, or toe-holds, of a permanent and stable community. Inadvertently, however, they posed a threat to the sojourners' way of life. Habitual attendance at a café, for example, while helping that business, also represented a potential threat to sojourning, for it was a first step from the migrant's maximizing of savings and his spartan life. Most conscientious migrants went to coffee-houses only once a week, usually on Sunday. As the majordomo of a well-run boarding-house would ask of an impressionable young charge, 'Who goes on weekdays to the coffee-house? Only the loafers, the bumbi.'[14]

INDUSTRY AND SETTLEMENT

The three districts with substantial numbers of Macedonians – Cabbage-town, Niagara Street and area, and the Junction – grew within ward 2 (divisions 1A, 1B, and 2), wards 4 and 5, and ward 7 (divisions 1 and 2), respectively. The early residential boundaries (1903–9) of the initial, East End settlement area were King Street East to the north, Trinity Street to the east, Cherry Street to the west, and Lake Ontario, industrial sites such as Gooderham and Worts and the National Iron Corp. Ltd, and the railway areas to the south. The area quickly grew and expanded after 1910. In the period 1910–19, the group moved above King Street, settling the area above and below Queen Street East, and after 1920 the northern boundary moved north of Dundas and Gerrard streets to Carlton Street. Between 1910 and 1919, the western boundary moved rapidly beyond Trinity Street to include Berkeley, Ontario, and Princess streets. Movement to the Sherbourne Street area came primarily after 1920. By 1919, Cherry Street had ceased to be the eastern boundary as the group settled in the St Lawrence and River streets area. The years after 1920 marked the group's movement and involvement in life east of the Don River.

In the city's West End, from 1909 to 1919, Macedonians congregated in the Niagara Street settlement. Queen Street West formed the northern boundary, and Spadina Avenue the eastern one. Macedonian residences by Stanley Park on Niagara Street and Walnut Avenue helped to create the western residential boundary. Wellington Street West, the Municipal Abattoir, and the Grand Trunk and Canadian Pacific Railway (CPR) lines made an impenetrable southern boundary. Macedonians moved into the area north of Queen Street West after 1920, settling on Augusta Avenue and McDougall's Lane.

Also in the West End, eager young slaughterhouse workers helped to establish 'The Junction' – formerly the Town of West Toronto Junction before its annexation by the city in 1909. During the First World War, Macedonians settled an area bounded by St Clair Avenue West to the north; Annette Street to the south; Weston Road and Miller Street to the east, and Keele Street and the CPR terminal and complex to the west.

After 1920, the settlement rapidly expanded into the area around Jane Street and Runnymede Road, and so Macedonians eventually found themselves in suburban areas.[15]

The chronology of Toronto's industrial development helps us to understand the respective growth and development of these settlements. The Macedonians' initial and most heavily populated settlement area was in the East End. This district both attracted and provided a large Macedonian labour pool for the local sheet-metal industries, iron and steel foundries, slaughterhouses, and leather- and fur-processing companies. Indeed, the group exhibited a special perverse sort of pride in its ability to endure near these smelly fur-dressing and dyeing works. Macedonian sojourners found work at the National Iron Corp. and the William Davies Co., a Front Street East pork packer and slaughterhouse, and at the Kemp Manufacturing Co. The large number who ended up working at the Kemp sheet-metal plant irritated the editor of *Jack Canuck*, a muck-raking journal of the day. Macedonians were also to be found in the city's slaughterhouses – Harris Abattoir Co., at 35 Jarvis Street, and Gunn's Ltd, at 74–80 Front Street East. It was a natural step from slaughterhouses to working with hides at such tanneries and producers of staple and leather goods as A.R. Clarke and Co., Clarke and Clarke Ltd, and Wicket and Craig. The group also worked in the various soap works in the district, especially at Taylor Soap Co. and Lever Brothers.

The Junction and the Niagara-Wellington streets areas were established later, as the West End became the site of Toronto's meat-packing industry. The emergence of West Toronto Junction as a slaughterhouse centre began in 1903, with opening of the Ontario Stock Yards on Keele Street, just north of the CPR's terminals and shops. Stockyard officials and promoters saw the area as ideal for this unpleasant industry, because it stood apart from the city and its residents. In the beginning, the stockyards stood alone, since no packing plants were set up near them. Livestock was first unloaded a block or so east of the yards and then driven along Junction Road to the pens. Later, when the animals had been sold, the process was reversed, and they were driven down the street to the waiting stock-cars for shipment to packers in the East End. In 1905, opening of the Levack slaughterhouse next to the stockyards signalled the end of this difficult and inconvenient method of operation. In 1907, Gunn's Ltd shifted to the Junction; Swift's followed in 1911, and Harris in 1912. Macedonians, especially those already employees with those firms, made their way to new jobsites.

Development of the area of settlement along Niagara Street had a similar pattern. F.S. Tomev argues in his unpublished 'Memoirs' that the great fire of April 1904, east of old Union Station, scared the men – 'the flames had reached their [boarding-house] windows' – and the devastation in its aftermath forced them from central downtown to Niagara Street. Creation of the Municipal Abattoir in 1912 at the site of the Western Cattle Market at the foot of Tecumseth Street brought Macedonians to the district, as did work at Massey Harris, Ideal Bedding Co., and York Knitting Mills, on Queen Street West.

Each of the three settlement areas had industries with few or no Macedonians on payroll. The pattern of exclusion from certain jobs and firms is as important to the history of the community's development and occupational mobility as is the history of men's actual labour. Prejudice of employees and foremen, or their own lack of particular skills, prevented many sojourners from taking advantage of all opportunities for industrial employment. Macedonians did not find work in such large East End concerns as Gooderham and Worts, Elias Rogers, and British American Oil. They did not work for Consumers' Gas. (Macedonians did, however, go daily to the company's yard, at Front East and Trinity – to pick and choose reusable pieces of coal and coke from the scattered piles - which became an informal meeting-place. Oral informants remembered men sitting on the coal piles conducting classes in rudimentary English, planning erection of a church nearby, or conducting political debates.)

In the Junction, Macedonians did not work at the Weston Road factory of Canada Cycle and Motor or at the piano factories of Heintzman or Nordheimer. Members of the group were not employed by Gurney Foundry Co. on Junction Road or Campbell Milling at the foot of Cawthra Avenue. Although they worked at the East End soap concerns, Macedonians were not employees of Pugsley, Dingman and Co. Ltd and so did not yet work at its Cawthra Avenue Comfort Soap Works, and they never laboured at the CPR terminals. They were given work in the bush or were occasionally members of street construction gangs such as the crew that laid track from Bathurst to Simcoe Street. In the Niagara Street district, Cosgrove Brewery, Public Cold Storage Co., and St Andrew's Market did not welcome them as employees. A few Macedonians were labourers or factory hands at National Casket Co. at Niagara and Tecumseth streets.

In the Junction, indeed, the Macedonians were almost invisible. They coexisted with other and older residents. An examination of the suburban listings in the city directories for 1903, 1905, and 1908 – before the Macedonians' arrival – gives us a view of those older settlers, mainly

Canadian or from the United Kingdom. Labourers and tradesmen, slaughterhouse office and support staff – bookkeepers and clerks of the D.B. Martin Co., for example – and men of the railway and piano factories had established themselves on High Park, Willoughby, Pacific, Quebec, and Clendenan avenues and on McMurray, Annette, and Maria streets. Macedonians, when they began to arrive, lived at the undeveloped fringes nearest the livestock pens and cattle cars around Keele Street and St Clair West.

The Junction was a marginal and changing area, caught between its residential and commercial characters. Junction Road was the site of the Gurney Foundry Co. Ltd. The north side of West Toronto Street was taken up by the Union Stock Yards; the south side, by the CPR car shops. Benjamin Moore, paint manufacturer, could be found on Lloyd Avenue. Campbell Flour Mills Co. Ltd was located on the east side of Cawthra Avenue; the Comfort Soap Works occupied the west side. Macedonians displaced few people in this area. Keele Street, for example, which the directories had described as being 'not built on' in the period before 1907, was settled by Macedonians on the east side between Junction Road and St Clair West. Far from pushing people out, the sojourners and settlers, although it is difficult to establish the sort of housing that they found, were part of the urbanization of the city frontier. The limited size of the group and its failure to dominate in the Junction seem to have saved the area from rapid residential succession or inter-group hostility. For example, only half of the residences on Mulock Avenue were occupied by Macedonians even during the heyday of settlement. Other groups, including Anglo-Canadians and Poles – both antedated Macedonians as residents – lived in the other homes. Macedonians did not descend on the Junction in a single, disrupting wave. Men worked there as casual labour in the slaughterhouses before they moved there. Village chains, boarding arrangements, and brides caused a staggered pattern after 1920; people made their way to these streets in their own time and fashion. It was a steady movement of individuals over several decades.[16]

LIFE ON THE MARGINS

Study of Macedonians' migration about and between the three settlement areas in Toronto as well as of their forays to work in the hinterland and outlying regions of the province raises thoughts about the men's perceptions of geographical space and magnitude. For how large a region was Toronto the community's metropolis? A sojourner's mental map was rooted in awareness that he and his compatriots lived in three geographically disparate settlement areas. He quickly learned to appreciate physical and social or cultural hurdles en route as he walked or endlessly dodged his share of streetcar ticket collectors. The city itself and the Canadian community at large, which surrounded and separated the Macedonian enclave, usually failed to concern or interest him at first. His thoughts were of home – the family farm, political uprisings, the village church and bridge.

The sojourner was content, and even found it tactically useful, to remain on the edge of the Canadian way of life. He centred himself around the group settlement areas and depended heavily on the economic, cultural, and religious goods and services that they could provide. Even those in the distant hinterland behaved in this manner. Ignoring city life at large during forays to base camp Toronto, they depended on Macedonian entrepreneurial services (e.g. steamship agents, grocers, and bankers) and ethnic ambience as generated by the church, cafés, and boarding-houses for rest, relaxation, and psychic sustenance. Although an inquiring *Toronto Star* journalist, a student of Macedonian coffee-houses, expressed amused awe at 'a little man who had come down a hundred and fifty miles for the Sunday dance,' we should see it for what it was – a natural occurrence within an ethnic community.[17]

The sojourner's map of North America was simple. Macedonians were unfettered by political and geographical boundaries; they knew and spoke only of 'Upper' and 'Lower' America. An everyday reference tool, Malincheff/Theophilact's *Dictionary* (397–8) understood the needs of these men and so reflected their movement and crossing of boundaries:

Do you know where do Bulgarians live in this city?
Yes, sir. They are living on King Street.
On which part of the city?
On the east
On the west
On the south
On the north
Which car to take to go there?
It is not needed to take the car. It is close by.
You will take the King car.
Where to get off for Eastern Avenue?
Thank you for your kind information.

The next passage suggests how little the border meant:

Where is the Wabash depot?
What time does the train leave for Chicago?
When does the next train leave for Chicago?
How many hours does it take to go from Toronto to Chicago?
What is the fair [sic] from Toronto to Chicago?

Two early organizers of the church and participants in the men's cultural and athletic society Balkanski Unak left Toronto for Buffalo by 1915, as they felt that there was 'more work there.' The sojourners' continuous motion or openness to migration to seek opportunity was also understood and catered to by the sponsors of that first dictionary. Advertiser Vasil Pop Stefanoff, a steamship agent and restaurateur of 3 Morris Street, New York City, informed all Macedonians in North America who might visit that city that they could purchase their choice of steamship tickets and enjoy dining at his 'well-established restaurant where every Macedonian and Bulgarian will be most satisfied with our reception as well as our food and our price.'[18]

Guidebooks and 'letter-writers' were very popular among migrants. Respondents had cherished copies of both Yovcheff's and Nedelkoff's *Letters.* Also dealing with such typical sojourner themes as transience, employment, and varied and distant worksites, these publications offered sample letters of introduction: 'I take pleasure in introduction my friend Mr. H. Nicheff to you. He proposes to spend a few months in Illinois, and as he will be an entire stranger in Springfield any courtesy you may show him will be duly appreciated.' They also instructed men on how to request travel and lodging information (see Yovcheff's 'Information on Going to New York'), forward mail, and claim baggage. Samples included asking the postmaster in Sand Coulee, Montana, to forward all of Dontcho Krivoshieff's mail to Granite City, Illinois. Another request was directed to a landlord in Toledo, Ohio, by a former tenant and now resident of Chicago, M.P. Panoff. A George Valkoff could be seen graciously asking for the assistance of a Chicago baggage master.[19]

CONCLUSION

The multi-layered life of the Macedonian sojourner in Toronto revolved around fellow Macedonians in boarding-houses and cafés, work in or near one of the three settlement areas, and the possibility of temporary or permanent migration to Ontario's north or the United States in search of better opportunities. Informing all these sojourning activities, and decisions about them, was a desire to help family and village at home in Macedonia – and eventually to return there.

3

Seasoned Artisans

Early in the twentieth century, most Canadians believed that many of
the newly arriving southeastern European migrants were unskilled
labourers. Yet the majority of Macedonians, as pre-industrial villagers
and small homesteaders, had learned an assortment of artisanal skills.
For example, the need and desire to be as self-sufficient as possible led
men to acquire basic knowledge of agriculture and trading and such
trades as butchering, cobbling (which centred around fashioning a useful byproduct of butchering – practical pig- and cattle-skin moccasins),
blacksmithing, tailoring, and barbering.[1] These skills, too, would prove
invaluable in Toronto. Little in their lives to that date, however, had
prepared them for the working conditions they would have to endure
in Canada, and when their employers and other Canadians showed
indifference or hostility, they turned to fellow Macedonians for help.

The men's skills and occupational repertoires were also enhanced by
their migratory experiences before they reached North America. Working seasonally alongside the meisters (master builders), carpenters,
plasterers, and stonemasons at worksites in Greece, Bulgaria, and
Romania, young Macedonian helpers could gather a wide range of
apprentice skills within the construction trades.[2] Macedonians were also
prominent in the dairy industries of the cities of Bulgaria and of
Istanbul. Under the watchful eye of dairy owners, many of whom were
Macedonian, sojourners or multi-seasonal migrants cleaned and
scrubbed the copper milk vats and learned the pasteurization process
and the art of making good yoghurt. Younger men learned to peddle
among strangers by selling yoghurt in the streets.

The period of apprenticeship varied in length and was governed by a sense of obligation and a perception of additional opportunities. One migrant adolescent abandoned a three-year apprenticeship in a Bulgarian dairy when he heard of opportunities on the Californian railway. Another Macedonian worked in the building trades of Athens for two years until he had earned his passage money to North America. A different set of loyalties and priorities caused one Macedonian to complete a rigorous six-year tailoring apprenticeship in Istanbul before venturing to Canada.[3]

With their skills, brawn, and biceps, these seasonal sojourners would now help to ensure the industrial take-off of the city of Toronto. Macedonians, unlike Chinese, Italians, and Jews – Toronto's largest immigrant groups – were mainly factory hands and labourers. Even later, when hundreds of Macedonians ran shops or restaurants, factory jobs guaranteed – directly, or indirectly, through clientele – the community's income.

TYPES OF WORK

Macedonians in Toronto obtained work in tanning and fur-processing plants, slaughterhouses, metalworks, knitting factories, and street railways. Some men found jobs treating hides and furs. In the East End, they worked at the F.A. Hallman Co., on Logan Avenue. They also ventured westwards to the garment industry on Spadina Avenue to work at Hallman and Sable, Ltd. The majority of Macedonians in the fur industry, however, worked at the Frederick Schnaufer Co., in the city's West End, at 39–45 McMurrich Street. There Macedonians did the heavy and dirty work of dressing pelts and dyeing them for the city's wholesale furriers. On Eastern Avenue, some men worked in the tannery of A.R. Clarke and Co. Ltd, manufacturer of 'Gloves, Mitts, Moccasins, Leather and Sheepskin Coats ...' Others found jobs at the Wickett and Craig Co., a manufacturer of staple and coloured leather goods, on nearby Cypress Street. With a little experience, some ventured out to distant leather industries, such as Clarke and Clarke, Ltd, on Christie Street. Macedonians performed such strenuous tasks as stretching and spreading animal skins and hides. Some laboured in the factory support systems; as a coal stoker, one Macedonian tended to the demands of the factory furnaces while his countrymen were active in the tannery itself. Tanning was, of course, related to the abattoirs in the economy of using all the product of slaughtered animals; it was also an industry familiar on a small scale to 'greeners' and village men.[4]

It was in the dirty and dehumanizing slaughterhouses and abattoirs that Macedonians found most work. East Enders had begun as casual day labour at the William Davies Co., a pork packer on Front Street East, almost as soon as they arrived. In the West End, residents worked as butchers, water boys, hide-room labourers, and sausage and fertilizer makers at the municipal abattoir, the Swift Canadian Co. Ltd, Harris Abattoir, Gunn's Ltd, and, eventually, Canada Packers. As the business moved westwards in the city, Macedonians moved with it to work and often to live near the municipal abattoir in the Niagara Street district, or to the cluster of new slaughterhouses opening near the West End railway junctions.[5]

Although there had been blacksmiths in the villages, the jobs that Macedonians found in iron, sheet metal, tin, and stamping works were less familiar than tanning – cleaner, but more dangerous. Men served as industrial helpers and machine operators at such companies as the Toronto Iron Works Ltd and the Atlas Engineering and Machinery Co. Several were employed at the River Street complex of the Kemp Manufacturing Co., a large producer of sheet metal and tin goods. The proportion of Macedonian employees at Kemp's has been estimated by employee sources at as high as 75 or 80 per cent. Involved in every aspect of production, the Macedonians held labouring jobs in the firm's enamelling, inspection, and pickle rooms.[6]

Macedonians also found jobs in Toronto's silk mills and knitting factories. East End residents held positions at the Dominion Silk Mills and at the Berkeley Street location of Joseph Simpson and Sons, a popular manufacturer of knitted goods. Men from the West End settlement areas worked as spinners and yarn separators at the York Knitting Mills, 993 Queen West. Residents of Niagara Street and its environs also worked in manufacturing, especially at the Ideal Bedding Co. and at the Massey-Harris Co., where they unloaded lumber wagons, melted steel, and produced components of agricultural machinery such as screws and bolts.[7]

Casual work on the intercity and street railways, though regarded by Macedonians as the preserve of Bulgarian immigrants, opened up for them as well. Armed with picks and shovels, men could be found working on street railway projects around the city. The expansion of track facilities from Front and Bathurst streets to the area around King and Simcoe streets was one such endeavour, and many Macedonian labourers first began to get a sense of the commercial downtown and its opportunities while working at that site. Railways also drew Macedonians out into the Canadian bush to perform labouring tasks. Alongside Italians, Bulgarians, and Ukrainians, they worked in such northern areas as Hearst and Copper Cliff, Ontario, preparing and clearing tracts of land for the railway or for mine spurs.[8]

WORKING CONDITIONS

Working side by side in the city's abattoirs and factories, Macedonians generally performed the most unpleasant and physically disabling tasks. Young men, between the ages of fourteen and seventeen, were introduced to the slaughterhouse as water boys and sausage makers. Steeped in an irritating mixture of salt and perspiration, they laboriously produced casings by squeezing out the unpleasant waste substances from an endless stream of animal intestines. In other areas of the plant, able-bodied Macedonians worked feverishly on the 'killing beds,' a world of crowded pens, bellowing cattle, sledge-hammers, and death blows. Further along the line, other men quickly and systematically rid the dangling carcasses of their entrails.

This world of stench and blood took a heavy toll on 'the professional shoveller of guts.' The harmful effects of such work, let alone the psychological coarsening involved, took their toll. Lack of ventilation and constant exposure to coarse salt and the weight of cattle hides debilitated the men's lungs, skin, and backs. The demands of the bosses and the assembly-line system discouraged men from using the washroom facilities lest they lose their place in the line. In an anecdote that became a legend, a man named Stavro, who had his arm severed by a machine, tried to reject all offers of assistance. 'Never mind me. See that the machine does not stop so that the workers [do] not [have] to stop working.' Occupational dangers were not usually that dramatic but led to smaller and debilitating injuries and easy susceptibility to such diseases as tuberculosis, arthritis, and rheumatism.[9]

Macedonians fared little better elsewhere in terms of safety and working conditions. The men at tanneries such as Clarke's and Frederick Schnaufer lived with the pungent odours of animal hides. Indeed, the men at Schnaufer's exhibited a quiet pride in being able to endure the oppressive atmosphere of the 'smelly factory.' Daily exposure to the galvanizing process at Kemp's gave many employees permanently blackened teeth. Acid residue dripping from freshly treated iron and steel wares caused skin burns. The issue of job safety at Palmolive Soap came to a head in 1918 when a Macedonian was electrocuted either by a machine with faulty wiring or by standing in water and touching wires.[10]

On rare occasions, a job, despite or because of its inherent danger and unpleasantness, proved a source of good income or mobility for an unskilled Macedonian. As an employee of the Dominion Bridge Co., Nicholas Temelcoff, who had no apparent fear of heights, found that he could make good money as a construction worker on the Bloor-Danforth Viaduct building project during the latter years of the First World War. Temelcoff received about $1.00 to $1.25 per hour while he worked dangling far above the Don Valley. His countrymen in the factories were earning between 40 and 50 cents an hour.[11]

The immigrants' world of work was characterized by long hours. At Kemp's, for example, Macedonian labourers worked ten hours a day, six days a week. Such long days affected people more used to peasant rhythms, as well as their Canadian-born children: 'I can remember my father going to work when it was dark and coming home when it was dark.' In the West End, workers at Massey-Harris put in equally long hours – usually from 7 a.m. to 6 p.m. It was only in 1917 that the company instituted a fifty-hour work week and made Saturday afternoon an all-year-round half-holiday. Remembering his first job in Canada, F.S. Tomev spoke of his rare good fortune in having only a five-day week. His Jewish employers, Louis and Morris Soren, proprietors of a Toronto tinworks, rigorously observed the Sabbath and religious holidays. But Tomev was surprised and shocked that his countrymen were obliged to work on one of the great holy days of the Eastern Orthodox faith, the Elevation of the Cross.[12]

Factory working conditions for Macedonians were largely ignored by industry and government. Concerned almost exclusively with accumulation of profits, Toronto's industrialists gave little thought to, and made almost no provision for, the safety and welfare of their employees, especially the 'foreign element.' For example, a young Macedonian's request that repairs be made on a faulty machine was rejected by a foreman at Kemp's with the words, 'You can work or you can get your coat on and go home.' Men who lost limbs at Canada Packers could accept either a cash settlement of $2,000 or a pension of $16 a month for life. One Macedonian, Hristo Temovski, who had lost an arm as an employee of the Blackwell Abattoir, accepted a cash settlement. He then returned to the old country, where he used the money to buy a piece of farmland. Without the advice of counsel or consul, and with no government assistance, injured Macedonian workers were the most vulnerable of men during the settlement of claims and were little inclined to litigation. Since the companies alone established terms of settlement, men were wholly dependent on the manufacturer's goodwill.[13]

Employers' indifference often exacerbated those privations chosen by men, especially sojourners. Committed to saving money, intent on returning home with the optimum amount of cash, many men denied themselves assorted luxuries while even scrimping on such necessities as nourishing meals. Many Macedonian workers in abattoirs, factories, and railways barely survived on a meagre and unsatisfactory diet of bread, grapes, and cheese.[14]

The world of factory work, despite its physical and social hardships, could provide both lateral and upward mobility for Macedonian labourers as they moved through unskilled positions. Within eight months, one Macedonian worked at Kemp's and at Clarke and Clarke Ltd and then moved to Massey-Harris in the mistaken belief that he could make a dollar a day. Men also gradually acquired the skills necessary for upward mobility of occupation. At Kemp's, for example, Macedonians attained supervisory jobs in both the pickle and sample rooms as early as 1911. At Canada Packers, men assumed similar roles in the slaughtering quarters. Much later, by the late 1930s, Macedonians also became union stewards. Others who began as railway or factory workers built the nest eggs or confidence needed to strike out on their own and set up small businesses – the subject of chapter 7.[15]

Such self-sacrifice went hand in hand with unflagging commitment to working and earning at the highest level of efficiency. These men had, more often than not, come to Canada as sojourners, intent on sending money home to parents or wife. The threat of unemployment, of being idle or unproductive, when so much had been invested in their migration was their paramount fear. They were thus prepared to line up outside the slaughterhouse at the crack of dawn, risk injury and death at work, deal with padroni, both honest and dishonest, visit the labour exchange of the proselytizing Baptists, and listen tirelessly to the advice of friends and relatives for tips about jobs, or better jobs if they were already employed.

JOB MOBILITY

The Macedonian peasant-sojourners, no matter what their levels of education, were thinking men who set their own priorities and operated and moved according to their own perceptions of opportunity and success. If some never left their first jobs, many others were in motion, constantly changing jobs and moving around the city's three settlement areas. For example, a young Macedonian gave up his East End residence on Wascana Avenue and his steady job piling timber on the Toronto docks along Cherry Beach to move to Old Weston Road in the heart of the West End community and a job in a slaughterhouse there. Another sojourner moved among labouring jobs in the West End, at Massey-Harris, and in the East End, at Kemp's and at the Phillips Manufacturing Co., maker of mouldings, mirrors, and frames. When the Harris Abattoir Co. established itself in the Junction, a group of novice and seasoned slaughterhouse workers abandoned their Trefann Street boarding-house and followed the company to the West End. They took up residence at Keele and St Clair West.

Oral testimony offers insight into the choices that led to either internal migration in the city or clinging to the first migrant reception neighbourhood. Some men subordinated their feelings about households, living quarters, and neighbourhoods to their jobs, changing residences in accordance with work opportunities. Some sojourners were burdened, even frightened men who 'stayed put.' Working to pay off mortgages on farms and homesteads back home as well as to provide for other family needs and to plan households, they frequently bore uncomfortably the label 'birds of passage.' Happy to find a job with appropriate accommodation nearby, many fell into a pattern of surviving and enduring, not daring to risk much either entrepreneurially or by moving on. Several respondents in Toronto remembered feeling locked into their first jobs – dangerous, often brutal ones in slaughterhouses and industrial concerns.[16]

Some sojourners accepted years of long and costly commuting rather than give up ethnic companions and ambience. Many discarded the belief that accommodation should be near workplace. One group of young men lived with fellow villagers on Trinity Street in the East End while holding jobs at the Massey-Harris plant across town. East End residents also worked in such Niagara Street and Junction industrial concerns as Gunn's Abattoir, Matthews Blackwell Ltd, and the York Knitting Mills. For example, among labourers at Gunn's, Anton Vasil and George Chriss lived at 418 King East and 82 Berkeley Street, respectively. Two Macedonian spinners, residents of 122 Parliament Street and thus tenants of the former steamship agent and immigrant banker H.D. Peroff, made the daily trek to the knitting mills on Queen West. The 1919 Tax Assessment Rolls show a pork packer who lived at 362 King East and worked at Matthews Blackwell Ltd, at Niagara and Wellington, site of the Municipal Abattoir, the Western Cattle Market, and Livestock Exchange. West End residents, in turn, worked in the East End. The William Davies Co. employed the services of a Tecumseth Street butcher. These patterns existed even though each of the three neighbourhoods had some Macedonian presence. It may be, however, that village ties were different in each of the three areas.

Sojourners also moved freely between the two West End areas. Junction resident Tony Chriss, a boarder at the Keele Street restaurant of George Aceff and Mite Todoroff, was a spinner at the York Knitting Mills. Niagara Street residents also worked in the Junction slaughterhouses. A Richmond Street butcher, Cosma Djidroff, and labourer Argie Velcoff, a resident of the venerable Bull's Head Hotel, also had jobs at the Harris Abattoir.

If the majority of Macedonian men continued to live in boardinghouses close to work, then the above examples reveal forces other than employment defining choices about community. Bonds of family, village friendship, and fellow-feeling, for instance, might outweigh the convenience of living close to work. A well-developed public transit system and the sojourners' spirited and daring use of it also helped keep people where they first settled: '[We rode the] streetcar often for free [because] as soon as the ticket collector would come by [we would avoid having to pay by] jumping off.'

Some of the sojourners did challenge the group's emphasis on job security. A young East End slaughterhouse worker defied a boardinghouse rule: 'No one quit a job unless it was to go to another, one with higher pay, or to go back to the old country.' He left the William Davies Co. after only a day. Sickened by pungent odours and handling cattle entrails, and with hands reddened by salt and animal skins, he walked away from the slaughterhouse and his more docile countrymen for ever. The young man's father was also among the sojourners and had secure work, which allowed the son the breathing space to look for a more appropriate position. Few arriving migrants had such a safety net.

Other sojourners did not confine their movements to the settlement areas or the city proper. They ventured into Ontario's hinterland and used Toronto as a base camp. Many of them, along with Bulgarian migrants, laboured on the railways and took to bush life in northern Ontario. Men joined the work gangs formed during spring and winter. Macedonians especially sought winter employment because the wages were higher. Migrants went into the outlying regions during the economically lean years of 1907, 1912, and 1913 in search of the jobs that the city could not provide. Failing to get a position in Toronto on his arrival in 1913, one sojourner found employment in a Copper Cliff bakery. As well as receiving a good apprenticeship, he got seven dollars a month, food, and sleeping quarters. He later improved his skills at other Macedonian and Bulgarian bakeries in Sudbury and Sault Ste Marie before returning to Toronto, his initial destination.[17]

Employment took Macedonians into southern and western Ontario as well. A sugar-processing plant in Kitchener offered seasonal employment and good wages, and the men in Toronto soon heard of it. When the York Knitting Mills decided to open a plant in Windsor, many of its Macedonian employees followed, grateful for work and excited by the proximity to Detroit and its industrial opportunities. Some left the mills to work in Detroit steel plants for four or five months. Macedonians also helped construct the Welland Canal; according to oral testimony, 'Some made a lot of money, some killed.'

Railway labour in northern Ontario was both seasonal and difficult. Most men worked long hours during summer, only to be laid off with the coming of winter. Many returned to Toronto in the off-season in search of day positions in factories until the railways again needed them. Men made their choices between the hardship and higher pay of seasonal work in the bush and the drudgery and lower but steadier pay of factories and slaughterhouses. Some chose to pass up urban opportunities in favour of remaining at northern railway sites throughout the winter season. A group of Macedonians and Bulgarians, for example, found winter work in the forest areas near Sudbury.

Work conditions in the north were more primitive than those of the city. Macedonian railway labourers were often forced to lodge in boxcars and eat poor food. Eager for bread baked in the familiar Old World style, hungry navvies slept alongside balls of dough in the hope that their blankets and body heat would cause the dough to rise before baking. A Macedonian immigrant summed up his spartan boxcar life: 'Not pleasant hearing the howling of the wolves.' In time, he and his comrades abandoned the railway campsites for the permanent jobs and living quarters of the city.[18]

Still other sojourners searched for work elsewhere. Operating on the by–then firmly established concept that 'America is where the jobs are,' they rode out across North America on family and village chains. One Macedonian's life shows the pattern: he worked in a shoeshine parlour in Detroit, a restaurant in Ann Arbor, Michigan, and a bakery in Mansfield, Ohio, only to end up in Toronto, his original intended destination, as an independent milkman. Later, as a settler, immigrant, and family man, he owned a restaurant in Hamilton, Ontario.[19]

The guidebooks and dictionaries that appeared in the 1910s reflected practical aspects of the men's peregrinations. Malincheff/Theophilact's *Dictionary* (1913) emphasized the ever-present question of travel and transportation costs:

> How much do you want to drive me to this address?
> One dollar
> That is too much
> How much would you give?
> Take fifty cents.

It also dealt with some of the physical realities of distance from the base-camp city: 'from Toronto to Hamilton there are thirty miles.' Yovcheff's *Letters* contained a thoughtful discussion on the relative cost and time of travelling from New York to Chicago on the Pennsylvania and the New York Central railways. All of 'Upper America' and 'Lower America' was but a train ride away, and the sojourner's search for work could encompass an entire continent. Many Macedonians, however, came to Toronto and stayed.[20]

ANGLO–CANADIAN ATTITUDES

When many Macedonian sojourners found themselves without jobs during the recession of 1907, a series of events told them a lot about the ambivalent attitudes of Canadians towards them. That year a gang of some three hundred Macedonian and Bulgarian railway navvies returned to Toronto at the conclusion of a long summer working in the north. Their employer had reneged on its promise to provide free transportation to and from the worksite and charged the men for their trip to Toronto. They therefore spent the bulk of their hard-earned wages on the train tickets home. Exhausted and virtually penniless, the men hoped to wait out the winter in the city before heading out with newly formed construction crews in the spring.

The labourers fanned out to find drab quarters in the East End colony. Most often they paid about $8 a month to rent empty houses. Groups of men settled into squalid cottages along Eastern Avenue, Eastern Place, King Street East, and Front Street East. They slept on bare floors and huddled together for warmth. They rationed their money, often restricting themselves to two or three cents' worth of bread a day. Others existed on a subsistence diet of uncooked oatmeal, purchased by the handful in desperation. One of these labourers ambled up to the counter of a Macedonian grocery store and spent his one remaining

'American copper' on a single clove of garlic which 'he attacked ravenously.'[21]

The city's reaction to this group, even under these was extraordinary circumstances, offers some insights into official attitudes. By the end of November 1907, the men's situation had deteriorated to the point where an appeal for assistance was made on their behalf to the city's relief officer. Emergency assistance was offered: the House of Industry distributed coke for fuel, hot soup, and bread along Eastern Avenue and the nearby streets. Archibald MacMurchy, chairman of the board of the House of Industry, stated: 'The case is very difficult to deal with, for the whole three hundred are in need. Our plan for years past has been to take in anyone who needs shelter, give him his supper, a night's lodging and breakfast and then in the morning have him break stone to earn what he has received ... However, our building and yards are far too small for all these men.' During the wait for assistance from the board of control, the House of Industry was prepared to send daily provisions of food and heating materials to the men in their existing quarters.

Prominent and often sympathetic newspaper accounts of the men's plight inspired many kind-hearted citizens to donate food supplies. A resident of Sunnyside called the office of the *News*, offering a box of food for the men of Eastern Avenue. A couple from the East End came forward with two parcels of food. Speaking to a reporter from the *News*, the woman said simply, 'We read about these people starving, and I just said, well, here we are warm and comfortable anyway. I think we had better take something down.' An East End Macedonian grocer and restaurateur provided meals and foodstuffs on credit to the men. A grocer on Eastern Avenue told the press: 'See, I have a book and write down their names ... They will pay when they get work.'

The stranded navvies accepted the boxes and bags of food with gratitude. A rudimentary organization emerged among them to distribute food equitably. In celebration of their good fortune, the men lit candles and listened to the music of the gaida.[22] The mayor and board of control pledged assistance to the House of Industry in providing fuel, food, and shelter. The city had considered housing the men in the Dairy Building on the grounds of the Canadian National Exhibition, but the Office of the Parks Commissioner soon found that it was unable to remove the show and display cases. The city then prepared the Exhibition Park's Dining Hall to accommodate one hundred men. However, kindness was tempered by Anglo-Canadian fear of an unwelcome flood of pauper immigrants. The mayor and board of control cabled the dominion minister of the interior, Frank Oliver, to inform him of the men's presence and to request assistance. The superintendent of immigration dispatched E. Blake Robertson, assistant superintendent, to investigate and report back.[23]

With the help of translators, Robertson discovered that the majority of the men had been brought out by the Cunard Line, and the others by the Allan, Donaldson, and Dominion lines. Asked why they came to Canada, the men stated that the steamship agents in the Balkans and the Bulgarian press had painted an encouraging picture of opportunities in Canada generally and in Toronto specifically. Robertson suggested to Ottawa that they had been lured to Canada by false reports given 'to them by Gregor Ivanoff, a Macedonian in the employment of N. Christoff, a steamship agent for the Cunard Line at Belgrade. Some of the parties of Bulgarians arriving in Toronto had in their possession a letter of introduction from George Ivanhoff to his father Ivan Stoyanoff who runs a grocery store at 14 Eastern Avenue, Toronto. In the letter Ivanhoff asks his father to procure work for the parties presenting the same.' The dominion government cabled its agents in Britain and on the European continent to discourage further immigration from the Balkans.[24]

Robertson then turned to the problem of finding employment for the men. Immigration officials cabled the Eastern Construction Co., of Dryden, Ontario, to ask if it needed three hundred able-bodied labourers. Eastern replied that it did not: 'plenty of labour here.' Robertson did, however, obtain an offer of work for about fifty of the men on the Temiskaming Railway at $1.50 per day. When informed of the wage rates and living and travel deductions, the majority of the Macedonians turned down the offer. Perhaps they feared further abuse from a railway employer, but their independent decision astounded and angered Canadian officials. 'What do they want – a clerkship in the City Hall?' asked an angry Controller Hocken at a meeting of the board of control. 'Perhaps some of them intended to run for the Mayoralty,' the mayor suggested. At the request of an exasperated city government, the dominion Ministry of the Interior began making arrangements for deportation of the navvies as undesirable public charges under section 33 of the Immigration Act.[25]

As this incident reveals, the highly visible presence of immigrant workers in the city's factories and at railway worksites drew the attention of uneasy and latently xenophobic Canadians. In an attempt to 'open the eyes of the too trusting public,' the muck-raking weekly review *Jack Canuck* took strong exception to the predominance of foreign labour in Toronto's industries. *Jack Canuck* approved of the fact that 'one factory west of the Don is discharging and will not employ any more Macedonians.' It condemned another enterprise: 'Another soap factory, east of the Don is engaging them. It is supposed to be an English firm. They have laid off British hands to get cheaper labour.'

Jack Canuck also objected to the large number of Macedonians employed at Kemp's Manufacturing Co. Evaluating owner A.E. Kemp's bid for a parliamentary seat in the next dominion election, the paper carried one of the most overt attacks on the Macedonians as an immigrant group: 'We have no doubt that you will conduct your campaign like a gentleman ... also that you will give anyone who chooses the privilege of examining the payroll of your factory, where so many natives of that turbulent, throat-cutting country of Macedonia are employed.'[26] The paper represented the nativist fear of competition for jobs among Toronto's artisans and labourers. Capitalists and businessmen were, for their own reasons, more sympathetic to the Macedonian workers. The sojourning men were counted model employees, both hard-working and easily controlled. For that reason, Macedonians continued to outnumber other ethnic groups in the work-force at Kemp's and its successor, Sheet Metal Products Co.[27]

The First World War was to heighten tensions between Anglo-Canadians and Macedonians in Toronto, as we see below, in chapter 5.

INTERNAL ASSISTANCE

Given the indifference and not infrequent hostility of Anglo-Canadian citizens, 'caretakers,' and employees, Macedonian workers came to rely heavily on internal sources of information and assistance. Men frequently secured jobs on the railway and in the factories through the services of the padrone, or labour agent. A description of a Greek padrone fits the Macedonian case as well: 'This designation runs all the way from the petty faction leader who happens to know English and acts for a few, or some unscrupulous exploiter of his people who has got the upper hand, to the really great and enterprising contractor. The "agent," however, defies exact definition because of the manysidedness of his agenthood.'

Many Macedonians obtained jobs at Kemp's Manufacturing through the efforts of two company employees, Lazo Evanoff and Staso Filkoff. Among the earliest of Macedonian employees, these two carefully learned the manpower needs of the factory's departments and then directed compatriots to them. It is not clear whether Evanoff and Filkoff profited in more than reputation and status for playing this role – or whether the company encouraged them as a means of imposing social controls on the recruitment of labour. As if to dehumanize the men who turned to them for work, the padroni at Kemp's also renamed the new immigrant employees. A Macedonian immigrant states simply: 'Lazo Evanoff told them [the employers] my name "Charlie" because English people ... don't want the foreign people of those days. Proper names [such as Dono] they don't want. They want names that are easy for them. I was called, "Charlie Johnson."' As long as he remained at Kemp's, this immigrant was known to his friends and employers as 'Charlie Johnson.'

Jobs on the railway were, similarly, obtained through the good offices of the padrone. Andrew Dimitroff and James Georgieff, partners in a dry-goods store on King East, acted as labour agents for railways. The padroni at Kemp's were said to offer their services without fee. In contrast, Dimitroff and Georgieff required job seekers to pay one dollar and purchase their 'railroad clothes,' such as boots and overalls, from the bosses' store. Railway jobs were also available through the elusive 'man from Florina' – Chris Tipton. Macedonian labourers believed that Tipton was an agent of the Grand Trunk Railway. He was an important figure, a go-between with much informal power, but little is known about him. Tipton travelled north from Toronto taking gangs of Macedonians, Bulgarians, and men of other nationalities to jobsites along the route.[28]

Other sources aided Macedonians in their search for work. Railway navvies in the United States and Canada from the village of Buf in Macedonia received funds to tide them over and were kept informed by villagers about seasonal and permanent jobs in Toronto; in Columbus and Mansfield, Ohio; and in Detroit and Ann Arbor, Michigan. The Toronto steamship and banking agency Slave Petroff and Co. offered the services of a labour office especially for all those whose migration it brokered and to the Macedonian community. The Baptist church in Toronto also established a labour exchange and information bureau at its East End Macedonian and Bulgarian Mission Hall. The reluctance of many Anglo-Canadians to perform certain tasks opened opportunities for 'less fastidious' immigrants. Macedonians accordingly found jobs at the 'smelly factories,' the fur and dye works of the Frederick Schnaufer Co., or the W. Harris Co., which made, imported, and refined vast quantities of 'Glue, Fertilizers [and] Tallow Greases.' Canadian experience also gave men the confidence to search for and obtain jobs. After he 'learned the trick' of making soap at the John Taylor Soap Co., one

Macedonian found greater benefits as an experienced workman at the rival Palmolive Soap Co.[29]

The guidebooks of the 1910s reflected a decade or more of work and experience in the New World and made job-hunting and dealing with authorities much easier for sojourners. Malincheff/Theophilact's *Dictionary* (1913) aimed to protect Macedonian newcomers from undue hardships by enabling them to comprehend the nature of potential work. It showed the men how to ask a foreman or a company representative, in English, for a job: 'Good morning, sir. Have you any work for me?' Macedonians then learned how to ask about wages:

How much do you pay per hour for this work?
How much do you pay per day for this work?
How much do you pay a week for this work?
How long will this work last?
Fifteen cents per hour
Dollar and a half per day
Nine dollars a week
I am satisfied with this wage.

Also: 'How many hours do we work a day? Is there overtime?' Formal phrases dealt with job advancement and employees' privileges:

Dear Sir: –

As my present work with the ——— does not give me an opportunity for advancement. I regretfully beg to make application for a change to some other kind of work ...

Men learned how to request a day off because of illness or to attend a relative's funeral.[30]

Nedelkoff's *Letters* (1911) and Yovcheff's *Letters* (1917) offered more detailed and comprehensive instruction and assistance. Nedelkoff's volume presented sample letters requesting financial compensation or an occupational adjustment for injured employees. Varied levels of directness and intensity allowed men to choose the form that most suited their temperament and predicament.

In the best tradition of such industrial critics as Upton Sinclair, one such letter boldly demanded restitution from an insensitive corporation: 'I appreciate that a corporation is a soulless being, and hence what I ask, I do not ask as a matter of charity, but as a matter of justice.

Neither do I expect to gain a fortune therefrom. You will agree with me that as I lost my finger at your work, it is nothing more than fair for your company to allow for this loss, at least the twenty-five days of labour, which I so unwillingly lost, and amount, at $1.75 per day, to $43.75. I hope you will see way clear to grant this petition of mine.'

In contrast, a request for a change of occupation because of after-effects from a work-related injury was humble in tone: 'I recently applied at your plant for re-employment and secured my old job. However, even the first day, my head began to ache, my eyes got dim, and I was forced to quit. In a few days, I tried again with the same results, in fact, I was dizzy and unable to work. I am a poor man, without means of support with a wife and [three children] to keep. I must work. Will you be kind enough to find me a different place in the plant, where it would not require so much lifting and exertion as at moulding? Anything you may do for me will be appreciated.'

When an industrial accident killed a Macedonian worker, quick provision had to be made to notify kinfolk and countrymen. Yovcheff's model telegram – 'Nestor Parmakoff was killed in a coal mine yesterday. Funeral March 10. Please notify his relatives and friends' – provided his readers with a brutally simple and efficient example. The guidebooks also dealt with such combustible and delicate issues as relations with co-workers of other ethnic origins. Nedelkoff's guide contained a form letter of protest over the preferred position of Italian navvies in a railway camp.[31]

The three guidebooks/dictionaries became popular with Canadian Macedonians and their families. They were invaluable compilations of collective wisdom and experience – one of the community's first public expressions of its sense of its place in Toronto and in the New World. They occupied a special place in each household and were consulted frequently, if not acted on, by one and all. However, Macedonians were quick to grasp their limitations. These guides could only alleviate the heavy dependence on go-betweens, both in and outside the group. People met the need to provide for themselves, in what we would now call social insurance and workers' compensation, by creating a range of community institutions, a process explored in detail in the next chapter.

4

Village Societies, National Church

To help ease unemployment and provide camaraderie Toronto's Macedonians set up village-based brotherhoods and benevolent organizations
which obliged working members to assist their needy comrades in finding a job. The well-publicized plight and deportation of the 300 or so
unemployed Macedonians in 1907, described above in chapter 3,
spurred organization that same year of the first such group, the
Oshchima Benefit Society St Nicholas.[1] And fellow-feeling and mutual
support soon found expression in creation in 1910 of a *national* parish
in Toronto, centred in SS Cyril and Methody Church.

MUTUAL AID SOCIETIES

In times of illness, the brotherhoods and benevolent societies encouraged members to seek the counsel of physicians and to submit to hospital care if necessary. The organizations were prepared to pay for such
medical aid. The Oshchima Benefit Society St Nicholas would also
assume the cost of transporting a sick member back to the old country
if that were his wish. The member, once recovered and suitably
employed, was expected to repay the society.[2]

Many Macedonians greatly feared being buried by strange men in an
unknown land. They wished traditional burial in sacred and familiar
ground among friends and relatives. Brotherhoods and benevolent societies would pay the full cost of members' burial. The Oshchima Benefit
Society assumed as well the burial costs of non-member villagers in
Canada. It purchased a burial plot in Toronto's Prospect Park Cemetery

for this purpose. The parish burial records of SS Cyril and Methody reveal funeral provisions made by other groups of Macedonians. The society also included the Old World in its scope of activities. Its *Fiftieth Anniversary Almanac, 1907–1957* stated, 'Many times our Society sent financial help to poor families in the village, and a few times for public works as well.'[3]

The communal bodies raised operating income in a number of ways, including 'voluntary sacrifices' (donations), dances, picnics, the sale of name-day greeting cards, and group festivities such as the celebration of a patron saint's day. In this way, they became major centres of ethno-cultural intensity, rivalled from 1910 by the church and from 1921 by the Macedonian Political (later Patriotic) Organization (MPO). Membership dues, however, provided the bulk of their income. Members of such groups as the Banitsa Benevolence Society Hope (founded 1911), the Gabresh Benevolence Society, the Zagoriskoto Benevolence Society Peace and the Zhelevo Brotherhood were all initially required to pay a monthly fee of twenty-five cents. The Gabresh and Zagoriskoto societies opened membership to women for ten cents a month. Memberships in the brotherhoods and societies were open, despite the apparent village-based clannishness of their names and emblems, to 'anyone' wanting to join and able to pay the required fees. Anxious to gain the support of all fellow Zhelevtsi in Canada, many of whom had strong and conflict-ing ecclesiastical viewpoints, the founders and initiators of the Zhelevo Brotherhood boldly announced that the organization would be both non-political and non-sectarian. Members had to pay their dues regular-ly, attend the biannual general meetings and the special and extraordi-nary sessions, and cast their ballots on the issues and elections of the day.[4]

The articles governing the rights and obligations of societies' mem-bers acknowledged and made allowances for the frequency of the men's migrations and their transitory ways. For example, members of the Gabresh and Zagoriskoto benevolence societies and the Zhelevo Brother-hood retained the rights and privileges of full members on return from the old country or from localities outside Toronto. The Zagoriskoto soci-ety later allowed absentees to authorize proxy voting. Each village brotherhood and society had a three-member executive committee: a president, who presided over meetings of the executive committee and the membership as a whole; a secretary, who recorded the proceedings of every meeting and issued all formal correspondence; and a treasurer, who kept a strict account of financial transactions. Cheques issued on behalf of an organization were duly signed, however, by all members of the executive committee. The Zhelevo Brotherhood set up another financial safeguard, the controllers' commission – three elected members who verified, at least twice a year, both the accounts and supporting documentation.[5]

Who were the leaders of these mutual aid societies? Leadership appears to have been diverse; it came from among entrepreneurs and work-ingmen. Bojin C. Temoff, an employee of the York Knitting Mills, helped establish the Oshchima Benefit Society St Nicholas on 26 October 1907. This literate and self-educated man drew up its first constitution. The Banitsa Benevolent Society Hope, founded 26 June 1911, received hearty support and direction from the community's leading steamship agent and banker, Hadji D. Peroff. At this distance, it is difficult to know how altruistic his role was.[6]

The Zhelevo Benevolence Brotherhood was apparently founded in 1907 and active for a number of years. Trpo Stefov, a labourer at the Ideal Bedding Co. and a committed member of SS Cyril and Methody Church and of the men's athletic society, Balkanski Unak, started the drive to resurrect it in 1921. His proposal gained the immediate approval of the proprietor of the Bull's Head Hotel, Vasil Stoyanov Popovsky. The meetings and social gatherings of the brotherhood were held at the hotel; the owner provided accommodation free of charge. It may have brought him more customers, but the memory culture recalls him as totally committed to the society's work. Trpo Stefov later reflected on the nature of leadership: 'I proposed that we organize a Benevolent Zhelevo Brotherhood. Vasil [Stoyanov Popovsky] accepted my proposition. We mediated and [were] determined to find a way to call our people to a meeting, but who? I was afraid, because I consi-dered our people would not follow me. I was too young. Vasil also was afraid to take the initiative, because the Zhelevtsi might not respond to his invitation and he would be disappointed and humiliated. Our hesi-tation did not prolong. We both decided to call Zhelevtsi to a meeting.' Neither success in business nor good reputation among fellow-villagers at first seemed enough to assert a leadership role or initiate social action, but both men persisted.[7]

The charitable activities of SS Cyril and Methody Church (founded 1910) assisted or complemented the good works of the benevolence societies and brotherhoods. The good works of the church included pro-vision of financial assistance to the needy. At a meeting on 28 July 1918, the church's executive committee agreed to the request of Evan Miloshoff, a 'sick boy' in the Weston Consumptive Hospital, who wanted to buy some clothes. The young man, originally from Bitola, received an unspecified amount, between $15 and $17, for clothing purchases. Many other such specific instances of charity are recorded. Cooperation between the church and the societies became a tradition. On 14 March 1937, for example, the church's executive committee, in conjunction with the MPO's Toronto local, Pravda, and its ladies' and youth sections, decided to make the parish hall available to those benevolent societies 'who are on good terms with the Church and Organization' for a modest rental of $20 and two weeks' advance notice.

The church, with the approval of the general membership body, also issued official letters of introduction which requested financial assistance for their needy bearers. On 28 March 1929, Traian Dimoff received a letter from the church 'to seek help for his sick and suffering brother.' Eager to return home to Prilep, S. Andreev, who had lost both an arm and a leg, was endorsed by the congregation when he tried to raise his fare home from within the community. SS Cyril and Methody also established a visitation program in 1937. The church appointed two women members, Mrs Toleff and Mrs Zolumoff, to call on the Macedonian ill and infirm in the city's hospitals. Members of the church committee were later appointed to continue such friendly and supportive rounds among the Macedonian ill in Toronto.[8]

A NATIONAL PARISH

In their homeland, Macedonians had long viewed the church as the 'interpreter of self-consciousness and self-respect.' Acting as a bulwark of national identity, the village church was the centre around which Christian villagers who spoke Macedonian rallied. In North America, Macedonians looked to the church to re-create its traditional role as the protector and 'monument to our consciousness.' In Toronto, the new parish faced the task of uniting an immigrant flock from many different villages into a single religious community.

SS Cyril and Methody, the church that the Macedonians organized in Toronto, became the centre of ethnic existence for a community in psychic transition from a temporary way of life in Toronto to one of permanence. The little church that they built on Trinity Street in the East End settlement area not only tended to their spiritual matters but also served to focus their political and communal actions and their loyalties.

In the United States, Macedonian immigrants founded churches in the first decade of the twentieth century, with the assistance of the Bulgarian Holy Synod. Lacking a religious base of operations in North

America, the synod dispatched its representative, the abbot, or hieromonak, Theophilact to the United States to help organize parish
communities. Despite its help no parish was possible unless the immigrants themselves showed enthusiasm and willingness to pay the costs.
Dedo Kone of Steelton, Pennsylvania, acknowledged the hard work and
sacrifice of fellow immigrants: 'I was appointed to collect donations for
the building of the church. I was not literate however, I took a cloth
tied the four corners together and went from person to person and
everyone dropped money in the cloth. Receipts were not given, since
no one knew how to issue them. Their generosity and trustfulness was
amazing. In a short time we collected the necessary funds and built a
church.' As a result of such efforts, churches were built in Steelton and
in Granite City, Illinois, by 1908.[9]

Macedonians in Toronto learned of their American co-nationals' success from articles in Macedonian-American newspapers and correspondence. They began on the difficult road to building a parish in 1910.
The impetus came from a group that included both businessmen and
workers. Men such as banker and steamship agent Hadji Dimitar Peroff
undertook to gather the support of the entire Macedonian community.

The decision to set up a national church stemmed from the villagers'
growing New World sense of themselves as Macedonians – members
of a single ethnic community within the city and within anglophone
North America. In the Old World, people had carried out their religious
obligations and rituals within the strict confines of the village church.
Arriving in Toronto, both migrants and immigrants had tried steadfast-
ly to perpetuate their customary loyalties and outlook through creation
of village mutual benefit societies and brotherhoods. But now men from
such villages as Armensko, Banitsa, and Verbnik saw the logic of
moving beyond their village loyalties and differences in order to work
together for a common church.

A series of preliminary meetings in 1910 and 1911 served as a catalyst
to a remarkable upsurge of lay and youthful initiative. The first church
protocols contained the names and ages of the early organizers and
committee members. In 1911, most of the men active in planning a
parish were in their mid-twenties and early thirties. The church had
long been a traditional area of concern for village elders. In North
America, however, men came of age sooner; the young sojourners and
settlers had no choice but to assume responsibility.

Macedonians had waged a constant and bitter battle in the name of
religious freedom against the Greek patriarch from the time of the
repression by the Greek Orthodox millet at Istanbul of the Ochrida

archbishopric in 1767. With establishment of the Bulgarian exarchate in 1870, they continued their struggle against the Greek clergy by supporting the exarchate. In old-country villages, men such as Hadji Pavel of Zhelevo had struggled to build churches in the name of the Bulgarian exarchate. Members of the initiating committee in Toronto also decided to place the proposed church and religious centre under the spiritual jurisdiction of the Bulgarian exarch and the Holy Synod.

They began a round of correspondence with Hieromonak Theophilact, who was still in Pennsylvania. He responded by promising support for any local initiative in Toronto. Eager to put the church proposal before their compatriots, committee members raised among themselves the necessary transportation funds needed to bring Theophilact to Toronto for a general meeting of the community, which took place during the latter half of August 1910. Enthusiasm and patriotism abounded. Hieromonak Theophilact gave the major address to over two hundred people, who voted for creation of a parish under the aegis of the exarchate.

The alliance with the Holy Synod meant that Macedonians would share the church with those in Toronto from Bulgaria proper but not with fellow villagers who called themselves Patriarchists and owed allegiance to the Greek patriarch. Few in number, members of the latter group probably did not attend that eventful meeting. The Patriarchists first conducted informal meetings in their homes and residences and then began to attend the Greek Orthodox parish in the city. Their identity, or at least that of their children, as Macedonians atrophied.[10]

A committee of village delegates launched a campaign to gather funds to purchase or build a church 'in the name of SS. Cyril and Methody' – the ninth-century Thessalonican brothers who Christianized several Slavic peoples, gave them an alphabet called Cyrillic, and translated the Bible. Both peasant democracy and lay initiative characterized the effort, as the community prepared to tithe itself according to each man's village of origin. Acting as the ethnic group's own census, the tithing system was used and supported by approximately 1,090 Macedonians in the city. A uniquely 'interior' and precise 1910 census of Toronto's gave numbers of Macedonians by village of origin: 'Kostursko, Macedonia – 514, Lerinsko – 332, Prespansko-Ochridsko – 121, Bitolsko – 42, Kalyarsko – 32, Dimir-Hisarko – 15, Bulgaria – 38.'

Fundraising centred around villagers from the districts of Kostur and Lerin. Of the $2,591 amassed between 1 October 1910 and 2 March 1911, $1,249 came from the men of Kostur and $1,075 from Lerin; the district of Kaliary raised $158. Forty-two men from the village of Gabresh, for example, donated $227 to the parish fund, and 93 men from Zhelevo contributed $227. Men from Old World city centres also participated. Two men from Prilep donated a total of $12, and two from Bitola gave $15. Villages and individuals seem to have given according to ability. Those from Lerin, Kostur, and some of the larger villages, most heavily represented in the Toronto migration, saw their town or village as the central support of the new church.

On 29 November 1910, the Macedonian community in Toronto negotiated the purchase, for $5,000, of a house at Trinity Street and Eastern Avenue. Acting on behalf of all Macedonians, ecstatic members of the initiating committee put down $1,500 as a first payment. They arranged to cover the balance owing, at $300 every six months, at interest of 6 per cent per year.

The regular meeting of the village delegates agreed that a permanent church committee would be created. The protocol describing the process again reflected both democratic, lay initiative and the place of village sub-ethnicity within the larger religious and national identity:

1.   The incoming committee will be comprised of 7 members.
2.   The Church Committee will be elected from the village delegates, who in turn will elect a committee from outside of the village delegates and from among themselves.
3.   A member shall be elected by majority vote and with the voting of not less than one third of the voting village delegates.
4.   Each village with 10 members shall have one delegate; from 20–40 members, two delegates; 40–60 members, three delegates. Every village up to 20 members shall have one delegate. A village with less than 10 members shall be joined with other villages. Each delegate shall have a letter certifying his right as an elected delegate.
5.   The village delegates shall be elected not later than one week prior to the election of officers.
6.   The delegates and the church committee shall have a mandate of one year. For the following years, the election of the delegates will be held during December and in January for the church committee.
7.   The church committee and the auditing committee shall give a solemn oath before the people that they will serve honestly and faithfully. The oath shall be given in church during the service.

The church committee was chosen on 11 April by 31 village delegates from Armensko, Banitsa, Besvina, Debretz, Dolno Kotori, Gabresh, Gorno Kotori, Konomladi, City of Lerin, Nevolani, Oshchima, Pozdivista, Roula, Smerdesh, Statica, Ternava, Tersie, Verbnik, Zagoricheni, and Zhelevo. A later protocol provided that the 'Gospel will be read in Slavonic, Russian, Bulgarian, English and Greek'!

The new church – which later became SS Cyril and Methody Macedono-Bulgarian Orthodox Cathedral – stood in the heart of the Macedonian section of the East End – the earliest and most stable and organized of the settlement areas, according to the community's memory culture, and the natural and appropriate location for the church. By contrast, the West End was portrayed as an area of turbulence and conflict, not least because of uneasy relations between the Patriarchists and the Exarchists there. Whatever the truth, creation of the church confirmed the pre-eminence of the East End among the city's Macedonian neighbourhoods.[12]

After its purchase, the interior of the two-storey lathwork-and-plaster structure immediately underwent alterations and repairs. Macedonian volunteers and Canadian workmen began by knocking out the walls and partitions of the ground floor to create space for the congregation and altar, which was erected on the east side. It was then handsomely decorated with iconic lithographs, believed by many parishioners to have been imported from the Russian port city of Odessa through the good offices of Hieromonak Theophilact. Similar renovations prepared the upper floor for use as a parish hall, where meetings, socials, and athletic and educational endeavours could be held. Church services were first conducted on 2 March 1911, following completion of renovations. On 24 May 1911, the church was consecrated (in the absence of a Bulgarian ecclesiastical hierarchy in North America) by the Russian Orthodox metropolitan from New York, assisted by Hieromonak Theophilact.

Improvements followed, and over time the exterior of the building changed. The single entrance door was replaced by a larger set of double doors. Above the doors, in the 1930s, was placed an impressive icon – oil paint on galvanized steel – created by Foto S. Tomev, of the parish's patron saints, Cyril and Methody. A steeple was erected on the roof. A wooden cross, fashioned according to Orthodox tenets, was placed on top of the steeple's gilded dome.

Purchase and alterations of the church generated a debt of about $7,000, which was paid off over four years and four months. The compilers of SS Cyril and Methody's *National Calendar* for 1916 proudly pointed out that, except for $15 from a supporter in Detroit, all monies were raised for and within Toronto's Macedonian community.[13]

Payment of the church's first round of debts strengthened the immigrants' resolve to maintain a cultural and religious identity. The community's confidence grew, and in April 1916, when the original edifice was proving too small for the growing congregation, it decided to purchase the adjacent house and property. The purchase price was $4,200. After making a down payment of $1,000, church trustees arranged to pay the remainder over five years. The deed was issued in the name of a group of trustees including Hieromonak Theophilact, Done P. Lazaroff, Hadji D. Peroff, Naum Phillips, and Tipe Tipoloff. The house at 95 Trinity became the priest's living quarters and headquarters for the church's executive committee meetings, held previously at Theophilact's Parliament Street residence, which also housed the protocol books and a large work table.

The Macedonians of Toronto devised fundraising measures in order to pay the mortgage on the new addition and to meet the church's operating costs. Not content to rely solely on village tithing, the church appointed a collector, 'a proper person,' 'to visit the families, the restaurants, the businesses and the wards where there is our people to collect help.' The collector was given a formal letter of introduction, or 'trust,' and a brass collection box; the box remained locked at all times, and the key was held by the treasurer. He was expected to conduct his visitations once a week. One East End collector closed his King Street butcher shop in order to perform his canvassing duties. Mindful of the expense and effort, the church committee for 1914 decided that the collector would be paid two dollars for each of his rounds.

Faced with the need to raise $1,200 annually for mortgage payments, officers of the church frequently asked members to lend money to the church. In 1918, for example, the committee raised $1,040 in loans, including $20 from Pasko Atanasoff; $40 from Koste Giamandoff; $50 each from Pavel Dimitroff, Nako Gecheff, Dencho Kraeff, Nikola Misikoff, Vasil Sterioff, Dimitar Stoyanoff, Evan Tosheff, Mitre Velianoff, and Dimitar Zhivkoff; and $100 each from Georgi Dineff, Stase Filoff, and Hadji Guleff. The list may represent men making a sound investment within their ethnic group, but it may also speak to levels of piety in the community.[14]

Hieromonak Theophilact had accepted the invitation to become the first priest of SS Cyril and Methody Church at the January 1911 meeting of church and village delegates. By the end of 1912, he returned to Bulgaria to appear before his spiritual leaders at the Holy Synod.

Pleased with Theophilact's missionary work and his role in establishing four North American parishes, the Holy Synod had promoted him Archimandrite. It was a mark of Toronto's importance. Early in 1913, Archimandrite Theophilact returned to SS Cyril and Methody to take up his post, for which he earned about thirty dollars a month. He combined his spiritual duties with more secular ones. He was church president during 1912, 1913, 1915, 1917, and 1921. He resigned as parish priest in 1921, the year he completed his medical studies. Now Dr Demetrius Mallin, he had come to believe that he could serve his immigrant flock better by tending to its corporeal rather than its spiritual and cultural needs.[15]

The early years also saw a revolution in women's role in religious and community life. Women, as wives and fiancées, came in numbers to Toronto after the Balkan and First World wars. The church's executive committee for 1918 considered adding women's washroom facilities during basement renovations that year.

Church and religious matters had long been the preserve of village priest and male elders in the old country. Women had entered the church as worshippers, candle makers, and caretakers, dusting and washing the walls regularly, especially after weddings and other religious celebrations. While they continued to make candles in the church backroom on Saturday afternoons, Macedonians women in North America enjoyed considerably more participation and influence. As members of the parish and, from 1921, the Macedonian Political Organization, they became enthusiastic participants and instructors in SS Cyril and Methody's educational, athletic, and cultural programs. Young women in the Bulgarian-language school and Macedonian Unak came under the spiritual tutelage of more emancipated women such as Vera Matova and Mary Evanoff. Opportunities arose for performing in plays and concerts, and the church choir now welcomed women.

Women took part as well in the church's decision making; they helped to determine who would be tenants of the parish hall. They also gave the larger host community some sense, albeit at a minimal, folkloric level, of Macedonian culture; they showed that behind the half-acculturated and rough ways of labourers and countermen lay a sensitive and aesthetically rich culture. The women mounted popular and prize-winning embroidery displays at the Canadian National Exhibition.[16]

As a centre of ethnoculture in Toronto, SS Cyril and Methody felt its responsibility to the community, and members became involved in its activities to further religious and/or local/national Macedonian causes. The 1910 group census had found eight families within a community of 1,090 people. By 1915, there were forty-three families, with forty-nine children, most of them under the age of five. The growing number of pre-schoolers prompted the authors of the church's financial report for 1914–15 to raise the issue of community responsibility and sound the cultural alarm: 'These children are growing up in a far away and foreign country. Left without care, they will not be able to read or write their own language, nor will they know a thing about their religion, church and nationality.' The report urged the church community to create a Bulgarian-language school. For their own good and that of the ethnic group, it said, Macedonian children should learn to balance the lessons of the 'city's English schools' with those in Macedonian history and the Bulgarian (written) language and religion.

Prosveta, a Macedonian educational and cultural society dedicated to building cultural institutions free of Greek domination, agreed to sponsor such a school in Toronto. It formed the first Bulgarian-language school in 1915, in collaboration with SS Cyril and Methody. The church and the society had come to terms over accommodation, income, and representation for the church's executive committee, which made the upper floor of SS Cyril and Methody available to the society rent-free. Prosveta was also to retain the income generated from its popular Sunday lecture series but was to pay five dollars a month and assume costs of electricity and minor repairs to the upper floor: major repairs were a joint responsibility. Later, from 1921, a Prosveta activist, Simo Velianoff, was present on the church committee to speak for the society.

Between 1911 and 1921, the varied activities of Prosveta and the athletic society Balkanski Unak, along with church teas, dances, entertainment evenings, and the major religious celebrations, animated the little church on Trinity Street. More often than not, church committee members coped with lack of space by renting local rooms and halls. Neighbouring Trinity Anglican Church generously made its meeting-rooms available on the Macedonians' request.[17]

There were potential class, as well as regional, rivalries to be reconciled in the running of the church and, through it, of the community. The executive committee remained largely in the hands of the businessmen and entrepreneurs. The committee elected on 14 April 1911 contained, for example, night-school instructor and principal Apostol Kalavasoff, banker and steamship agent Hadji Dimitar Peroff, grocer and merchant Grigor Stoyanoff, baker Simo Velianoff, and butcher Stavro Zolumoff.

Butcher-turned-steamship agent Naum Phillips was church president in 1919, 1924, and 1925, and master butcher and successful entrepreneur Lambro Tenekeff in 1930, 1932, 1933, and 1936.

Membership on a committee of the church was a mark not just of piety but of concern either for the welfare of the immigrant community, or for the Macedonian national cause, or both. Acting on matters of substance that often went beyond either religion or nationalism, the newcomers would show a degree of lay initiative that had not been necessary in the homeland but that equalled that of their Protestant Canadian contemporaries. The church and the affiliated cultural associations and school were forging a national community that transcended the local loyalties that had led earlier to the creation of village-based mutual and fraternal societies.[18]

5

Preachers, Teachers, Soldiers, War

Various Anglo-Canadian institutional 'caretakers,' particularly Protestant churches and public schools, sought to acculturate Macedonians in Toronto. The immigrants' response was more studied and complex than has often been realized. The First World War, which cut them off from their newly partitioned homeland, highlighted for Macedonians their uncertain place in the land that choice and/or circumstances increasingly made them think of as home.

The sources and literature created by the 'caretakers' are revealing, but only oral testimony can tell us about the Macedonian side of the encounter. Historians concerned with only the caretakers' perspective, usually in written form, have exaggerated, for example, the role of Protestantism. Oral testimony shows that Macedonians made use of all things Protestant that aided them in the new land but for the most part remained Eastern Orthodox. Of course, many of the ways and habits of mind of the 'North American religion' (Protestantism) entered their lives through the social missionaries, schools, and neighbourhood encounters.

PROTESTANT CHURCHES

It was some of the Protestant churches, especially Baptist and Presbyterian, caught up in the enthusiasm of the 'Social Gospel,' that moved first to help the newcomers; Anglicans and Methodists were much less active. The Social Gospel called for a functional and aggressive Christianity; its adherents responded to the needs of people within an urban and industrial society. The growing number of city slums, for example, claimed the attention and energies of the reformers. The presence of alien immigrants in the city also warranted a large-scale, institutionalized response. Macedonians provided a good target for this new form of Christian witnessing and reform politics. Protestant missionary efforts, confused religion and culture absolutely. A 1908 Methodist missionary publication offered their operating creed: 'It is our duty to meet them with the Open Bible and to instill into their minds the principles and ideals of Anglo-Saxon civilization.' Perhaps, the caretakers reasoned, the entry of immigrants into Canadian urban and industrial life could be eased if the church established a strong presence among the newcomers. Unfortunately, introducing people to the Canadian way of life also brought, more often than not, the demand that those people abandon Old World religious beliefs and practices.[1]

Having concentrated its 'New Canadian' work for many years on the Scandinavian immigrants of northern Ontario, the Canadian Baptist Home Mission Board shifted its attention to the Slavic immigrants crowding into urban southern Ontario. Reverend John Kolesnikoff was asked to spearhead the program. Kolesnikoff was a fascinating figure – preacher, fanatic, and organizer. Some said that he was a Russian Jewish convert to the Baptist sect; others, that he was a Macedonian. He had worked successfully among various Slavic groups in the coal-fields and towns of Pennsylvania. He came to Toronto in 1908, known for his 'sunny smile, his winsome word, his hearty handshake,' and his total dedication to evangelism. He arrived to survey the opportunities for Baptist missionary work among the Macedonian residents and other Slavic immigrants. He found over four hundred Ruthenians in the city's centre ward and more than four hundred and fifty Macedonians and Bulgarians in the East End, but he did not discover the many Macedonians already living in the Junction and near Niagara Street.

Aware that the Presbyterian and Methodist churches were concentrating their home mission efforts on Italians and Chinese, Kolesnikoff urged the Baptist Home Mission Board to recognize and take over this new and unconquered territory, to 'open the door for preaching' and commence missionary work among the city's Slavic immigrants. Impressed with Kolesnikoff's findings, the board set up immigrant mission halls on Elizabeth Street and on Dundas Street West to serve the area's Russian, Ruthenian, and Polish immigrants. A hall was rented at 426 King Street East at Sackville Street to serve the 'Bulgarians, Macedonians, Servians, Montenegrins, Turks and Greeks.' The generous donations of affluent Canadian Baptists paid for rental fees (to the estate of George Gooderham) and furnishings. One member of Jarvis Street Baptist Church, for example, gave $300 towards the annual rent for two halls. The hall soon became a centre of intense evangelical and social activity, though not a competing centre of Macedonian ethnicity. On Sundays, the indefatigable Kolesnikoff, preaching in at least three Slavic languages, tried to communicate with the city's eastern European immigrants. Testimonials and prayer meetings took place twice a week.

Street meetings brought religion out of the mission hall and squarely into the Macedonian urban presence. In the East End, Kolesnikoff preached at the corner of Trinity Street and Eastern Avenue every Sunday evening to a crowd, according to Baptist sources, of approximately two hundred. He frequently aroused the emotions and interest of spectators, who were encouraged to participate by singing hymns such as 'Good Words, Good Words, Sing unto Christ.' The eighteen amateur immigrant musicians that made up the Macedonian Brass Band, a Baptist-sponsored ensemble, provided spirited musical accompaniment.

The missions dealt with more than just the religious needs of immigrants. A night school at the mission on King East was established out of concern for the newcomers' educational needs. There, young volunteer instructors recruited from Toronto's Baptist congregations held English language classes, frankly religious in character, for the mission faithful. They taught immigrants the language, laws, and customs of Canada only after they had been 'taught the laws of the "Upper Canada" – Heaven.' The program included prayer and scripture reading.

The missions tried to help the settlers as well with their employment problems. The labour exchange and employment bureau at the King Street mission challenged the monopoly over brokering work held in the East End by the Macedonian steamship agents and labour bosses.[2]

Although the Baptists made the first ethnically specific effort to reach the Macedonian community, Presbyterians soon followed suit. Under the direction of Reverend Atanasoff and Reverend Katsunoff, they established missions in the East End, on Parliament and Sumach streets. Sermons, Wednesday evening prayer meetings, and English-language classes were offered. Services at the Parliament Street mission were well attended not only by committed Macedonian Protestants but by interested parishioners from SS Cyril and Methody. Indeed, a member in good standing of the latter frequently played the piano during services. Macedonians attended because of Atanasoff's personality and viewpoint. One member of SS Cyril and Methody, who attended the mission regularly, summed up his popularity and ability: 'You learn something [from the sermons]. He talks slow but every word is worth something to a young fellow.'

Atanasoff encouraged members of his immigrant flock to become 'good citizens, honourable and honest men.' Unlike the fiery Baptist Kolesnikoff, Atanasoff proselytized Macedonians very subtly. One respondent observed: 'He tried to point out his religion was better, but, not pushing you.' Atanasoff kept polite, even warm, relations with the clergy of SS Cyril and Methody and the Macedonian community. The former priest of SS Cyril and Methody, Dr Mallin, treated the sister of Atanasoff's associate, Reverend Katsunoff, after he became a physician.[3]

The Church of England in Canada, unlike the Baptist and Presbyterian faiths, did not seek to minister to Slavic, non–English-speaking immigrants. It fully acknowledged its duty to minister to all racial and ethnic groups only in the late 1950s. Generally, its acts of fellowship and concern towards other immigrant groups were 'rare achievements.' However, a strong bond grew up between Macedonian East Enders and the pastor of the neighbouring Little Trinity Church, Reverend Canon Hilliard Cameron Dixon. The minister saw fit to lend a helping hand to his Macedonian neighbours. Using membership lists from SS Cyril and Methody, he provided Christmas packages of fruit and candy to needy families. He also allowed Macedonians to use his parish hall for concerts and plays when they needed a larger space than their own hall provided. Oral testimony asserts that Dixon's role as a good neighbour never included proselytizing. The encounter between the two communities was that between two self-confident ethnic churches; there was no room nor need for raiding or poaching souls. 'To him you were alive in one way or another.'[4]

The major Protestant denominations of Toronto, except for the Anglicans, sought to woo the city's Macedonians away from their ancestral faith – with rather little effect. The immigrant group did not look kindly on these efforts. 'As though we were heathen,' one old immigrant remembered, still smarting with indignation. Kolesnikoff's forceful attempts to convert the settlers, coupled with his repeated attacks on the Eastern Orthodox faith, angered Macedonian lay people and clergy: 'He tried to force people [to join the Baptist church]. He knocked our church, our religion. That was no good.' In a famous incident, Archimandrite Theophilact allegedly discredited Kolesnikoff by exposing his fear of the power of Orthodox icons. Theophilact not only defended Orthodoxy ably but knew modern science. Many people say that none the less Kolesnikoff on his death bed asked for Theophilact (by then Dr Mallin) to pray for him; Orthodoxy and the Macedonian community were held to have scored a final and all-important victory. Opposition to Protestantism did not come from clergy alone: families recognized that conversion meant conflict and quicker of assimilation. One Macedonian was stopped from entering the King Street Baptist mission by his angry brother and a friend. The Protestant intrusion forced Macedonians to size up the situation and act on it. They shrewdly decided to use the educational and work opportunities offered by the proselytizers. The majority did so without abandoning either faith or heritage.[5]

Several immigrants recalled enjoying and appreciating the English-language classes taught by Baptists and Presbyterians. One pragmatic woman even chose to christen her children in a Protestant church because, unlike SS Cyril and Methody, it had no baptismal fees. The Baptist missionaries went so far as to claim that approximately 75 per cent of all the Bulgarians and Macedonians in the King Street community had been assisted by the local mission. Such estimates were, of course, exaggerated because of the missionaries' need to retain the continued assistance of their church.

If they were 'sober reflections of reality,' the rates of return – that is conversions – for Baptist good work were remarkably low. Despite the fanfare and the fact that social good accomplished, few Macedonians became Protestant. Decisions to leave the Orthodox faith were not made lightly, especially since it was so central to ethnic identity in both Canada and the Balkans. Archimandrite Theophilact bluntly told those who loitered around the Baptist mission that they would lose their standing in family and community. 'Boys, don't go,' he would say.

The Macedonian Protestant sub-community was small. Moreover, many of its members had been exposed to Protestantism in the Old World. Some had converted even before their arrival in Canada, especially those from around Monastir (Bitola), where a large Protestant college with Canadian connections had long operated. The Protestant sub-community also included those few individuals who had attended one of the Old World mission schools, such as the American Agricultural and Industrial School in Salonica. Similar factors influenced some of those drawn to Baptist witnessing. Some Macedonian navvies just arrived in Toronto left bunk cars in the railway yards at the foot of the East End neighbourhood to join in one of Kolesnikoff's street meetings; they had been crypto-Protestants in Macedonia, according to a Baptist account. One man had found the faith as a result of the distribution of Bibles by missionaries in a Istanbul jail.[6]

What of this Protestant immigrant sub-community? Did its members enjoy more mobility and acceptance in Toronto by virtue of their membership in a more 'mainstream' faith? It depended on which denomination they chose. Those who joined the Baptist or Pentecostal churches were inserting themselves into the lowest socioeconomic and status level of Canadian Protestantism. Joining the Methodists or Presbyterians, or (later) the United Church, opened up a very different process. One Macedonian, who had become a Protestant in the Old World, found that a mission school reference letter from the old country, which characterized him as a 'young man of excellent Christian character, temperate, faithful, industrious, and [in] every respect worthy,' gained him entry into Albert College, a Methodist institution, and, subsequently, into Victoria College in the University of Toronto. Adoption of Protestantism apparently increased mobility and speeded up acculturation. Perhaps it broke through some Anglo-Canadian barriers of prejudice. Or perhaps different mores and contact with urban Canadian ways, which came from already thinking in Protestant modes and being marginal to the main Macedonian-Canadian community, hastened assimilation. It is difficult to say.[7]

ENGLISH-LANGUAGE INSTRUCTION

The city's Protestant churches were not the only agents of assimilation. School officials were also worried about the newcomers' adjustment to urban life. In 1913, the city's Board of Education articulated its role: 'If these people are to be assimilated and made good citizens it must be largely through education.' Even before that, the board offered English-language classes to immigrants as part of the night-school program. Classes were organized in 1900 at the Elizabeth Street school in response to the demands of Romanian immigrants. In 1907, the board established classes for Italian immigrants at the Agnes Street mission. That same year, English-language instruction, mainly for Macedonians, began at the Sackville Street night school under the direction of Reverend G.M. Atlas.

As sojourners, few Macedonians had wanted to learn English. They saw acquisition of the language as unnecessary or a threat to their migrant frame of mind and way of life. An immigrant summed up the situation: 'If the father had a son and he wants to go to school, he [the father] thinks as soon as he [the son] learns English he would leave the father and won't go to the old country. He'll stay for good.' Another young Macedonian had his English-language texts burned in the stove by a concerned brother who feared that schooling would make the young man unfaithful to his pledge to return home or send money home.

The decision by any man to become a settler brought about a change in his attitude towards acquiring English. Learning it, especially for those emerging as entrepreneurs, became an immediate and important matter. Such men did not flock to night-school language classes at either Sackville Street or Niagara Street Public School, but many adults tried to adjust to the confines of a classroom and the embarrassment of showing their language ignorance in public. In 1909, a Bulgarian immigrant, Apostol Kalavasoff, became an assistant master at Sackville Street. He taught both oral and written English to a group of thirty Macedonian men. Later that same year, he was named principal of the Niagara Street night school. As principal, he instructed a class of over forty men.[8]

Industrial and business concerns and individual Macedonians also initiated English-language instruction. For example, Dominion Glass Works conducted classes during lunch breaks. Anglo-Canadian workmen, acting as teachers, introduced immigrant workers, among them Macedonians, to the fundamentals of English. 'He [the workman teacher] reads, he ask you to pronounce the words.' John Grudeff, an arts student at the University of Toronto, set up two classes for his countrymen in 1917. For one class, at the Bull's Head Hotel, the enthusiastic proprietor, Vasil Stoyanoff, provided free space and encouragement. In the other, in Mitre's grocery store, at Keele Street and St Clair Avenue West, young Macedonian men learned arithmetic, English, and Bulgarian grammar.[9]

Classroom attempts to teach English met with only moderate success. Macedonian factory labourers and small shopkeepers had little time or energy for steady attendance. One slaughterhouse worker remembered learning English 'through the air' – by years of trial and error and listening. Other Macedonians shunned the classes simply because they feared a public display of their uncertainty and verbal clumsiness. Such people – the majority of the immigrant generation – learned the language imperfectly and helped maintain the ethnic ambience; they needed it for social comfort, and their accents helped to define its boundary with the larger society.[10]

Macedonian women did not make use of night school or group-organized classes. Timidity, fear of embarrassment, and responsibilities to families and boarders prevented attendance. Women, however, did receive an education. As part of their Canadian Christian Fellowship Programme, Baptist women, moving away from the confines of the church and mission halls, ventured into the immigrant community and offered basic English-language instruction to Macedonian women in their homes. A Baptist missionary wrote: 'When a Macedonian woman opened a homemade book which had [the] lesson "Setting the Table" with a picture of a table prepared for a meal ... she said, "I learn English now!"' Macedonian women, as a result of missionary efforts and learning 'through the air,' acquired a rudimentary grasp of spoken English. The Protestant encounter had some unexpected results. Macedonian women established long-standing friendships with some of their missionary English-language instructors. Some even tried to reciprocate their teachers' efforts – 'We taught Macedonian to Miss Evans [a Baptist missionary].'

Women picked up English informally during the course of daily living. They learned on the job; wives of entrepreneurs developed their language skills working in their families' restaurants, butcher shops, and grocery stores. Children and sympathetic Anglo-Canadian neighbours also helped. The urge not to learn was also there. The new tongue spelled the end of Macedonian household familiarity for some of them – an admission that they could not do things their way in Toronto. Some women really preferred not to learn English. They would fulfil their New World obligations by using their husbands and children as emissaries.[11]

PUBLIC SCHOOLS

Although Toronto's Protestant churches and its Board of Education had organized night-school classes for adults, teachers and professional educators directed the bulk of their energies towards the immigrants' children. Canadian educator J.T.M. Anderson observed: 'It should never be expected that the older people will become "true Canadians" ... The children of these newcomers [should be] given every opportunity to receive proper training for intelligent citizenship. They, along with those who enter our country while still quite young, are the material upon which Canadians as nation-builders must work. They are the "New Canadians."' The city's schools, both elementary and secondary, and the churches demanded that children adopt 'a new national loyalty: to prove [they were] different from [their] parents – to think, act and speak "English," "White" or "Canadian."' A good Protestant stood to be created as much in school as in the church.[12]

The teachers of immigrant children felt that they had a two-fold responsibility. They first had to provide core academic training, a basic public school education. The teachers, who saw their young charges either as slum children – this was especially the view held of East End residents – or as offspring of the working class, believed that few of them would proceed beyond public school. 'It has naturally been the case at Sackville Street School,' a *Toronto Star* journalist noted in 1916, 'that a large portion of the children drop out at fourteen years of age and go out to work.'[13]

Teachers also had the additional and important task of Canadianizing them. On their arrival at school, immigrant children had to learn the new language; but despite their special needs, few English-language classes had been organized for them. Teachers, at Park and Sackville Street schools, seated Macedonian youngsters at the front of the class and repeated key words during periods of blackboard instruction and class discussion. One Park School instructor even brought a variety of household items and foodstuffs to class to use as visual teaching tools for his Macedonian students. One student recalled: 'He would say to me that this is salt, and this is sugar and this is pepper.'

Macedonian children who had gained adequate command of the language were frequently appointed informal instructors. They helped new and younger students get through registration procedures and spent evenings assisting other children in mastering the new language and completing homework assignments. Older immigrant children were also placed in the lower grades amid the younger. Teenagers felt profoundly uncomfortable sitting at a small desk in a grade-one class. Macedonian children encountered many tangential aspects of Canadianization and began early to have the symbols of their own ethnicity and nationalism crowded out. They prayed for the British royal family and studied the growth and development of Canada and the British Empire in their history and geography classes.

Not all school Canadianization was Anglo-conformist. Teachers at Niagara Street School invited their Macedonian students to educate their classmates by reciting Old World poems, songs, or stories that they had learned from their parents. They also encouraged children with academic or athletic skills. A teacher at Niagara Street tried to keep a bright Macedonian boy in school; he spoke to the boy's father in an effort to gain crucial support for further education. He kept an eye on the student's progress throughout high school and university. An East End principal pressed a Macedonian butcher to allow his daughter, who was a talented athlete, to have some time off from her job in order to play in a crucial girls' volleyball championship game.[14]

BETWIXT AND BETWEEN

The Macedonians' plans for a temporary stay in Toronto were altered by the Balkan Wars of 1912–13 and then by the outbreak of a general European war the new year. The Ottoman Empire's long-standing and oppressive domination of Macedonia now gave way to the rigours of Greek hegemony and a repressive regime. Hopes for a freer homeland faded quickly when Bulgarian-language schools and churches in Macedonia were ordered closed by the Greeks. Villages were forced to billet Greek soldiers, who conducted comprehensive searches for the hidden rifles and ammunition of rebellious peasants. The confused and unhappy situation in the old country convinced the men abroad that their future and that of their families lay in the New World. So the faraway Balkan Wars, much as the earlier Ilinden Uprising, shaped men's sense of their permanence in Toronto.

It was against this turbulent background that sojourners began to grapple with the business of becoming settlers. Given their North American presence, Macedonians had to decide where to live, either in the United States or in Canada. In *The First Bulgarian-English Pocket Dictionary* (1913), Archimandrite Theophilact outlined and compared the citizenship requirements of both countries. In Canada, the author observed: 'You are not required to know the English language as in the U.S. There is not examination.' For some men, the choice was unimportant. They had made a settlement pact with 'America' and so kept up their sojourner ways and outlook as they and their families moved between the United States and Canada in search of work and business. For example, a successful East End restaurateur left his Trinity Street establishment and moved to Buffalo with his family for what he perceived to be abundant opportunity. Marriage and the search for success would, in turn, bring his children back to Canada.

Men now had to deal with the realities of the new Greek regime in Macedonia and how it affected their relationship with the villages that they had left behind. Once again, the priest's new dictionary proved helpful, warning readers about the uncertain protection provided by an American or Canadian passport in the homeland. Return visits to villages under Greek rule could and did sometimes result in a demand that a returnee fulfil his military obligation as a Greek citizen. A man who returned to Zhelevo in 1918 was conscripted into the Greek army and forced to fight against the Turks in Istanbul for two years before being allowed to return to Canada. Arger Mishailoff, a resident of Toronto and a British subject, had his passport impounded on arrival in Macedonia in 1920. Greek authorities refused to recognize him as a British subject and demanded that he enter the army.

Despite such problems, the majority of Macedonians were unhappy at the prospect of remaining permanently in Toronto. Some had quietly made the decision to stay during the heyday of migrant adventure. 'As soon as I set my feet in Canada,' a respondent said, 'I never thought to go back.' Early economic success and the potential for even more changed men's minds about going home. A few even drew strength and were motivated to settle by the New World example of other groups – 'Watch the Jews and others bring wives.' So attitudes and behaviour changed, sometimes imperceptibly, as the indefinite stay of the sojourner became the permanent stay of the settler.[15]

Even though many immigrants were already naturalized, the First World War brought confusion. As subjects of the Ottoman Empire or Bulgaria, Macedonians, whose passport problems of identity we have already discussed, were sometimes treated in Canada as enemy aliens. They were required to report monthly to the Office of the Registrar for Alien Enemies on Adelaide Street in Toronto. A Macedonian immigrant humorously recalled his registration duties by saying: 'The officials asked "What are you doing?" "Where do you go?" They think you were doing spy work. We Macedonians didn't know nothing about spy work in those days.'

Afraid of imprisonment, this immigrant and his countrymen dutifully reported their activities and whereabouts. According to the memory culture, a half-dozen Zhelevtsi and some other Macedonians served in the Canadian forces overseas. These men felt that they gained some respectability in Toronto for their actions. It was ironic that men who met and conspired in the hope of Macedonia emerging from the Turkish ruins as a free and autonomous state should be treated as Ottoman loyalists. The war reminded all Macedonians of the contradictions between their Old World heritage and their New World life. It also, in small ways, continued the refining of their identities. Canadian authorities were apparently harsher in their treatment of Bulgarian nationals as enemy aliens than of Macedonians. Macedonians received a reminder of their statelessness, however, when Serbian recruiting officers approached their Serb neighbours with the blessing of Canadian authorities.

One wartime incident, now shrouded in the memory culture and unclear in the mainstream Canadian press, also helped define a separate Macedonian-ness in Toronto. When Great Britain and the Allies grew incensed with the Greek monarchy for its apparent collusion with Kaiser Wilhelm II of Germany, this anger trickled down to the wartime jingoist press of the empire. As a result, Canadian forces bivouacked at the Canadian National Exhibition grounds in Toronto went on an anti-Greek rampage along King Street. Restaurateurs, if they were uncertain about their identity at all, found for the first time that a declaration of Macedonian-ness brought fraternity rather than anger or dismissal.[16]

The extraordinary manpower needs of the First World War broke, at least temporarily, some of the existing barriers to work. John Inglis Co. took on Macedonians from the Niagara Street district. One respondent vividly remembered his fears and worry about his brother's job – 'I felt sorry for him working amid the the big guns, big shells' – in the Inglis munitions works. Oral testimony also shows that many of the men were subsequently forced out when veterans returned home and reported for work. One Macedonian who worked at an office specialty company on Wellington Street West had to give up first a position as a saw-man and then one as a wood-planer when former soldier employees, especially one 'who had been wounded in battle,' returned home.[17]

STARTING THE TRANSITION

Having taken the psychic step from sojourner to settler, Macedonian men often had to express their feelings and go public with their decision in the boarding-house. When the tax assessment rolls repeatedly listed 'Macedonian' as the sojourners' occupation, they were unwittingly correct. Ethnicity, occupation, and inclination about length of stay merged to form one visible 'eth-class type' in Toronto. Escape from any part of the identity affected the rest of it. Very often the actions of the new settlers served notice of their decision and intentions.

Writing about his increasing commitment to life in North America in *The Eagle and the Stork*, Stoyan Christowe recounted his co-residents' reaction to him as he entered the boarding-house in his American-style suit: 'As I climbed the steps toward the porch I heard the clatter of the spoons. And then six pairs of astonished eyes glared unbelievingly at the apparition at the door; and six spoons, some filled and some empty, wherever they happened to be in their journeyings from bowl to mouth, remained suspended in mid-air. Only Klement's mouth continued to chew absently; all others were frozen as if by sudden paralysis. Klement gulped down the half-chewed food and attempted to speak, but he found himself voiceless, like a stork. My footsteps as I walked in were cries of derision and defiance. "Shut up, shut up," the footfalls on the floor kept repeating.'

A decision to remain in Canada frequently was expressed by the effort to learn English at night school. Those who chose to attend classes had to endure either hostility or the humorous barbs of their relatives and countrymen – 'What do you want to be? A teacher?' Afraid and suspicious, sojourners saw acquisition of the English language by any of their number as an unsettling and disruptive force threatening the workings of the migratory process. As one early settler summed up the situation: 'If the father had a son and he wants to go to school, he [the father] thinks as soon as [the son] learns English he would leave the father and won't go to the old country. He'll stay for good.' Another young Macedonian had his English-language texts burned in the stove by a concerned brother who feared the impact of the acculturating influence of schooling on the family.

Novice settlers soon moved out of the boarding-house as differences in attitude emerged and hardened between them and those who still thought as sojourners. Vasil Dimitroff rented a room for himself because 'I like private [quarters] and I like to read a lot.' A young man from Zhelevo left his East End boarding-house for the cleanliness of the nearby Dominion Hotel – 'the beds were nice and clean, they clean every day.' For both men, the sojourner's priorities – maximizing savings, being with one's own kind – had faded.[18]

EMERGENCE OF THE BACHELOR SETTLER

Eventually all Macedonians found themselves making this psychic transition in their own time and fashion. The psychological shift from migrant to immigrant – from sure knowledge that one worked towards a return home to a new and often uneasy commitment to life in the New World – slowly altered, among other things, disposition of available capital and the type of entrepreneurship possible in the community. Boarding-houses became less central than eateries, hotels, and other services.

The emergence of the bachelor settler helped, for example, to trigger the rise of the Bull's Head Hotel as a central Macedonian establishment. The hotel, at the corner of Niagara and Wellington Street West, was own by Vasil Stoyanoff, a Macedonian. He provided accommodation, food, and drink for the many cattle dealers and traders doing business at the neighbouring Municipal Abattoir. Macedonian residents of the area also frequented the hotel – one respondent fondly remembered 'the great bar,' youthful good times, and, as an unshakeable counterpoint, the discomfort of being a foreigner in a sea of Canadian cattlemen: 'We were afraid to speak any other language, because of criticism – "Hey, what the heck kind of language is that you speak?"' Rooms could accommodate either one or two people at a time; such privacy was luxurious after the boarding-houses, and its purchase might have seemed spend-thrift a few years earlier. Rent was at least two or three dollars a month (excluding meals). In contrast, bachelor boarding-house fees were generally kept under two dollars per month per person by the usually large number of residents, and they covered food and heating.

Housekeeping duties at the Bull's Head – changing of sheets and beds – were performed by Stoyanoff's sister and sister-in-law. Stoyanoff's wife cooked for the hotel's restaurant/dining-room guests. Residents were expected to eat there without fail. Stoyanoff became angry when residents ate out occasionally at nearby Niagara and King Street cafés. 'You live here. Why do you eat there?' The bar/saloon now did duty as a coffee-house, as the proprietor adhered strictly to liquor regulations. Hotel residents carried their room keys on key chains bearing the twin-bulls'-heads motif.

The ambience of the hotel and the activities that it offered and sponsored made it a natural gathering place and focal point of the Niagara Street settlement area. It was the site of John Grudeff's English-language night school classes and the meeting place of the Zhelevo Brotherhood, a village mutual aid society, until that organization built a hall of its own. The hotel was also a place to go when life in the boarding-house became too tense as a result of political or personal arguments – or burnt onions in the stew.

Men who saw themselves as settlers were now also willing to invest both their time and money in vacations and rest. Junction bachelors went to the Muskoka Lakes north of Toronto. One East Ender spent the summer of 1912 at a resort in Burlington, Ontario, after working at a hectic pace on a shift from 6 a.m. to 12 midnight daily as a short-order cook. Vacations did not stop following the arrival of the families from the Old World. One East End candy-store owner and restaurateur had a cottage on Highland Creek. Several Niagara Street district residents went en masse to Stoyan Duke's farm in Osaka/Port Hope each summer and stayed a day or two in residence at the big family farmhouse.[19]

UNEASY TRUCE

Macedonians were part of and yet distinct from their Canadian urban labourer/urban poor neighbours. They often did not work in the same factories or at the same skill level. The East End, for example, housed Anglo-Canadian labourers, teamsters, and drivers for Gooderham and Worts, the distillers, and for the Consumers' Gas Co. There were also caretakers, sailors, lamp trimmers, carpenters, painters, moulders, clerks, motormen for the Grand Trunk Railway and the Toronto Railway, firemen, brewers, porters, inspectors, and proofreaders. None of these was Macedonian. Among entrepreneurs, the differences were obvious as well. Butchers, grocers, and barbers existed in both communities, often side by side, but the small tradesmen – such as blacksmiths, harness makers, potters, and shoemakers – and merchants – such as jewellers, dressmakers, and second-hand dealers – were not Macedonian.

Macedonians differed from their Anglo-Canadian neighbours in their attitudes and use of public transportation, reflecting deeper divergences in life-style. Macedonians continued to walk to work over distances for which their Canadian neighbours rode the trolley. The act of walking dramatically affected daily life. To save streetcar fare, men invested as much as two hours of their time, walking to from work each day. This decision, coupled with ten-hour workdays, may not always have been wise or efficient, but it demonstrated the primacy of work and saving in their thought. Their bodies and time were the free commodities they had to give. Such small, ethnocultural choices tell us of priorities and of thought and planning about how best to use twenty-four hours.

In the beginning, the act of migration itself, the state of bachelorhood, and the suspension of family life that migration imposed were strange, frightening, even a source of anger to the migrants themselves. Some Anglo-Canadian residents of the settlement areas, who saw young foreign men as restless 'corner-boys,' competitors for jobs, non-participants in society. The following excerpt from an issue of *Jack Canuck* (22 June 1912) gives form to some of those feelings: 'A Macedonian dropped his purse the other evening. Being the purse of a foreigner who makes his money in Canada, but doesn't spend it here, it contained a substantial sum. Little girl found it and returned it and was rewarded with the magnificent sum of 15¢.'

Local and city-wide awareness of the Macedonians as a community grew, and with it stereotypes began. No doubt, neighbours noticed the surge of humanity coming out of the church and onto the street after holiday and nationalist celebrations. In 1911, the accidental wounding of an Anglo-Canadian worshipper in a neighbourhood Anglican church during Orthodox Easter celebrations, which included a traditional firing of guns, proved especially newsworthy.

The Macedonians were victims of the xenophobia and nativism endemic in early-twentieth-century Toronto. One Macedonian respondent remembered his shock and sadness at being greeted by children pitching stones at him as he made his way from the Don Station. Moreover, failure to form the largest ethnic group in any of the three settlement areas meant that there was no totally safe enclave, or 'home turf.' One only has to hear accounts of the fear that men had of moving beyond King Street East, the early boundary of the East End settlement area: 'We were not daring to go above King Street. Farthest we could go was up to Power and Queen, that was the limit for us because the boys at that time were prejudiced against us and were throwing stones, tomatoes and all that and so we took precautions, can't go, can't go.' As their English improved, their fear declined. 'They [Macedonians] didn't give a damn after [they learned the language]; they could give back what ever they [their tormentors] said.' In the early days, their tendency to travel in groups of young males – without English, and warily – was both cause and effect of trouble. 'A bunch of us, otherwise couldn't go by yourselves.'[20]

CONCLUSION

In the turbulent period before 1920, the Macedonian community in Toronto began to take shape. Macedonians in Toronto had set up boarding-house, cafés, small businesses, village-based mutual aid societies, and a national parish; they had found work, often in very difficult conditions; and they had responded in evolving ways to their neighbours and to Toronto's Anglo-Protestant 'caretakers.' It is in those years, as we have seen, that most of the strategies – and not a few of the scars – that fashioned the emergent Macedonian-Canadian ethnoculture, its boundaries, and its contents first became apparent and were reflected upon and articulated. The 1920s and 1930s saw the maturing and expansion of the non-settler community and its responses to new, more complex and subtle pressures both from within and without.

6

Settler Households

Marriage and new households – especially when young wives came to Canada as their men passed from sojourning to settling – were the central fact of the Macedonian group in Toronto in the 1920s. They created a community of families but involved a peculiar cultural lap. Many brides had been left behind in the period before 1910; it had been easier, quicker, and more profitable to have men migrate seasonally or sojourn than to make arrangements (passports and so on) for a couple or family to emigrate. The First World War had further delayed the emigration. Typically, a tailor from Gabresh, who had married in 1914, recalled that he could bring out his wife only in 1920, after the 'roads opened up.' The women arriving about 1920 had lived through a further decade of Macedonian history; they lacked their husbands' sense of the New World and needed the linguistic and cultural reassurances of an ethnic community.[1]

Married men who had left brides behind at the beginning of their sojourn made provision after the war ended for their wives and families to join them. Many of the wives migrated to Canada reluctantly. Sorry to leave friends and relatives behind, frightened at the prospect of living in intimacy with men whom they had not seen for a decade, they came because the ethnoculture required them to do so, or because they feared trying to survive without a mate. Some wives simply refused to move. Recalling the reluctance of her mother to venture to the New World, an immigrant woman said: 'Father [a former sojourner] wanted to bring the family to America. Mother scared. Nobody here. She never come.' Such women watched their children come of age and leave for North America to marry and take on family obligations. For them, the migration system and the myth of 'America' meant only loneliness and broken families. In other cases, husbands who chose to stay in Canada did not send for their wives in the village. Some women made the decision to emigrate in spite of their husbands. They mortgaged property or borrowed passage money from relatives and travelled to husbands in Canada who had, perhaps, become too fond of bachelorhood or found other female companionship.

Children born in the old country mirrored the reactions of their mothers in many ways. They regretted leaving behind all that was familiar and had little comprehension of the political and ethnic despair that was an unspoken factor in most adults' decision to leave Macedonia. One respondent remembered her disappointment at being called to live in the New World instead of Bulgaria, a country touted as free from Turkish or Greek oppression, but near and familiar. Many young migrants feared meeting their fathers again or for the first time. The tradition of migration had made some men a fleeting presence or strangers to their offspring. Children, unlike their mothers, did have a resilience that helped them face the new situations of migration. On the voyage to Canada, one village child started a lifelong love of films from watching the movies that were being shown; another dreamed of climbing the ship's stacks.[2]

SELECTION, MIGRATION, AND MARRIAGE

The majority of bachelor settlers chose to write to their families, asking them to select and dispatch acceptable girls. Characteristics and attributes demanded for Old World unions now became the stuff of New World marriages. Prospective brides were expected to be chaste and come from families of good reputation; as residents of Zhelevo argued, 'Even when you choose a dog it must be from good stock.' They also had to demonstrate a flair and capacity for hard work. Gina Petroff's hard work at the riverside (for example, fetching water, washing clothes) and in the fields during planting and harvesting made her one family's choice as a bride for its son, a barber thousands of miles away in Toronto's Junction area. Similarly, Tina Vassil found herself sent as bride-to-be to an East End restaurateur. Her diligence and good nature so impressed the restaurateur's landowning family that it was willing to overlook the sins of her father, stripped of his share of the family holdings because of his marriage to a Greek.[3]

Few, if any, girls immigrated on their own initiative to seek their fortunes or find a husband. A Macedonian village woman went from being a man's daughter to being another man's wife. Fathers – and husbands-to-be – wanted their women to stay within these perimeters, and older females abetted this system of a male-centred society. Female conduct was monitored; men made their thoughts and expectations known. Preparing to leave for Toronto, Gina Petroff was cautioned by her father: '[You] find some trouble, the boy don't want you, I can take you home when you come. But if it's trouble from you, you say I don't want this boy, I'll go home, I'll gonna put your head in the stove.' A woman who is reputed to have declared on her arrival at Union Station, 'So this is the country where the men work and the women are bosses!' was immediately bundled back on the train and sent home by her aghast fiancé. Believing that the New World held many temptations and dangerous freedoms and opportunities for their womenfolk, thinking men felt that they had good reason to worry.[4] Moreover, to the extent that women had worked as field hands in the old country and the men emulated comitadjiis, like a warrior class, there were adjustments to be made in Canada.

The young women who were selected as brides remember making their way to the New World in a state of combined fear and happiness. They were glad to escape political turbulence, the unwanted attentions or brutalities of billeted Greek soldiers, and back-breaking farm chores. They also feared marrying men whom they knew about, usually from fellow villagers, but did not know personally. As a Junction bride re-called: 'When I came over here [Toronto] I'm lost. I never know even my husband. I know his people, but I never know him.' Many tears were shed between Cherbourg and Halifax.[5]

The women journeyed to the New World over well-worn chain and travel routes. Indeed, the business of bringing out brides became just that, allowing some men to make money as go-betweens. These guides were men who had the time and opportunity to travel along the Toronto-to-villages communications network. Many possessed English-language skills and Canadian final citizenship papers, both of which facilitated flow along the migration route. Stavro Gemandoff, a West End slaughterhouse worker, took up the role shortly after losing an arm in a stockyard accident. The small service fees paid by waiting husbands and fiancés to Stavro for going back and forth to Macedonia to shepherd out prospective brides tided him over until he was able to take up light duties at the slaughterhouse again.

Such go-betweens guided women through the train stations and port cities of Europe. Gemandoff escorted Gina Petroff – 'like a little child going to buy candy' – and a friend from Bobista to the Junction. The teenaged brides-to-be had never been outside their village area. This flow of human cargo suggests the size, complexity, and precision of the 'mental map' of the Macedonian sojourners and settlers. Other go-be-tweens worked only the North American port cities, escorting wives and brides-to-be from Halifax and Ellis Island in New York to the inland settlements. Using the Hotel Balkan in New York City as his temporary base of operations, Vasil Trenton, a Toronto restaurateur and part-time go-between, arranged with officials of the 'Canadian Office' to escort twelve women from Ellis Island to Toronto.[6]

Most of the newcomers got a rude introduction to Toronto after the clean and open spaces of the village – smoke, grime, and identical squa-lid and box-like houses greeted them as they met urban industrial life and Canadian society head on. A new bride arriving in the West End summed up her first impressions: 'Most houses look same to me, only [the] numbers are different.' A woman who came to join her brothers in Toronto was appalled at having to inhabit a 'shack on Tecumseth [Street].' In Zhelevo, she had lived in a six-room house with two bal-conies, paid for with the money that her migrant father had earned in the New World. Female Macedonian newcomers often demonstrated a critical sense and eye to match that of the city's medical officer of health, Dr Charles Hastings. Seasoned sojourners, men who had worked in or near European towns and cities, accepted matter-of-factly the less attractive aspects of the new urban way of life.

For the brides-to-be, marriage took place soon after arrival. (One can only wonder whether being reunited with husbands after a decade apart was only slightly less traumatic for those married before the sojourn.) In the Old World, weddings – elaborate, week-long celebra-tions – included processions and receptions held by the parents of the bride and groom. In Toronto, lengthy ritual gave way to the demands of urban life and the workplace; there evolved a spartan custom of a one-day celebration. Married on a Sunday, a Junction barber opened his shop for business on Monday morning. An affluent East End butcher and his wife honeymooned by taking evening drives after work. Most weddings were conducted either at SS Cyril and Methody, in the church itself and the parish hall, or at residences, with the priest in attendance, in the three settlement areas. As late as 1930, Christo Andonoff married Vena Christova in his home. In times – not infre-quent – when there was no priest at SS Cyril and Methody or when theological politics flared, Macedonians wed at Christ the Saviour (Russian) Orthodox Cathedral, on Manning Street. In June 1922, for example, steelworker Lambo George of King Street East married Marie Christova there. At most weddings, guests and friends of the couple prepared simple foods for the reception. Celebrants danced to the music of a gramaphone or of the gaida, the native pipes, if an accomplished player were present.[7]

Photographs of early Macedonian-Canadian wedding parties are instructive. They record the community in transition – a settlement process under way. The group, though top-heavy with men, usually includes some women and children. New households and new families affected all those in the ethnic group, not just the contracting parties. For fellow villagers, at least, endogamous marriage in Canada confirmed something akin to a community of extended family. The photographs also document changes in clothing and outward appearance. The brides may wear a Canadian-style wedding dress, not traditional bridal clothes. Knowledgeable friends or relatives took them shortly after arrival to the downtown department stores to make their quick and inexpensive selections. 'Who's going to see you dressed like a gypsy?' they were told. The men in the photos, with moustaches either trimmed or shaved off, demonstrate their willingness to embrace the way of the Anglo-Canadian 'sports' for at least a day by wearing suits and ties. Thus the attire and the tempered but happy celebrations tell us something of the intricate shifting of mental gears, the complex interplay of adjustment, accommodation, and maintenance.[8]

There were variations on the selection and marriage process. Macedonians from the United States came north to marry Toronto-based women either at the church or at the home of friends or relatives. Andrew Demitroff of New York City, for example, arrived to marry a Queen Street West resident in 1929. In 1930, a Toronto woman, Milko Kirigieva, married Phillip Purdoff of Milwaukee in a ceremony performed by the priest of SS Cyril and Methody at an East End residence. Some US-bound brides-to-be had been stranded in Toronto by changing American immigration laws; others were misdirected there by steamship companies. Some Macedonian men who came from 'Lower America' were redressing such failures of the migration chain. Others were acting on intelligence from fellow villagers in the Balkans and North America about eligible candidates as mates.

Ranging throughout the continent for brides seemed natural and perfectly suitable for men who spoke of Toronto and Chicago's Wabash train station in the same breath, as we have seen from Malincheff's phrasebook. These marriages tell us a lot about group linkage; they were yet another set of bonds that formed between the Macedonians of 'Upper and Lower America.' Along with village ties and an increasingly distinct Macedonian-Canadian identity, immigrant society had a continental aspect. The activities of the Macedonian Political (later Patriotic) Organization (MPO) from 1921 reinforced this sense of a common Macedonian community in the New World.

There were also a few out-marriages to Anglo-Canadians and members of other ethnic groups. SS Cyril and Methody's marriage register for 1916 records the union of a Macedonian chocolate maker to Miss Dorothy Burton of the Church of England. In 1923 a resident of King Street East wed a Polish girl, Mary Lenin. There were naturally more out-marriages contracted by Macedonians who lived in Toronto's hinterlands. For example, in 1924 Nicolas Blagoi of Guelph married a fellow resident, Helen Grand Dunlop. This and other ceremonies were conducted in Toronto in the presence of Macedonian and Anglo-Canadian witnesses. One interesting variation was the 1915 marriage of a Macedonian tailor, resident in Toronto, to Gladys Knox of the village of Inglewood, Ontario. The couple wed in Inglewood in a ceremony conducted jointly by a Church of England minister, Frank Herman, and the priest of SS Cyril and Methody, Archimandrite Theophilact.

Did marrying out mean leaving the group identity? Certainly the Macedonian community did not show any official or theological hostility to any outsider married within its church. No ethnic barriers had to be lowered or overcome from the Macedonian side, especially given the small pool of eligible Macedonian females. It is hard to detail the nature and scale of slippage. SS Cyril and Methody's records, of course, do not tell us of civil ceremonies or weddings conducted in other churches without Macedonian clergy present. If slippage was seen as a serious cause for group concern, it does not seem to have penetrated the consciousness of the memory culture or writings and notations of the priests and members of the church's executive committees.

Did the bridegrooms in these out-marriage unions possess a greater sense of social mobility, an earlier formed and deeper commitment to things Canadian? Maybe so. Oral respondents remembered how proud some men were to have married urban Anglo-Canadian working women, milliners and clerks. It was seen as some sort of act of mobility. One respondent recalled that men who married outside the group 'used to think they were much smarter because these women would marry them.'

Macedonians who left Toronto for the hinterland felt less community coherence and were more likely to have unencumbered encounters with women of other ethnic backgrounds. Decisions to marry outside the group, and efforts to marry within the church in the company of friends and family, speak to a Macedonian-ness as well as the church's commitment to life and survival in the New World.[9]

FAMILY-RUN BOARDING-HOUSES

Like all greenhorns, the newly immigrated womenfolk had little time for reflection. Each had the private task of coming to grips with mates whom they sometimes barely knew and an ambience totally foreign to them. They were required to adjust quickly and take their place in the family as an efficient economic unit. The arrival of women affected the bachelor households and the sojourning way of life. The boarding-house was an unsuitable residence for newly married couples. One man's story is typical: he left a boarding-house at Keele and St Clair West and, with his new wife, found a flat on nearby Mulock Avenue. He remained close to work and to his fellow villagers but, by taking a wife and moving into a flat, removed himself from both the migrant and bachelor ranks. Women who joined men who already ran functioning bachelor boarding-houses were more often than not expected to become part of the operation.

Family-run boarding establishments began to appear everywhere in the settlement areas. They varied in size. Families appear to have housed anywhere from one to ten boarders, depending on the couple's energy, business commitment, and ethnic network, as well as the size of their building. Boarders began to reside with families in four- or five-room houses on quiet side streets. This pattern began to replace the earlier sojourner pattern of renting collectively big old houses on main streets. Two boarders – one a restaurant worker, the other a Queen Street peanut vendor – shared a house on Tracy Street with a confectioner's family of five. The men occupied the living-room; the boarders slept in two bedrooms upstairs and on couches in the dining-room.[10]

Men were also housed in cramped upper and back residence rooms on streets such as King and Queen East, sites of immigrant businesses and commercial enterprises. Living in a three- or four-room flat above his store, a King East clothing merchant and his family took in boarders, too. Whether such a practice was to maximize income or from a sense of fellow-feeling for the bachelors is difficult to ascertain. The profit motive was rarely absent, but the sense of ethnic fraternalism usually pervaded as well. Occupying the smaller rooms, the family chose to rent out the larger to the boarders.

Boarders were also found in the larger Macedonian residences. Men occupied the third floor of a house on Wyatt Avenue in the city's East End. In the Junction, seven or eight boarders shared rooms on the second and third floors of a nine-room house on Keele Street. In the same building, barber and grocer Noe Petroff and his wife slept in the front room on the second floor – the first floor contained the kitchen, dining-room, and barber shop – while their friends Mr and Mrs Steve Gemandoff also occupied a room on the second floor.[11]

Life in the boarding-house was complex; it was a household, both structured and informal, and it was also a well-organized business enterprise. Payment was expected and made for services rendered. Services offered reflected both the demands of the men and the priorities and responsibilities of the operators and boarding-house–keepers. Many women prepared meals for boarders, washed their clothing, and provided fresh linen and frequent bed changes. One East End woman also performed banking duties, depositing in the men's accounts pay packets entrusted to her. In the Junction, Gina Petroff and her friend Mrs Gemandoff cleaned and dusted for their boarders. They also changed their linen, but they did not cook for the men. It appears that the men enjoyed doing this; they appreciated freedom in the choice and preparation of food. One resident was particularly known for his ability to pickle peppers – treats that he sometimes shared with his boarding 'missus.' If the system had any drawbacks, they were more often the result of crowding and pre-urban modes of thinking than of personal or economic conflict. The toilet in one house was frequently blocked as a result of the men's efforts to flush away spare-rib bones and other food scraps.[12]

That family–operated boarding-houses were very much a business is reflected in the selection and choice of boarders. In the beginning, boarding-houses operated as a logical extension of village and kinship ties. An East End Zhelevtsi catered to the New World needs of her relatives and fellow villagers. Summing up her mother's philosophy, a respondent said, 'You're trying to help out so he [a fellow villager] can set somewhere too.' Later, when two women, from Bobista and Zagoricheni, took on household duties for boarding men from different villages, including Smerdesh, Vumbul, and Zeleniche, they did so as their contribution to their family's earning power as a unit. No other obligations of kinship or village were involved.

The residents carefully monitored the outlay of expenses and the integrity of the boarding-house–keepers. The parsimonious use of coal by an East End keeper was recalled by her daughter: 'She didn't dare use a bit more coal because everything went halfers with the boarders.' Junction men placed money under their pillows to determine whether the operators were honest while doing their daily housekeeping chores. Gina Petroff recalled: 'We fix the bed, we put the five dollars where they been and when he come in the night time – used to work in the Swift – I say ... it's nothing to me ... we found 'um five dollars in your bed, we put them back over there. Next morning you gonna find some coppers on the bed. We fix the bed and leave coppers.'

Disruptions or threats to the spirit and working order of the house simply could not be tolerated. An oral respondent recalled the story of Nick 'Coca Cola,' an unsuccessful resident of a Junction boarding-house: 'Any way he been sleeping on the third floor. Not working. He never get up two days, just sleep and stay there day and night ... There's depression and nobody give work to you. So anyway they [the boarding family] they kept him for a little while over ... and they kicked out.' Carrying a blanket, Nick set up residence in one of the larger sewers near the Swift's Canadian Co. The community, despite a sense that it was just that he should be evicted, now concerned itself with his plight; the other men who met him at the Balkan Cafe humoured him and soon cajoled him into returning to the old country.[13]

When boarders dealt with expenses promptly, this type of enterprise could survive and succeed, but it was more than a business. Although families often depended on this money – for example, to help with the cost of rent and mortgages – 'we put so much roomers over there and we make a little rent and we pay the rent' – there was also much warmth between the boarders and the boarding 'missus' and her family. The men who ran the integrity tests by leaving cash around were also the ones who allowed diapers to be dried in their quarters, bought Christmas presents for the children of the house, and solicitously purchased old country–style bread to help appease the particular food cravings of a pregnant boarding 'missus'.[14]

But good feelings coexisted with personal tension and human difficulties. 'Older boarders were called uncle by the young women who, after marriage to a boarding-boss, found themselves wives and keepers of boarders.' The use of such terms was respectful, but it also helped establish household decorum. The term 'uncle' was also used by the children of the boarding operators. The etiquette mirrored an ordering of proprieties about sexual relations. The selection of boarders was often made carefully by a young husband uncomfortable with the economic necessity that made him bring other males into his household. Recalling his father quietly sizing up potential residents, a man said, 'You get a young women into a place with ten roomers, my father would pick.'[15]

The arrival of brides, wives, and families brought change as well to such sojourner and bachelor-settler institutions as the coffee-house. The proprietors of such places had little choice but to accept the presence of families in the community. The owner of an eatery in Ann Arbor, Michigan, advised his customers to 'Keep Your Wife As Pet' and to continue eating at the Buffalo Lunch. To cater to the new situation, the International Restaurant in Toronto held weekly family nights in summer. The Balkan Cafe in the Junction and the East End's Geneva Restaurant remained male strongholds and sought the business of the remaining bachelor settlers, new arrivals, and family men on a night out. Most husbands and fathers found time for an occasional visit to their former haunts but revelled in normal family life. A Junction resident was only too happy to eat his wife's cooking after a steady diet of Balkan Cafe food. The proprietor's annoying habit of scooping out daily specials, such as macaroni and cheese, with his bare hands – after stroking his pet cat – often made dinner a less than enjoyable experience.[16]

GETTING THEIR BEARINGS

Women built their new world around the stores, hospitals, and neighbourhood clinics so central to their domestic role and duties; their sense of focal points differed from the men's, and from that of their children, too, as they matured. Women became city-wise on their own. One West End woman ran some distance after a streetcar before she realized that there were designated stops. A first trip to the city's major department stores at Yonge and Queen streets became almost a rite of passage; women longer in the colony baptized newcomers into the Macedonian class structure and 'store-bought' consumer society. A Niagara Street resident remembered moving endlessly between her home and the Hospital for Sick Children, as illness and poverty affected her offspring: 'Take one child [in] bring the other home.' As wives of businessmen, or if they themselves offered a special skill or service such as midwifery, they came to view themselves and their geographical presence in terms of business or 'professional' obligations.

A woman's understanding of the city was affected also by her and her family's nationalist sense. In the 1920s and afterwards, loyal attendance at annual conventions of the Macedonian Political Organization (MPO) drew many people to various North American urban centres and so expanded their sense of the Macedonian diaspora. For example, Toronto butcher Lamb (Louis) Tenekeff and his family went to all such conventions as Toronto delegates. In contrast, a number of women used their children and husbands to deal with the New World. They dispatched men to do the shopping, enrol children at school, and so on. For such women, Canada amounted to little more than the street on which they lived.[17]

Macedonian women also got their bearings by comparing their situations with those of people around them. In the Old World, Macedonian women had distinct social and economic roles, obligations, and restrictions. As Christian village women, they had assessed their lives in the context of the Vlach mountain women, the Greek and Jewish town women, and the veiled Turkish wives around them. They knew that there were many ways of being a woman – roles to accept and reject, status to aspire to or refuse.

As their new lives took shape in Toronto's three settlement areas, Macedonian families cast a critical and evaluative eye on themselves and the non-Macedonians around them. Women took stock and compared themselves with others as mothers and housekeepers. They believed that they were more concerned and involved in the lives of their children than Anglo-Canadian mothers were. A Macedonian mother was 'more warm for the kids. The mother dies for the kids. The English don't like their children that much.' Macedonians clucked and were suspicious of the morals of Polish and Ukrainian women who worked in factories; they saw Polish and Ukrainian men as hard workers – a positive trait – but also brawlers and heavy drinkers. Macedonians also saw themselves as good and efficient housekeepers with a commitment to cleanliness that pleased both landlords – 'she [landlord] look around ... her new house clean. First time the house clean' – and visiting public health nurses. In *Cabbagetown*, novelist Hugh Garner gives an interesting account of 'European immigrant women' who aired their mattresses and 'washed down their front porches and steps every day.' He was writing about Toronto's East End Macedonians.

The immigrant women prided themselves, often long after economic justification for such parsimony was gone, on how carefully they could budget and still put out a good meal for their family. Macedonian children were always clothed adequately, even if their garments were often crafted out of the adults' used clothing. The memory culture recalls that some other ethnic groups were not as concerned with this. Items like bedsheets and curtains were made from flour and sugar sacks provided by family and restaurateurs. First cut and split along their seams, sacks were then washed and bleached; these prepared pieces were joined together to make different sizes of clothes and sheets. Macedonian women were thus proud of their ability to survive, if not thrive, in poverty, when compared with non-Macedonians.[18]

What emerged in Toronto was neither a father-dominant nor a mother-centred household. Gender roles were distinct, but authority and duty in the family were fluid or blurred, since they related to the constantly changing ethnoculture itself. Although women stayed out of the coffee-houses and nationalist debates, they played an active and often opinionated role in the running of family enterprises and households. No one of the immigrant generation questioned that the nuclear family should be a single economic and entrepreneurial unit; it was, however, more often 'a joint stock company' than a venture owned and run by the male family head.

Macedonian-Canadian children in the first Canadian generation generally accepted the immigrant's view of family roles and elaborated upon them. They were proud of and secure in the fact that their mothers were always home and available. Living above or behind the family shop or restaurant meant that working women could also be at home. At the same time, however, Macedonian children were envious of the freedom and lack of parental supervision enjoyed by the offspring of working parents from other ethnic groups. They appreciated and respected fathers who went to work early in the morning and returned late at night.

Formation of a child's sense of the community began early. Visits to the church on special family and religious occasions and socializing with parents around the three settlement areas effectively taught children Toronto's Macedonian geography. While growing up, a child forged a unique set of bonds with the area in which he or she lived. The street, the school, and its playground all conspired to make children of the Junction, Niagara Street, and Cabbagetown identify with those areas in ways that their parents did not. The offspring of Macedonians who lived outside Toronto developed their own sense of the relationship among settlement, space, and ethnicity. At first their understanding of Toronto and the community at large was generally limited, based on occasional or special forays to the city. Changes came when their parents moved to the city, or they themselves moved to Toronto as young adults to work.

First-generation Macedonian children were raised in households that operated as a single work and financial unit. With parents running a boarding-house, shop, or restaurant, or fathers working long hours in factories, young people quickly entered the work world. Children were expected to shop and carry out other duties. One man remembered his dealings as a boy with Macedonian merchants at King and Wilkins Avenue: 'I would do the shopping with [a] wagon [and] $5.00. [I'd] go from store to store [and] check the price [of] beans, cheese, whole wheat, olives.' He and other children culled unburnt coal from the Consumers' Gas Co. yard. Parents expected them to be at the yard by 5 a.m. each and every day in order to be assured of a good collection. A woman recalled her efforts and those of her sister: 'We'd go home and we'd dump that [the first load]. If we had time we'd go back for another load. If we didn't, we'd go home and get washed up and get set for school.'

As they got older, children got either summer jobs or work after school. The offspring of entrepreneurs joined their parents at the restaurant or store. They washed dishes, served at the counter, waited on tables. A daughter of a community steamship agent worked in the agency as a file clerk after school. A butcher's daughter helped to grind meat and lost a finger in the process. The children of factory workers went to work either in the establishments of family friends or relatives or in non-Macedonian businesses in the neighborhood. All were expected either to go without a wage per se or to be willing to turn over any pay that they earned. A woman who once worked in both the family enterprise (a candy store) and a factory stated: 'We [the family] got the store. [I] didn't get no money there. It all went to the family – even the pay from the factory I turned over to my parents. They gave me 50¢ a week out of a total pay of $12.00 ... They bought my clothes.'[19]

Work and the responsibilities that it brought led older children and teenagers to see the settlement area and city as their fathers did – in terms of Macedonian settlement and work. For the families of shopkeepers and restaurateurs, entering the labour force often meant travelling only from the family living quarters to the store downstairs or in the front of the house. Even a short trip to responsibility, however, cast the neighbourhood in a different light. Young workers started thinking in terms of distance to work, its relationship to housing, time lost travelling, and the comfort of neighbourhoods lived in or passed through. Storekeepers' children learned to think about and appeal to clientele, both Macedonian and Anglo-Canadian. Was it better to put ham and eggs on a menu than sausage and peppers? Which passers-by on a street in the East End each day could be lured in for lunch?

Dating and marriage complicated images of the environs still further. The desire that their children date and marry within the Macedonian group meant that most parents encouraged them to go to the church to meet and mingle at various social events. Working children could now cover transportation costs on their own. Niagara Street and Junction parents who had previously felt that they could not afford the time or transportation costs for weekly attendance at church services or Bulgarian school now exhibited different priorities for their young people. They did all they could to foster marriage within the group, even sharing willingness to attend youth events as chaperones. Maintenance of identity and survival of the ethnic group were all-important – high enough stakes to overcome problems of space and distance.

Marriage began not only to cross Macedonian village lines but also to unite the peoples and local histories of the three settlements. When a Junction man wed a woman from the Niagara Street district, new links were created between the settlement areas. Questions of residence arose and were resolved. A Niagara Street woman moved to the Junction; she and her husband had obligations to in-laws in each neighbourhood. Views of Macedonian Toronto thus shifted, changed, and developed. At the same time, as in this case, the marriage linked villagers from Bobista, Oshchima, and Zhelevo, thus strengthening the larger identity, that of being a Macedonian, both in terms of the ethnic group as a minority in Canada and in terms of a more national consciousness about the Balkan homeland.[20]

RENTING AND BUYING PROPERTY

The arrival of families after the First World War launched a profound change in Macedonian attitudes about housing. The 1920s and 1930s witnessed the heyday and the decline of the family-run boarding operation. By the late 1930s, many such establishments had outlived their usefulness – boarders left because they had gotten married and were starting their own households. Even die-hard bachelors left, finding more comfortable private space with non-Macedonians elsewhere.

Once a man made the decision to strike out on his own, he might enter rooming-houses or take a single room, often in Anglo-Canadian or Jewish households. Macedonian slaughterhouse workers in the Junction, for example, rented quarters in Jewish households on Maria Street. Malincheff/Theophilact's *First Bulgarian-English Pocket Dictionary* (1913) taught many men how to make proper inquiries of a prospective landlord:

Good morning, lady
I want to rent a room.
How much do you want per week?
Alright, sir. Please come in
I would like to see the rooms
Have you a front room for rent?
rear room quiet room
not very expensive
I want a small room
I don't like this room
I will move in tonight
Where is the water closet?
Please, give me the key.[21]

Prospective boarders, essential for the enterprise, declined drastically in number because of new immigration restrictions and the Depression. The Depression also caused the boarding-house business to go underground, at least when the family running a place was also collecting relief. One respondent vividly remembered the need to 'take the bed apart so they [city welfare officials] wouldn't know we had a roomer' each time a welfare worker was seen making his or her way up towards the house on Adelaide Street West. Families that had kept successful boarding-houses changed their housing and income pattern as the business declined. For example, in the late 1930s, Noe and Gina Petroff bought a smaller house in the Junction, not just to avoid the rising rent on their nine-room boarding-house but because they were left with only one rather than seven or eight boarders by then.

   Few Macedonians had sought purposely to acquire Toronto property in the early sojourning period. Sojourners did not want to own property, to spend large amounts of money, and to make the kind of commitment and responsibility that ownership caused. A group of Niagara Street sojourners had a chance at one time to buy for $700 the house in which they were living. They knew that it was a reasonable and attractive offer but felt that the purchase would bind them to Canada and make them 'forget home.' Ownership of residential property lacked the central importance for Macedonians that it acquired for other immigrant groups. The reason was not lack of initiative, but rather the practical extreme of initiative. The guiding priorities of many were summed up in the proverb: 'A business generated income and financial returns; it was a productive entity. Houses – unless boarders were added – demanded too much upkeep and attention to tenants and so on. Like barns, they always needed tending and filling.'[22]

Well into the 1920s, and even later, many Macedonian labourers and entrepreneurs preferred to rent accommodations. As we have seen, labourers and workmen tried to minimize the cost of rent by taking in boarders. In that sense, the easy distinction that North American historians of mobility and labour historians make between unskilled worker and entrepreneur is, at best, naïve. Many families also chose to share living quarters and expenses with relatives and friends. A house on Mulock Street was shared by three Macedonian families; each paid rent of ten dollars a month. A Macedonian soap-factory worker and his wife shared a house on Niagara Street at Wellington with their friends, two couples.

A commercial enterprise, with families living in the rented quarters above the store or restaurant, was seen as a shrewd way to live and work in the city – much preferable to mere ownership of a family homestead and a daily trek to work for someone else. Such entrepreneurs also tried to share the burden of rent with boarders, relatives, or business partners and their families. A King Street East haberdasher and his family shared the three or four rooms above the store with boarders. Two energetic partners in a Keele Street restaurant shared their living quarters above the eatery with at least ten men; three of the men were employed by Gunn's, and a spinner worked at the York Knitting Mills. Only a very subtle eye could notice and understand the differences in contractual terms and personal freedoms that made those quarters neither a boarding-house nor a hotel, but a shared rental.

As in the boarding-houses, this sharing of housing and of living quarters brought on human tensions and personal disagreements. Three couples who shared a house in the West End disbanded when the women 'started [acting] kind of funny; [they] never got along together.' Couples even split when their children did not get along. An angry Mr and Mrs Steve Gemandoff left the bungalow that they had shared with Noe Petroff and his wife after their young sons fought and proved sadly incompatible – 'the kids will kill each other.' Maybe as the young acculturated, they simply could not feel or understand the same mutual need and ethnic bond that their parents did.[23]

As circumstances began to change in the 1920s and 1930s, many Macedonians bought property, symbolic of a new attitude towards Canada. Both small businessmen and labourers – where that distinction can be made – did so.

The process had begun earlier. In 1913, after renting two locations, a restaurant and a dry goods store on King Street East, Naum Phillips, one of the community's steamship agents, had purchased the property and buildings where he had his dry goods store. A few men began to acquire property in the manner of Turkish beys and pashas back home; property became for them a commodity, not a patrimony. By 1913, the community banker, grocer, and one-time steamship agent Hadji D. Peroff had bought homes at 18 and 20 Eastern Avenue and a rear residence at 24 Eastern Avenue. By 1915, Peroff, in partnership with Simo Velianoff, was also a property owner and landlord on Parliament Street for fruit dealer Natale Catalino and various Macedonian tenants. That same year, merchant Tipe Tepouloff and his partners became landlords in a budding housing business, and Anglo-Canadian confectioner George F. Dowson became their first tenant, at 472–474 King Street East. By 1927, businessmen Dimitre H. Paul and Jovan Nicoloff appear as the freehold owners of a lunch-room on St Clair Avenue West and a confectionery on Mulock Street.

Businessmen bought property generally as both a dwelling and as a base for operations. Purchase of a building, especially in less residential areas, freed an entrepreneurial man or family to use the rooms and building space to maximize income in any way seen fit. One could work all day for a packing-house and at night run a smokehouse and sausage factory of one's own, preparing sujuk for favourite customers. The Petroff family, for example, bought on Keele Street a small bungalow with a big front, which could be and was effectively converted into a storefront. Mrs Petroff offered a rationale for the purchase: 'We bought them [the house] for the front and not for the house ... If we were going to buy a house we would have bought a home in Baby Point [a swank neighbourhood].'[24]

Macedonians of many occupations and income levels bought property in all three settler areas. Ever-increasing rent spurred the process. Rising rent forced one Macedonian worker and his family to abandon a house in the King-Sumach Street area. In their effort to accumulate a small pool of capital for later use in Toronto, they moved down to less attractive quarters, first to Wascana Avenue and then to Trinity Street. They eventually bought a house in the East End. Macedonians made decisions about buying or renting obviously in much the same way as neighbours from other ethnic backgrounds, but there were typically Macedonian considerations as well.[25]

Several factors affected their choice of residence and location – and whether they rented or bought – inside or outside the settlement areas. The structure of anti-immigrant prejudice served to define their choice of lodging and the availability of housing. An early Macedonian woman settler recalled with some bitterness her first and lengthy search in Toronto for a house to rent: 'Many places told me. They said, "You said you a foreigner." They slam the door.' In the Niagara Street district, angry Anglo-Canadian renters, on more than one occasion, protested when landlords sold the building in which they were renting to Macedonians – 'Why should the foreigners come and take our house?'

Commercial and residential jostlings of other ethnic groups in the Macedonian areas also could affect the choice and purchase of a house. One respondent recalled her family's aborted purchase of a house in the East End: 'He [father] bought [a] house from English people but was rented to Italians. They would not go because they used to keep bananas downstairs to [go] ripe.' Landlords' objectives influenced acquisition of housing and property. Some oral sources cite the unwillingness of owners in existing settlement areas to sell while property values were rising. Many landlords, it seems, were prepared to retain their holdings for the lucrative rewards of rumoured commercial redevelopment and institutional expansion. Corporate landlords, such as the Union Stock Yards and the Swift Canadian Co. in the West End area and the Canadian Northern Ontario Railway in the east, seemed equally unwilling to sell. Lands held by the big firms on Keele Street, St Clair Avenue West, and Eastern Avenue were withheld from the market at least for a time for company development projects.

By the late 1920s, people were willing to buy a house just as a residence, when an agreeable home started to become a status symbol. The importance of residence also shaped the group's movement to the peripheries of the settlement areas and beyond. Immigrants in the East End moved north of Queen Street East and east of the Don River; Junction residents to Fisken, Priscilla, and Willard Avenues, for example; and Niagara Street residents to the area above Queen Street West and to Parkdale. They were moving away from industry and increasingly sought distance between home and workplace. This new attitude marked the passing of one aspect of the village mentality brought from the Balkans.[26]

The original Macedonian settlement areas can barely be discerned now. In the East End, for example, commercial and industrial development has destroyed many of the little streets of working-class housing that characterized the Macedonian neighbourhood. The growth and development of housing projects such as Regent Park pushed out of the area most of those who had stayed. Two Macedonian churches stand as lonely sentinels over the northern boundary of a once-thriving neighbourhood. The community's first and second generations were being drawn by opportunity and acculturation out to suburbs as much as they were leaving because of the area's industry and decline. Since the closing of the Lake Ohrid boarding-house on Eastern Avenue, no visible Macedonian presence remains.

Macedonian neighbourhoods were then never as visible as Chinatowns or Little Italies, but in each of these three settlement areas, networks of loyalty from the Old World villages and shared New World conditions were elaborating an ethnic group. Toronto's Macedonian colony was a centre of nationalist politics and religious ferment. Few outside the group could understand how large these humble neighbourhoods loomed on the mental landscape of Macedonians everywhere in the world.

7

Cooperation and Competition

FINDING A WAY

A number of Macedonians climbed into the merchant class in Toronto through various routes. A few newcomers had been merchants or entrepreneurs in the old country. The urban experience acquainted many others with the economic opportunities that dotted the city. Many men soon realized that it would be not only more profitable to operate their own business than to toil as labourers, but also physically safer. They served part-time or full-time apprenticeships in the shops of their families and friends. Cooperation and competition with non-Macedonians helped to shape the emergent Macedonian businesses, and, as with boarding-houses, families also played a major role.

Some immigrants found the chance to use their merchandising experience in Toronto; then worked their way up. Nako Grozdanoff, for example, who had been a dry goods merchant and proprietor of the general store in Verbnik, set up as a butcher and grocer on King Street East in Toronto after a brief stint as a slaughterhouse worker at Gunn's. One young man, while he worked at a sheet-metal factory by day, helped friends run their butcher store in the evenings. He received both valuable training and a small payment in goods, such as a pound of butter or lard. Others, such as Nicola Bittoff (Bitove), Dimitar Foteff, A. Kuzoff, and A. Stavroff (Stavro), served full apprenticeships under the watchful eye of butcher Lambro (Louis) Tenekeff. Tenekeff gave them his financial and moral support when they established their own shops, and they in turn honoured their mentor and recognized the value of his good repute by adopting the name of his shop, Louis Meat Market, for their own.[1]

Prospective restaurateurs gained experience as waiters and busboys in their countrymen's restaurants. Some also worked in Greek-owned restaurants – sometimes a difficult and uncomfortable experience. One Macedonian restaurateur said about a Greek boss: 'If they know your a Macedonian, he kill you. [He] won't let you touch nothing, [won't] let you sit down or have a cigarette or coke. You have to pay for it. Pushing you, pushing you.' Greek restaurateurs became the unwitting instructors of budding Macedonian competitors. The new Macedonian owner of the Dufferin Grill, for example, sent his young son to steal the menu from a popular Greek-owned eatery in order to emulate it.[2]

Other Macedonians underwent a sort of apprenticeship running Coney Island–type hot-dog stands and confectionery stores. The Karsto Mladen Confectionery, 'about two furlongs from the clubhouse turn of the Greenwood Raceway in East End Toronto,' enlarged on its service of packaged sweets and tobacco goods by serving hot dogs, coffee, and doughnuts to neighbourhood residents and racetrack spectators. In time, its lunch counter expanded into a complete restaurant-tavern, the Mecca Steak House and Tavern. It has long served toast and coffee to racing luminaries such as E.P. Taylor, the Toronto industrialist and horse breeder.[3]

Some Macedonians became entrepreneurs partly because of their nagging fear of personal injury. After witnessing a friend lose an arm in a grinding machine, a young slaughterhouse labourer, Noe Petroff, and his friend vowed never to return to the dangerous world of the abattoir. They decided to become barbers and went for six months of formal training and instruction at the Moler Barber College. They eventually formed a partnership and opened a small shop near St Clair Avenue West and Weston Road. Another Macedonian, after almost severing a finger in an industrial accident and witnessing his first cousin lose a limb at work, sought to escape danger by opening a shoeshine parlour in the West End.[4]

Ironically, partially disabling injuries, as often as the fear of them, propelled men on to the entrepreneurial stage. Loss of an arm in a slaughterhouse accident, acceptance of the meagre compensation in a lump sum, and a successful return trip for a bride launched Stavro Gemandoff on a career as go-between and informal travel agent between Toronto and the villages of Macedonia. The city's Macedonians paid Stavro on a commission basis to oversee the travel safety and welfare of their wives and fiancées en route to Toronto. The fact that he was maimed made him especially reliable for the role.[5]

Quitting jobs as railway navvies and industrial labourers, other men, often with no relevant experience at all, simply plunged into business. Some purchased functioning businesses. The very successful merchant Dimitri Petroff had bought his store from the previous owner, grocer Henry Armstrong. Another Macedonian learned his trade as a haberdasher by entering into a partnership with an established businessman. In time, the young partner 'became a gentleman, more or less,' and struck out on his own. He dissolved the partnership and opened his own store 'a few doors up' from his ex-partner.[6]

Lack of business sense or knowledge of a given trade might hurt a young entrepreneur, but ascriptive ethnic trust in the immigrant colony often compensated. One merchant put it simply: 'If you speak the language you bring them in.' For the skills of a trade, one could always turn to non-Macedonian hired help. A West End restaurateur and his son, for instance, received considerable advice and assistance from their Chinese cook in the art of preparing a variety of hearty soups.[7]

The majority of men, however, learned through the often costly method of trial and error. Macedonian businessmen ascertained their clientele's tastes and folkways through reflection on daily requests and with the assistance of their customers. Restaurateur Vasil Trenton had his customers come behind the grill to show him the proper and money-saving preparation of steaks, fried eggs – 'Hey, break it [egg] and put in on there [grill], but don't stir it'– and cold beef sandwiches. The proprietors of the Dufferin Grill depended on neighbourhood children for the correct spelling of such menu items as pea soup and cabbage.[8]

Customers' help and learning by trial and error affected more than menus and food preparation. The owner of the CPR Barber Shop, in the heart of Toronto's Junction, was urged by his convenience-minded customers to start selling a few tinned goods in his shop. In time, the barber and his wife, encouraged by their modest success as 'grocers,' purchased and remodelled new business quarters and established a well-stocked grocery store alongside the family barber shop. Greenhorn entrepreneurs got assistance as well from the community's guidebooks and language aids. A.C. Yovcheff's *Various Bulgarian-American Letters* (1917), for example, taught men how to write a letter of recommendation for a former employee. It also explained the art of notifying customers about dissolution of a partnership, retirement or death of a partner, and changes resulting from transfer of ownership. C. Nedelkoff's *English-Bulgarian and Bulgarian-English Letters* (1911) helped men to correspond with wholesalers and distributors, make out a bill of goods, request a catalogue, and lodge an effective complaint against an error in the bill or the poor condition of shipped goods.[9]

Literacy in English and command of the written word often acted as an entrée into the non-labouring ranks. Clients were solicited by A.G. Raycoff, 'Official Interpreter Police and County Courts,' who was available to those who sought accurate service 'during the performance of any kind of case or needed assistance when dealing with companies and official departments.' East End book dealers Bistreff and Dimitroff, of 304 King East, offered a wide selection of literary works and language aids in both Bulgarian and English.[10]

While some Macedonians did indeed hawk peanuts, popcorn, and homemade confections around the city, other types of experience provided a more likely basis for entry into the business ranks. Street vendors' goods or products simply did not lend themselves to opening stable shops as dry goods did for some Jews or fruit and vegetables for some Italian pedlars. Macedonians saved up the means to open businesses through hoarding of their wages as labourers and by borrowing capital from family and friends. Men could often borrow, on trust alone, amounts ranging from one hundred to three hundred dollars from friends, relatives, or fellow villagers. Dimitri Nakeff, for example, proprietor of Jimmy's Meat Market, received financial help from his parents toward purchase of his shop and business, but few settlers had access to an older generation with savings to give them a start in North America.[11]

Few Macedonians, either as migrants or immigrants, had chosen to enter farming, but Toronto's Macedonian restaurants, groceries, and meat markets provided a market for those who did. Agricultural and seasonal work could not build savings quickly, and the Canadian countryside was cold and forbidding. A small but energetic group of farmers and their families did settle, however, near Port Hope, Ontario. These Macedonians tended livestock and practised mixed farming. They were market farmers, and Toronto's Macedonians bought their produce. They drove regularly to Toronto, selling 'all over [to] every Macedonian door.' Beans, peppers, and apples were the chief foodstuffs, along with farm-fresh feta cheese and buttermilk for Macedonian butchers and grocers, such as Dimitri Nakeff of Jimmy's Meat Market.[12]

Because the West End settlements emerged after the East End, they did not develop the same enterprise system. They had neither a Macedonian steamship agent nor banker. Junction and Niagara Street businesses did, however, serve sojourners, settlers, and non-Macedonian residents. Macedonians in the Junction, especially around Keele Street, ran diners and cafés, groceries and barber shops, most of them started during the First World War or shortly afterwards. By the late 1930s, Macedonian establishments were lined along Keele Street between Junction Road and St Clair Avenue West, among them the CPR Barbershop and George Petroff Grocery Market Lunch, the Balkan Cafe, the Stock Yard Lunch, and the Step-In Lunch.

An analysis of the clientele sought and served there helps explain the world of immigrant enterprise. The Junction's lunch-rooms, barber shops, and groceries, and the Exchange Hotel, a non-Macedonian venture, served primarily the farmers who came to town to strike deals with stockyard and meat-packing officials, cattle dealers, supervisors, and bosses of the railways and slaughterhouses. All those engaged in livestock commerce had the money and leisure to buy their lunches or wait in the barber's chair.

The labourers of Junction industries carried lunch pails and patronized the George Petroff Grocery, where they could buy such supplements to cold sandwich lunches as milk, pop, cigarettes, ice cream, and meat pies. Nearby, the Balkan Cafe catered exclusively and without apology to Macedonian sojourners and settlers. It was a coffee-house, meeting-place, and restaurant, although well-run boarding-houses and budget-conscious immigrant wives did limit the number of meals purchased. (Macedonian restaurants and groceries in the Niagara Street–Wellington Street area had a more ethnically varied clientele. They provided meal tickets and daily lunches to carry to work for many of the Polish and Lithuanian boarders who inhabited that factory district.)[13]

The entrepreneurial base of the Macedonians in the Junction included a few butcher shops. Slaughterhouse employees were allowed to select and purchase meats for themselves and their friends during the course of a working day. With a network extending from slaughterhouses to many small restaurants, Macedonians became involved in wholesale meat supply and street vending, but the Depression limited their mobility in this occupation. The proprietor of a Dundas Street West hot-dog stand summed up his difficulties: '[The] hot dogs are turning green; [I] keep turning them in water. [I] throw the coffee away'.[14]

The Macedonian presence in Toronto did not go unnoticed by other small businesses in the three settlement areas. Canadian entrepreneurs, for example, tried to win the settlers' patronage. J.H. Greenshields, an East End grocer (at King East and Berkeley), broke traditional store etiquette by allowing Macedonians to move about the place on their own, picking and choosing items on the shelves and counters. This system not only approximated open market shopping in the Balkans but also overcame a language barrier between merchant and clientele. When Mr Pacini, a St Clair Avenue West merchant of 'Fancy Fruits and Olive Oil,' and the proprietors of Manonis Italiano Cheese on Bloor Street West advertised in the Macedonians' nationalist political almanacs, they did so not only in search of customers but also in support of a cause important to their customers.[15]

The corollary was also true, as Macedonian entrepreneurs made comparable adjustments (such as choice of foodstuffs and range of butcher services) to attract and serve as many as possible of the area's non-Macedonians. The opening of the George Petroff Grocery was much appreciated by Junction neighbourhood women, especially those who were sick – 'One, she got asthma' – or elderly, for they would no longer have to run to Dundas Street West to make their daily and emergency purchases. The establishment of the Commissioner's Lunch on Cherry Street brought Macedonian business and food skills to the heart of the East End harbour industrial district and catered to the many needs of appreciative truck drivers, taking on the character of its customers. It was open only during factory hours and half-days Saturday.[16]

FAMILY BUSINESSES

The arrival of Macedonian women and children in Toronto after the First World War reinvigorated the 'traditional way of looking at things that made all family members try to make money.' Macedonian women in the old country had reared children; baked breads and pastries and made large quantities of butter and cheese; prepared and spun sheep and goats' wool; sewed and mended garments; bred stock and also raised chickens, lambs, and goats; and planted and harvested wheat, hay, tomatoes, peppers, and potatoes, working the fields primarily by hand and hoe (the men alone used plough and scythe). All these activities had minimized use of cash, brought in money, and defined the family's economic status. Women particularly skilled in knitting or embroidering had often produced clothing for other village families; creation of a trousseau – bridal linens and embroidered shirts and handkerchiefs – had provided the optimum challenge to the women's patience, energy, and skills. Poor harvests had sometimes led the women of Tersie to obtain additional employment as harvesters on the more affluent holdings of a Turkish landowner.

With mass migration, women's roles changed. They might supervise the family property and do heavier labour, plough or manage hired help, and conduct family business outside the village. Tight social control of their movement eased, and trips to neighbouring centres increased in number and frequency. For example, groups of women from Tersie led horses bearing chopped wood to city markets for sale – work previously done by men.[17]

Macedonian women were ready to work when they arrived in Toronto, as chapter 6 makes clear. Some of them became boarding-house–keepers. Young brides oversaw the resources of the house, cooked meals, washed clothes, scrubbed floors, and tended to other family and tenants' needs. Through collecting boarding and rent money and by minimizing household expenses, women helped to build their families' income. The wives of storekeepers also assisted their husbands at work. At first shy and lacking a working command of the English language, they found it difficult to deal with strangers and with business practice. Describing her first attempts to help her husband in the family grocery store, a woman recalled: 'That time everyone worked with scales and pencil. I wasn't very fast in counting. Then my husband bought a cash register for me and then we was both happy.' Only sheer persistence and great effort allowed immigrant wives to succeed. Over time many seemed to usurp their husbands as chief proprietor of a small business or free him for other business or leisure activities. The wife of one West End shoeshine-parlour operator made herself indispensable by mastering the art of cleaning and blocking hats. Another woman managed the family's haberdashery business so well that her husband was freed to work at the A.F. Schnaufer fur and dye works to supplement the family income. The wife of a West End barber and grocer, as she learned English, made it possible for her husband to concentrate on his barbering duties while she took charge of the grocery's everyday operations. She served customers during the factories' lunch breaks, ordered and arranged an endless stream of tobacco, refreshments, and confectionery supplies, and made trips to the nearby slaughterhouses with a wagon in tow to purchase ice-blocks for the store's cooler.[18]

Macedonian women generally did not enter domestic service – an occupation that drew other female immigrants – in part as a result of recruiting practices. Responding to the demand for servants, the National Council of Women, the Young Women's Christian Association, and church organizations in Britain and Canada recruited almost exclusively British and Scandinavian girls. They probably considered southeastern Europeans unsuitable. Few Macedonian women came to

Toronto except as brides and wives, and their menfolk found ample scope for their productive energies within the family entrepreneurial unit.[19]

The growing movement of Macedonians from factory work to keeping shops and restaurants offered many opportunities for younger members of the family as well. Parental pressure and economic necessity forced children to obtain summer and after-school work. Many young boys and girls served as attendants in family-owned shoeshine parlours or as dishwashers, sometimes doubling as translators, in family restaurants. The daughter of an East End butcher remembered working from a very young age at her father's store after school each day and every Saturday. She would arrange foodstuffs on the counter, take cash, and place pieces of meat in the grinder, a task that eventually robbed her of a finger.

Macedonian children, especially those of factory workers, found work at larger businesses owned by relatives or fellow villagers. Youngsters at Davenport Public School were earning two and one-half cents a line as pinboys at M.T. Bunda's West End bowling alley. After completing the compulsory eight grades, many young people moved into the permanent labour force. 'It has naturally been the case at Sackville Street School,' a *Toronto Star* journalist noted sadly in 1916, 'that a large proportion of the children drop out at fourteen years of age and go to work.' Financial need triumphed over eagerness to learn and over assimilation. Many Macedonian breadwinners were of high-school age. Many a boy who wanted to continue studying succumbed to parental pressure and went to work to assist his parents at family candy stores, hot-dog stands, and restaurants.[20]

Those unmarried daughters who did join the work-force found employment in the city's meat-packing houses. At the William Davies Co., one woman was involved in the production of sausage casings, fancy pickles, and olives. Macedonian women did join the needle trades, though on a much smaller scale than Jews or Italians. At the Beaver Cloak Co., York Knitting Mills, and Joseph Simpson and Sons, they fashioned sweaters, coats, and buttonholes. Some young women worked in factories often because of economic necessity; working in the stores and shops of their husbands and fathers perhaps seemed more natural. But a countervailing opinion held that a woman's place was in the home, preparing for marriage or performing the duties of wife and mother. One immigrant woman recalled bitterly the stinging criticism that she received from a friend working in her husband's shoeshine parlour. She was chastened for not remaining home and accused of wantonly seeking the attentions of her male customers.[21]

Few first-generation Macedonians went on to complete high school and enter university; the cultural and economic incentives, unless one broke completely with the ethnoculture, were simply not there. Those who were able to did so as a result of great personal determination, academic achievement, and exceptional parental support. One young man recalled: 'I got no support at home ... The whole load fell on my shoulders.' He sustained his educational desire alone. Fiercely determined, he completed undergraduate and graduate degrees in engineering at the University of Toronto. Another informant credited the model of outstanding teachers at Jarvis Collegiate and natural ability in mathematics for his decision to go to university despite parental protests. By the late 1930s and the 1940s, some Macedonian women were attending commercial and secretarial schools after high school and became secretaries and stenographers. In general, the community remained remarkably impervious to higher education 'among the English' and was under-represented among professional people until the third generation. Upward mobility moved many Macedonians and their families from the worst labouring conditions to a comfortable place in the merchant class – and then ceased. Most were content to expand and solidify their position within the middle classes. By 1940, some Macedonian restaurateurs, for example, owned several establishments. One built and maintained three outlets of Paul's Lunch, in both the East End and the West End.[22]

A few younger immigrants or children of immigrants – those who came of age in the late 1930s or early 1940s – made a parallel but quantum leap into the professional world and the higher levels of commerce and industry. Until then, the Macedonian professional world was comprised of two individuals, whose deep commitment to Protestantism, though atypical within the community, gave them early access to the English language and higher education, as well as entrée to the status and power of Anglo-Canadians. Encouraged by her father, who was a practising Protestant in Strumitsa, Miss Parashka Stamenova studied and taught at the American Mission School in Bitola before coming to North America. Her continuing interest in the welfare of infants and children inspired her to study paediatric nursing at a New York City hospital. After migrating to Toronto, Stamenova became a public health nurse at the invitation of the director of nursing services, who was a fellow parishioner at Jarvis Street Baptist Church and organizer of the local Health Department's ethnic community nurses. John Grudeff, a young Macedonian Protestant, after attending the American Mission School in Salonica travelled to Toronto to seek his fortune, armed with 'a polish which one receives in America after having lived there for some years.' His faith and determination gained him entry into Albert College, a Methodist institution, and, subsequently, into Victoria College and the Law School in the University of Toronto.[23]

While ambition and ability did much to further a young Macedonian's academic achievements, religious affiliation also affected educational attainment. The children of Macedonian Protestants received the dual support of both parents and Canadian society in their quest for educational and social mobility. Having attended Sunday school classes as a child at a Toronto Protestant church and mission hall, a Macedonian physician and psychiatrist vividly remembered the high level of achievement among Macedonian Protestants. Many of his classmates went on to become doctors, dentists, and lawyers. At this distance, it is difficult to know whether shared Protestantism allayed prejudice and opened doors of access not open to the Macedonian Orthodox or whether Protestant Macedonians aspired to and achieved Anglo-Canadian norms and folkways far quicker than their co-nationals.[24]

In the 1930s, as we saw in chapter 6, Macedonians began moving out of the three original settlement areas. Confidence and experience, ambition and nerve put the small entrepreneurs and restaurateurs in the forefront of that network of movement as they searched for new opportunities. Some opened businesses outside the neighbourhoods but continued to live there. While always maintaining his residence in the Niagara Street area, Alex Martin, a barber, set up beauty salons at Carlton and Jarvis streets and at 1182 1/2 Queen Street East, between Jones Avenue and Curzon Street in the area east of the Don River. Martin also owned the Metropolitan Lunch at 3481 Yonge Street, site of the TTC's radial station at the city's boundary with North York.[25]

Other merchants moved their families along with their business ventures out to the new areas. When a former King East butcher, Nako D. Grozdanoff, set up home and shop on Jones Avenue, he attracted a diverse, non-Macedonian neighbourhood clientele. His customers, in the words of his daughter, were 'educated people ... government people, insurance [agents], policemen [and] detectives – no factory workers.' Tina Vassil and her restaurateur husband moved out of the settlement areas: 'In the thirties [you] couldn't get rich serving Macedonians.' He opened a restaurant on Danforth Avenue at Coxwell, where most of his patrons were Anglo-Canadians. The Depression merely capped a process whereby Macedonian working men, as more and more families were formed, ceased to eat out.[26]

Macedonians and their families affected these new areas of the city, and other parts of the province, as employers and customers. They had more contact with other ethnic groups as customers, employers, and workers. A Macedonian shoeshine-and-cigar-store operation at Yonge and Wellington, outside the Niagara Street district, employed Italians as shoeshine boys. One Italian fruit and vegetable merchant on Bloor Street learned the Macedonian words for a variety of foodstuffs, including rice, peppers, and grapes, from his neighbour, a Macedonian shoeshine operator. By 1940, a number of Macedonians had settled permanently in the city's outlying regions, as well as in the Ontario hinterland. Stable communities emerged; an entrepreneurial base formed. Men successfully ran restaurants and lunch-rooms in Hamilton, grills in Windsor, and hotel/taverns in Galt. There was even a Bulgaro-Macedonian outlet in Kitchener, where Peter Zlateff owned and operated the Victoria Fruit Market.[27]

Later, after the Second World War, Macedonians eventually employed their numerical strength within the food services industry as a springboard into larger and more sophisticated ventures. The proprietors of the Mecca Grill also formed the Christie Brothers Enterprise, an industrial catering firm that supplied coin music for restaurants. One of the owners of the Dufferin Grill abandoned his restaurant duties to become a full-fledged partner in the Macedonian-owned and -operated Parkdale Dairies, which supplied milk products to the city's Macedonian restaurateurs.

MACEDONIANS IN COMMERCE

A most unlikely source, the *15th Annual Convention Almanac* of the Macedonian Political Organization, published for its 1936 gathering in Toronto, illuminates the Macedonians' position in the world of commerce and the place of commerce in Macedonian immigrant life late in the period under study. The politically inspired and volatile almanac has, for example, advertisements containing passionate statements in support of Macedonian liberty, progress, and solidarity. The ad for the Louis Meat Market, at 1122 Queen Street East in Toronto, includes the declaration: 'The Macedonians Are Fighting for a Just Cause and Need the True and Honest Support of All of Us.'

The almanac was largely the creation of Macedonian shop- and storekeepers. Their subscriptions and advertisements financed its production.

Members of North America's Macedonian business communities used the volume to make known their existence and flog their wares. The almanac documents patriotic sentiment and provides a good picture of Macedonians in North America, but it also reveals the structure of Macedonian enterprise in Toronto, recording the sheer variety of businesses. Restaurateurs, grocers, and butchers aside, the business community was composed also of the proprietors of the soft-drink manufacturer Rose Marie Beverage Co., a coin amusement-machine distributor, an instructor in 'Hawaiian, Spanish and Tenor Guitar,' members of an eight-piece professional orchestra, and two photographers – Daylight Studio and the Queen Portrait Studio, which offered photographs and other artistic mementos of the towns and villages of Macedonia.

The world of Macedonian commerce in Toronto, as portrayed in the almanac, was permeated with a competitive spirit. The volume records the presence of no less than five butcher stores along Queen Street East, between Berkeley and Sumach streets, which formed a relatively small and compact business district. Macedonian butchers 'would go by' the stores of their countrymen 'to see how each other was doing.' The need to survive and grow challenged energies and abilities. Jimmy's Meat Market, of 378 Queen East, maintained a healthy share of customers by developing a reputation for preparing the best Macedonian spiced sausage (sujuk) and by the sale of fresh green peppers, black olives, and feta cheese. The store also provided free fancy butchering services which others did not.[28]

The desire to succeed often inspired entrepreneurs to expand their geographical horizons in the search for additional clientele. Shopkeepers were eager to conduct business beyond the bounds of the immigrant colony. Toronto tailor Norman Dimitroff, at 298 Sumach Street, informed almanac readers: 'We Travel for Orders [of made-to-measure clothes] All Over Ontario.' Stoyancho Mitseff, a Macedonian grocer in Akron, Ohio, declared: 'We want to inform our friends in the States and Canada that we always have for sale good, fresh, Hot Peppers, summer or winter. When you need peppers let us know'.[29]

The almanac also reveals the interpenetration of the Macedonian ethnic community with the business activities of the host society. Where small Macedonian entreprises were succeeding, especially food services, there were wholesalers from outside the group affirming friendship or sympathy for the group and looking for business. Firms such as the wholesale tobacconists and confectioners J. Shifman and Son, the Canadian Tumbler Co., and the wholesale fruit, produce, and commission merchants Stronach and Sons courted Macedonian grocers and restaurateurs by advertising in the political almanac. Proclaiming in boldface that 'Many of Your Fellow Countrymen Use Our Ice Machines and Are Entirely Satisfied,' the Toronto refrigeration-equipment manufacturer Perrin-Turner Ltd hoped to gain more Macedonian clients. The National Show Case Co., Toronto Dairies Ltd, and White Way Linen Supply went further, employing Macedonians as sales representatives in order to reach this lucrative ethnic market.[30]

Not all Canadian firms listed in the almanac were in the food service or related industries. Ambrose Kent and Son catered to the Macedonians' deep sense of village or to their larger community/national identification, offering 'Regalia, Society Emblems, Jewels, Medals, Trophies, Flags, Badges, etc., for Macedonian Societies.'

The almanac also documents the Macedonian presence within the restaurant business of the United States and Canada, which became stereotyped because it was so common. In the beginning, Macedonian restaurants were generally humble establishments, with a few chairs and tables. Homemade soup, stew, and an abundance of bread often constituted the complete menu. By the 1920s, Macedonian restaurants started taking on more modern features. Most of those in the United States and Canada, in search of more customers in mixed working-class areas, began to vary their menus. Unlike Toronto's International Restaurant, which had proudly proclaimed: 'We Cook Old Country Meals,' few continued to serve only spicy Old World meals.[31]

In the United States, the almanac revealed, Macedonian food service showed more diversification and lost both a Macedonian and a practical, working-class character sooner. Macedonian Americans established Coney Island hot-dog stands, lunch-rooms, chili parlours, cafés, and barbecue and grill operations. In Windsor, Ontario, perhaps because of its proximity to the United States, Macedonians did open a few barbecue restaurants. Before 1940, however, service in Toronto centred on lunch-rooms, sandwich shops, tea-rooms, and ice-cream and soda-fountain parlours. If Toronto had had less rigorous and restrictive liquor licensing laws, Macedonians might have followed more closely the pattern of their American co-nationals who became heavily involved in operating inns and taverns. As late as the 1930s, despite having the largest Macedonian population in North America, Toronto had few equivalents to the La Paloma Grille in Akron, Ohio, which invited almanac readers to enjoy an excellent fish supper and 'a Cool and Refreshing Drink of Beer and Ale,' or the Macedono-Italian Palmetto Beer Garden, in Dearborn, Michigan, which was described as the largest beer garden in the city and the scene of weekly boxing and wrestling matches.

Through the almanac's pages, we can also get some sense of Macedonian perceptions of other ethnic groups. Advertisements such as that of a West End Toronto fruit and olive-oil merchant, S. Pacini, upheld the prevailing stereotype of the Italian as grocer and fruit dealer and documented the residential and working presence of other immigrants in Toronto's Macedonian settlements.[32]

Contemporaries and Canadian historians have long been content to measure the immigrant work experience against a yardstick of their own beliefs and conduct. Little has been written about the immigrant's perception of his or her own accomplishments, of his or her own status. The hierarchy of trades status – the relationship of income to trade skills in defining status – could be explored properly only through extensive study of individual Macedonian work histories. Anglo-Canadian thoughts about occupational mobility further complicated the story. A Macedonian custom tailor and shopkeeper, for example, gave up his business to help his labourer brother establish and run a grocery store. Another Macedonian worked in northern Ontario as an apprentice baker and in Toronto as a construction labourer, dock hand, ice-cream–parlour operator, grocery-store butcher, and, finally, proprietor of a bakery. It is unclear whether these men read their mobility in terms of up and down, success and failure. Only the memory culture could answer that.

In the 1910s, the world of enterprise had been the preserve of a little group of men – the community's steamship agents and bankers. H.D. Peroff and Co., of 18 Eastern Avenue, had proudly offered a full range of goods and services in a manner that discouraged competing small, specialized businesses: 'Our firm's business is selling large and small Old Country foodstuffs and products, issuing ship cards with the best steamships, sending money to Bulgaria and Macedonia through express and exchanging Napoleons.' Unfamiliar with and suspicious of Toronto's banks, many Macedonians had deposited their money and conducted their financial activities under the watchful eye of this entrepreneur. Despite his incessant claims of 'honesty and accuracy in business,' banker Peroff's conduct had not been beyond reproach. Summing up his activities, one Macedonian stated: '[Peroff said] "I will keep it [money] for you" and then he don't give it to you.' By 1917 Peroff – following the route of so many immigrant bankers, honest and dishonest – declared his firm bankrupt, thereby causing his many depositors to lose their hard-earned savings.[33]

The 1920s marked the rise of the butcher Naum Phillips as the community's most popular steamship and travel agent. Calladine and Baldry Ltd, a Toronto travel agency seeking a foothold within the immigrant community, had encouraged and assisted the young butcher in setting up his new venture. Phillips abandoned butchering and quickly took on duties as a full-time agent helping Macedonians to send correspondence, cash, and steamship tickets to friends and relatives in the Old World. Like that of Hadji Peroff before him, Phillips's character became a subject of controversy. In 1929 the executive committee of SS Cyril and Methody Church discovered improper and unauthorized use of the church seal and stamp on group correspondence and documentation submitted to Canadian immigration officials. Although no one was formally charged with illegal conduct (such as forgery), Phillips and other members of the community who participated in the immigration process remained under a heavy cloud of suspicion for a considerable time.[34]

Despite the dominance of figures such as Peroff and Phillips, competition was sometimes rife among Macedonian steamship agents and bankers, as on the eve of the First World War. The venerable Hadji Peroff, for example, had had to compete with Slave Petroff and Co., which had a labour bureau, sold insurance, and offered a wide variety of first-aid preparations. And below the bankers were the men who filled out the community's entrepreneurial ranks – the restaurateurs, shoeshine-parlour operators, butchers, and grocers who form the principal subject of this chapter. All of them worked long and hard. The proprietor of Toronto's Royal Cafe, Stoyan Geleff, took great pride in his ability to serve meals 'at All Hours.' A West End shoeshine-parlour operator and his wife capped off a sixteen-hour workday with the time-consuming chore of cleaning and polishing equipment.[35]

The examples in this chapter show great occupational fluidity. Men moved with ease and no visible loss of prestige between labouring and commercial ranks. While a Macedonian business person might be congratulated for acumen and achievements, no rigid barriers of custom or class existed at the start among members of the community as a result of occupation; differentiation by money and class grew only very slowly in North America. Business success, wealth, or education did not guarantee a leadership role. Officers of the benevolent societies remained a mixture of every income and occupational status. Village peasants who had always been dominated by alien administrators and upper classes from other ethnic groups maintained a large measure of social egalitarianism even as North America began to elaborate income and occupational strata among them. Such egalitarianism, as the following chapters reveal, continued to shape every aspect of organized community life for the Macedonians in Toronto between the two world wars.

8

Community Life

The differing composition of their districts shaped the community life Macedonians developed in Toronto. Villages of origin, religious loyalties, and political inclinations affected relations in and among the three areas.

The East End settlement was heterogeneous – a target for migrants from many villages in the old country. Men and families from Tersie and Bitola settled on Wilkins Avenue. Before the First World War, Trinity Street had been home to men of many villages, including Embore, Konomladi, and Zigoricheni. No village patterns can be discerned for the commercial streets of the area, King East, Queen East, and Dundas. In the 1930s, for example, there lived and worked on these streets artists and photographers from Oshchima and Zhelevo; butchers from Gabresh, Gorno Kotory, Smerdesh, and Verbnik; and restaurateurs from Banitsa, Besvina, Dumbeny, and Zabrdeni. The Junction also had a diverse population, including slaughterhouse workers and entrepreneurs from Armensko, Bobista, Smerdesh, Sorovich, Srebreni, Vumbul, and Zeleniche. By way of contrast, the Niagara Street district was largely the preserve of people from just Oshchima and Zhelevo.

Proximity of clusters of migrants from different villages was a novel arrangement, but some Old World experience had prepared the newcomers for that. Bonds and links between villages had existed previously. Oshchima and Zhelevo, for example, were geographically close; intermarriage between their residents was common. New ties, in turn, were forged in Canada. Macedonian sojourners and settlers quickly got to know people from other villages in the coffee-houses, factories, and slaughterhouses. As new acquaintanceships and friendships grew on the street corners, in the church and athletic society, and on the shop floor, Macedonians became aware of their ethnic group at large and its presence in the neighbourhoods.[1]

The concentrated presence of Zhelevtsi around Niagara Street illustrates the nature and strength of the role of sub-ethnic networks, identity, and culture among the settlers; it also reveals the potential diversiveness of political and religious differences. Did the men in the area possess a stronger sense of themselves as a group than co-villagers in the Junction or the East End? At meetings of the Zhelevo Brotherhood, which initially took place at the Bull's Head Hotel in the Niagara district, Zhelevtsi from the two other settlement areas seemed as faithful in attendance as those from the Niagara district. Junction and East End Zhelevtsi may not have differed from Niagara district fellow villagers in their intense sub-ethnic identity. They did obviously, however, give the Niagara district more prominence on their psychic maps than would settlers from other villages in the Junction and the East End.

The Zhelevtsi experienced much more fellow-feeling around Niagara Street than elsewhere in the city. It was no doubt comforting for a man to know his boarding-house companions and neighbours – to have shared a village childhood, to know each other's families and ancestral histories. Yet the dynamics of this relationship went deeper and far beyond simple acquaintance and familiarity. Below the surface layer of fellow-feeling lay the villagers' political and religious differences. The majority of men were Exarchists – supporters of the spiritual jurisdiction in Macedonia of the exarch, the head of the Bulgarian Orthodox church. Others were Patriarchists, or Gurcomans, loyal to the Greek patriarch in Istanbul. There were profound differences of view about Macedonian identity and the proper political and cultural future for the village. Tensions that had existed in the village were exacerbated by the intimacy of the boarding-houses as well as uncertain news from Macedonia.

Exarchists and Patriarchists lived side by side in the Niagara Street area. They coexisted and yet, at the same time, remained separate. They rarely shared celebrations and social life. They, of course, attended different churches. The Exarchists went to SS Cyril and Methody, while most Patriarchists attended the Greek church on Bond Street. A few Patriarchists preferred informal religious gatherings at their residences. On special occasions, out of necessity, obligation, or respect to family members or relatives who were Exarchists, Patriarchists would go to SS Cyril and Methody. A Patriarchist restaurateur remembered his discomfort: 'I went to that church because my uncle and aunt, they belong to that and when she died I had to go in it for the funeral.' Nevertheless, his presence was accepted, not frowned upon, and tacitly understood.[2]

Men of the two faiths in the Niagara district were generally civil with each other on the street – 'we would say hello' – and in the shops and factories. Occasionally, however, the factional baggage proved too heavy and arguments or fights broke out on the job or on the streets. A memorable set-to at the corner of King West and Niagara drew jail sentences (six months to a year) for some participants, as a Canadian judge ignored the pleas of the priest of SS Cyril and Methody for understanding and decided to teach the fractious foreigners a lesson. This fight and other scraps that arose during the period under study affected Macedonian life both in Toronto and in the old country. Despite the tension and occasional bruises, however, few, if any, Macedonians of either allegiance felt compelled to move out of the area.

New lines of communication with the Old World were good enough to keep Zhelevtsi aware of the struggles between factions and Balkan states at home, but garbled enough to aggravate relations in Toronto. An Exarchist reminisced: 'The young people of the village danced with considerable enjoyment during a holiday celebration. We children just fooled around. A pro-Greek boy's nose started to bleed during these festivities. Those of us who did not attend the Greek school were blamed for the boy's suffering. Another Greek boy, with whom I was playing, ran to his uncle and told him that I had hit him. The boy's uncle quickly appeared from nowhere and slapped my face saying, "It isn't enough that your father beats us in Toronto, now you want to beat us here."'[3]

As we have seen, the East End settlement, in contrast, was not dominated by people from any single village, but the political differences divided people. There are no recorded instances of Exarchists and Patriarchists battling there; the villages of origin had settled that question long ago in the old country. In the East End, most of the populace was Exarchist, committed to a sense of themselves as Macedonians and hostile to the Greek church and government. Of course, there was a similar pride of village to that of the Zhelevtsi. The brotherhoods and fraternal organizations, such as the Gabresh and Banitsa benevolent societies, were proof of that. Angry Tersani villagers temporarily withdrew from SS Cyril and Methody when a favourite son failed to be elected parish priest. The incident speaks to villagers' pride and solidarity as well as suggesting that the continuum between village identity and Macedonian national identity was strained while expanded in sharing and creating institutions in the

New World. Such village partisanship in fighting for community office was frequent, and the powerful group from Zhelevo also lobbied openly for the (East End's) Exarchist priest to be one of their own.

Real tension in the East End was more often engendered by political than by village conflict. Members of the political left – the Progressives – were at odds with the majority of their neighbours, who supported the main-line nationalist Macedonian community. Residing in a discernible cluster on Sydenham Street, Dean Street, Sumach Street, Ontario Street, Wyatt Avenue, Blevins Place, and Wilkins Avenue, the Progressives helped to create and maintain the Macedonians' presence in the East End. They had departed parish life in 1918, thereby opting out of the religious, political, and cultural world of the Macedonian community at large. In turn, they created their own club on Ontario Street and sought to proselytize other Macedonians. These efforts caused controversy. Like some of the Patriarchists, the Baptists, and other Protestants, the Progressives formed what amounted to countercultures within a larger Macedonian-Canadian identity as it emerged. One nationalist family in the East End felt compelled to erect a high cement wall between its yard and that of its Progressive neighbours. As in the Niagara district's struggle of Exarchists against Patriarchists, the conflict rarely caused people to move from their area.[4]

Many people in each of the three settlements held stereotypes about the other two areas. The Patriarchist and Exarchist struggles on Niagara Street had caused East Enders to describe that area as more volatile and unstable. Most of Toronto's Macedonians viewed the East End as the bastion of community power and the focus of ethnic identity. After all, the only church was situated there, rather than in the West End or a compromise, central location. Believing that the community exists wherever the church is, some West Enders maintained that only the East End could be identified as the Macedonian community. As residents of Niagara Street and the Junction, even though both areas exhibited considerable Macedonian residential density and a network of informal institutions, they felt away from the community core. They lived in settlement areas; East Enders lived in the community.

Given its ethnic population density and its proximity to nationalist institutions, did East Enders have a stronger sense of their identity? Were they more intensely Macedonian than their West End compatriots? Macedonian identity, especially in the East End, was affected by the efforts of public health nurses who tended to the children at Park and Sackville Street schools, teachers who demanded conformity and adoption of

Canadian ways, and also Protestant evangelists, as shown in chapter 5. A Presbyterian mission and the spirited proselytizing of the King Street East Baptist Mission brought into question not just Eastern Orthodox faith but also Macedonian-ness. The presence of immigrants in the East End was then tempered by the efforts at acculturation that that very ethnic and immigrant visibility attracted.

Moreover, ethnic institutions and group density did not apparently mean that the young boys and girls of the community were willing to lose playtime or forgo the more attractive aspects of Canadianization. The memory culture suggests that as many played 'hooky' from Bulgarian-language school as went, or hid during the workouts of Balkanski Unak. At the same time, ethnic identity was reinforced among children by the bigotry that they encountered as 'Macedonian wops and greaseballs' in the schoolyard and streets. Canadian classmates and playmates were often cruel about the ways and accents of the children and their parents. That, as much as group institutions, led to ethnic persistence.[5]

Hinterland Macedonians resembled the Junction settlers in their sense of the East End community; they appeared at the church only for rites of passage or Christmas and Easter. They took part in ethnic associational life only sparingly. In 1922, for example, Macedonian couples from Oshawa, Port Hope and Richmond Hill, came into the city to have their children baptized at the little church house on Trinity Street. Nicholas Blagoi came from Guelph with his Anglo-Canadian fiancée, Helen Grand Dunlop, to be married in 1924. In 1928, two residents of Hamilton, Tase Vane and Gena Smiliakova, came to the city and were married by the priest of SS Cyril and Methody, Reverend Nicoloff. Hinterland residents and businessmen dutifully bought advertisements in the political almanacs and often attended the nationalist conventions. A Windsor restaurateur, Nick Kusitaseff, bought an ad to publicize his four establishments.

Relations between Macedonians working in northern Ontario and the Toronto community changed radically when city Macedonians, especially entrepreneurs, acquired automobiles in the 1920s. When Noe Petroff took his wife and son up to the mining town of Copper Cliff near Sudbury in the family Ford to visit a friend who was a railway navvy, the outing heralded a series of changes for all concerned. For those who had not been into the bush or the remote mining, lumber, and railway sites, a new sense of vastness, of the importance of networks, of the sacrifices made by the bachelor navvies came as the miles of wilderness passed. At the same time, such trips ended the isolation of those working in the north. The urban community could now go to the navvy, tying him back into village networks, planning his marriage, reaffirming his Macedonian-Canadian identity. Thus the three settlement areas in the city and the Macedonian work gangs in the hinterland came together to form a single Toronto-based community, ranking with or ahead of the area around St Louis, Missouri, and Granite City, Illinois, as the largest Macedonian settlement in the Americas.[6]

Each sojourner or settler, no matter how he or she shared the common history of the Macedonian colony, also experienced migration uniquely. Some operated in the small spheres of their village and then their boarding-house, while others thought on a continental scale of Macedonian settlements in Illinois or St Louis. Time of arrival heavily influenced these matters. For example, the growth of settlement around the stockyards soon drew people directly from Macedonia who did not know the East End or Niagara Street or at least did not share the deep loyalties to each other of those who first sojourned or settled there. Men who came to Toronto during economic hard times and had been forced to leave the city in search of employment elsewhere, or who came later, when immigration regulations demanded an initial stay in the agricultural areas outside the city, would have a different set of New World experiences to build on. Thus varying frames of reference emerged and were at work in the Macedonian community.

EXTERNAL PRESSURES

The group's presence in the three settlement areas did not go unobserved by the 'caretakers' and 'protectors' of the Canadian way of life, as we saw in chapter 5. Provincial and federal politicians were becoming aware of the Macedonians as a new block of voters to be wooed. Wilfrid Heighington, Conservative MPP (1930–7) for Toronto's St David riding, and Harry Gladstone Clarke, Conservative MP (1935–40) for Rosedale, took out ads in the 1936 convention almanac of the Macedonian Political Organization (MPO), in which they extended greetings to the Macedonian community. There is no evidence that they knew anything about the MPO's nationalist and revolutionary politics. No comparable interest by Canadian politicians in the Junction or Niagara Street can be found; apparently only the East End community seemed large enough to be worth considering.[7]

Prejudice, more or less intense, followed Macedonians throughout the settlement period. As we have seen, it affected the renting and purchase of housing. Rare but terrifying violent encounters became legendary in the community. One woman remembered being accosted by an Anglo-Canadian as she and her mother walked along Queen Street: 'This one individual – it was a man; he just stopped us – put his hand on my mother's shoulder [and] said, "Why don't you damn foreigners learn to speak English or get out of the country?"' Children of immigrants had to contend with the spill-over of prejudice into the schoolyard and the streets as well as the workplace. One East Ender remembered the frightening attempt, perhaps mock, by her Anglo-Canadian classmates to drown her in Lake Ontario because she was a Macedonian 'greaseball.'[7]

In contrast to the politicians, Protestant church representatives, especially Baptists, created a larger and more accurate network of contact with the community. Through its King Street Mission in the East End and its female volunteers and language instructors who combed the West End neighbourhoods in the 1930s and 1940s, the Baptist church attempted to aid, teach, and proselytize Macedonians in all three districts.

The Macedonian presence in Toronto also came to the attention of the police. For example, the police commended residents of a West End boarding-house for their good behaviour and good drinking habits. A former resident of a Junction household known as 'the Macedonian City Hall' remembered the words of a detective: 'So much liquor [residents favoured beer] but no trouble nothing. Polish people, they drink, mix liquor and beer. They don't know what they do, they start to fight.' One East Ender who had served as an informal court interpreter remembered an instance of men being charged and convicted of gambling as a result of playing backgammon in a coffee-house. So the cultural gap between Macedonians and the host society sometimes did cause trouble.[9]

Macedonians were not as obvious a presence as other groups in the city, such as Jews, Italians, or Chinese, even though their neighbourhoods were as dense. They did not require much entrepreneurship to supply their ethnocultural needs. In the absence of religious and dietary laws, for example, Macedonians did not need services like those offered by kosher butchers and poulterers. They dominated no single trade at first, so no special stereotype of them as pedlars, street labourers, or merchants arose at that time. Even when they came to dominate the city's small restaurant and diner business, they usually tried to play down the ethnic character of such places in the hope of serving a larger clientele. Coffee-houses, which served them alone, were few in number and subdued, at least when seen from the outside.

Because village-based brotherhoods and fraternal organizations for many years operated out of the homes and businesses of the leaders, the ethnic intensity of a site was not obvious to outsiders. Zhelevo Hall, for example, was built and completed only in 1948. The front lawns of Macedonian homes and residences were decorated with zdravets, a species of the geranium family. The plant was a subtle marker and recognizable only to the group. One respondent recalled: 'If anyone wished to visit another Macedonian and knew the street but not the number of the house, they needed only to look for this wonderful plant. When they saw the plant on the property they were then sure that this was the right house.'

Even the little church house on Trinity Street was a discreet presence: it was distinguished from other buildings in the neighbourhood only by its cross. MPO Pravda (the Toronto branch of the MPO) and the Balkanski Unak were housed in the church, and so they too failed to add to the visibility of the ethnic enclave. The Progressives' modest headquarters did not become a group landmark until later in the period. 'The Club' was located on Ontario Street, at the fringes of the East End community. It came into its own in the late 1930s and early 1940s, when it actively competed against the social programs and cultural activities of SS Cyril and Methody Church.[10]

COMMUNITY ACTIVITIES

Although work occupied the bulk of their time and energy, Macedonians also knew when and how to play and celebrate. Men relaxed in the company of other men – wives and families were excluded from the coffee-house. Outside the informal ethnicity of the male hang-outs, most leisure activities had specific ethnic content and emblematics. In the church, at the athletic society, at meetings, their gatherings were both consciously concerned with Macedonian nationalism and subconsciously an assertion of Canadian Macedonian ethnicity.

Women operated on a smaller and more familial scale. Their leisure activities were inextricably bound up with the business of minding children. Groups of Macedonian mothers socialized at Sunnyside and High Park as they watched their children play. They also met at each other's houses. East End women gathered to knit, crochet, and have coffee together. Although such gatherings were informal or connected with specific aspects of the liturgical year, women's leisure and ethnic in-gathering were not dismissed by the men. They were rather part of the coherence of ethnicity.

In the West End, the wife of a shoeshine-parlour operator could enlist her husband's help when it was her turn to entertain friends and neighbours. An accomplished performer on the gaida, the proprietor would close his store in order to 'play for the girls' as they drank coffee and ate zelnik. These social gatherings easily transformed themselves into a structure of assistance in times of illness or maternal confinement. Friends could come to visit as well as to perform the daily housekeeping chores, such as laundry, cooking, and cleaning, in order to keep households running as smoothly as possible and to provide the new mother with time for rest and recuperation. In that sense, women of a neighbourhood or from the same village had their own informal ethnic benevolent societies.[11]

Men, women, and children frequently came together to enjoy a picnic in one of the city's parks. At Lambton Park, for example, the colony monopolized a choice area of greenery by dispatching some young men to spend Saturday night in the park holding the site available for the weekly social event. Families made their way to the park carrying shopping bags full of fried peppers, cheese, and fruit. Many walked through the affluent Baby Point Road neighbourhood to get there. They were aware that they were an alien sight, and their response was both festive and defiant. One woman recalled these little processions: 'We walked by Baby Point Road with our shopping bags ... One day, I wore my hat backwards.' The gaida began to play once the families settled themselves at the picnic site. Canadians viewed such gatherings as something very ethnic, very outlandish. There is irony in the fact that such organized leisure, outside the seasonal or liturgical structure, was equally new and strange to the Macedonians themselves. They did not picnic in the Old World; they marked only the celebrations and feasts based on the religious, agricultural, and seasonal rites. Nevertheless they took to the western European picnic form and quickly made it their own. Attendance and participation at picnics soon became yet another ethnic and group obligation.[12]

Village-society or church-sponsored picnics were frequently held at such grassy and spacious areas as Lambton Park and Scarborough Heights. Announcements and circulars, in both English and Bulgarian, were widely distributed around the community to encourage the largest possible attendance. Transportation to and from the picnic site was arranged by the church's executive committee. The 1930 committee decided 'to telephone the TTC [Toronto Transit Commission] for buses.' The 1933 committee, however, decided 'to engage two or three trucks to bring the poor people to the picnic.' The trucks were scheduled to leave the church at 10 a.m. to go to their Dovercourt Road and Weston Road stops, where they picked up 'our people' en route to the festivities.[13]

The church-sponsored Ilinden Picnic, held on or near 2 August to commemorate the brave but ill-fated Old World attempt to overthrow Turkish rule in 1903, was the most important event of the summer and attracted Macedonians from Guelph, Hamilton, Niagara Falls, Thorold, and even Buffalo. The church committee arranged both the menu and the entertainment. The 1930 committee made the following provisions: '15 gallons ice cream, 2,000 cones, 15 watermelons, 10 cases of drinks, 10 loaves of bread and 100 pounds of ice.' Members of the 1933 committee purchased chocolates, one roast pork butt, cheese (bought on behalf of the church by butcher Lambro Tenekeff), and ten gallons of ice cream; merchant E. Stoyanoff donated buns.[14]

Entertainment at the Ilinden Picnic took the form of lotteries, music and dancing, races, and games. Lottery tickets sold for five cents a piece, generally with all proceeds going to the church treasury. One year, ticket holders were eligible to win 'gifts which were donated by the companies here' – Macedonian-Canadian firms that used the event as an opportunity to advertise. On other occasions, ticket holders were able to win such items as a portrait of the patriot and revolutionary Todor Alexandroff and a painting of the waterfall Voden. Such prizes themselves demonstrate the interweaving of Old World values and emblematics with that immigrant phenomenon, the organized picnic. Young people had the opportunity to compete in such events as foot and sack races.[15]

As Christians and adherents of the Eastern Orthodox faith, Macedonians also came together during the course of such religious celebrations as Easter and those held in honour of the patron saints of the church, Saints Cyril and Methody. Macedonians gathered in large numbers at the church for services on Palm Sunday, Good Friday, and Easter Sunday. Members were expected to participate during the services. For Palm Sunday, the church was appropriately decorated with flowers and greenery. In 1926, all parishioners and Bulgarian-school students were given prayer and music books so that they could chant during the Good Friday service. Easter Sunday was 'a time of candles and eggs'; the executive committee in 1929 ordered 480 eggs. One informant remembered eating these and homemade hard-boiled eggs for what seemed to be 'weeks afterwards.' Easter Sunday celebrations ended outside the church with men setting off firecrackers in the early afternoon.[16]

Celebration of the 'National' holiday – SS Cyril and Methody Day, 24 May – demanded even greater attention to ritual detail and preparation. The church was again bedecked with flowers and greens. In 1937, parishioners were given coat buttons that bore 'the image of SS Cyril and

Methody' as decorative remembrances. In the absence of a Bulgarian ecclesiastical hierarchy, the church called on the spiritual assistance of the Russian Metropolitan Platon for these occasions. In 1925, the metropolitan assigned the Russian bishop of Detroit to conduct services. The religious celebrations were often accompanied by concerts and afternoons of light entertainment provided by pupils of the Bulgarian school or by guests, such as the Russian church choir from Buffalo.[17]

EDUCATION

As we saw in chapter 4, the church and the society Prosveta had in 1915 launched a Bulgarian-language school. In the early 1920s, however, maintenance of an effective working relationship between the church and the society proved difficult. In 1922, the church's executive committee split over the level of support for the school's annual Christmas party. The society had asked for 'money and material help' in order to purchase a Christmas tree, and the committee responded by appointing district collectors to raise the money. It named Nikola Georgiev, Stavro Shamanduroff, and Simo Velianoff to canvass Niagara Street and the Junction; Pencho Novachoff and Nikola Stoicheff were to canvass along King Street East and 'around the church.' K. Brumakov and Vasil Georgiev were also appointed as East End collectors. The priest, Reverend D. Nakoff, and Naum Phillips arranged for a hall, rented a movie projector, and hired an operator to run 'religious showings' during the festivities.

When someone proposed that the church also give Prosveta twenty dollars, there were objections. Committee member Dine Sterioff argued that the gift was an unnecessary expense, especially since the church had made no claim against the party's proceeds; his suggestion that the church pay only for renting the hall encountered a storm of protest, particularly from Prosveta representative Simo Velianoff, a member of the committee. Members N. Georgiev and Naum Phillips also squared off in anger. The tempestuous meeting ended abruptly, with the dispute clearly unresolved. The scene hints at a confrontation between Macedonians concerned with their faith first and others committed to political nationalism; but our information allows only speculation.[18]

The often difficult relationship between the church and the society ended with dissolution of Prosveta in 1923. At a meeting on 13 December 1923, the executive committee and the general membership of the church decided to assume control of the Bulgarian-language school. The all-important business of educating Macedonian youth in the city was now totally in the hands of the church community. A committee acting in the name of SS Cyril and Methody and the Toronto Church Community School instituted a series of visits to all Macedonian families in the settlement areas. Committee men Stavro Giamandoff, Tashko Hristo, and Naum Phillips called on parents to sign up and send their children to the community's Bulgarian school. The Very Reverend Velik Karajoff, who succeeded Nakoff as priest in 1923, complemented their efforts by issuing pokani (printed invitations) to all Macedonians to support the venture.[19]

Classes, organized in grades from one to four, were generally held twice a week: each Wednesday from 6 to 7 p.m. and Saturday from 9 a.m. to noon. The students were also expected to attend vecherinki (entertainment evenings) where they were frequently called on to present concerts and poetry recitals. The subjects taught included Bulgarian grammar and literature and Macedonian geography and history – 'where it is, how big it is, how many people live under Bulgaria, how many people live under Serbia.' The church's executive committee purchased textbooks and primers and issued them on behalf of the school. Textbooks were ordered from Bulgaria and from ethnic community publishers in North America. The committee got reading material from the *Macedonian Tribune*, the MPO's US-based newspaper and publishing wing. It ordered texts from the publishers of *Naroden Glas*, the American-based Bulgarian newspaper – for example, in 1926, '12 first grade, 12 second grade, 10 for third grade and 2 for fourth grade.' Students were expected to purchase the texts. Primers, however, were given free of charge to those who could not afford supplies.[20]

The executive committee tried to attract the best possible teachers. It posted announcements on the church office door and distributed them throughout the immigrant community. It also advertised for teachers in the *Macedonian Tribune*, which enjoyed a large Macedonian readership throughout North America. The committee screened applicants, giving preference to those of the Orthodox faith who had documented teaching experience – in 1935, for instance, it rejected H. Govev because he 'was not Orthodox.' Members selected the appointee by majority vote in a secret ballot. In 1925, Mrs Elena Geleff defeated Mr Kuzo Temelkoff for the teaching post by a vote of eight to five. In 1931, the committee accepted K. Evanoff's application for further consideration because he had given proof of five years' teaching experience; two other candidates were told that they had to produce documentation or forfeit their chances.[21]

The church committee directed the school. It determined a teacher's salary; the amount could vary, even during the course of a year, reflecting the financial fortunes of the church. In 1925, Elena Geleff accepted the post for twenty-five dollars a month. In 1929, the teacher received thirty dollars a month. By 1932, the committee found itself asking the teacher, who had earned twenty dollars a month, to accept a five-dollar reduction as part of a larger effort to cut down operating expenses. Each year, it determined the opening and closing dates of the school and set the date for the annual examinations. It also issued pokani (invitations) to all church members to attend exams and the ceremonies for graduates. The committee monitored the academic progress and general conduct of both teachers and students. General membership meetings chose school inspectors 'to see that things go right, see that the teacher comes on time, see that the children are orderly and taught properly.'[22]

Some children found attendance pleasant and challenging. One woman recalled her joy in learning and performing a number of nationalist songs. The church committee tried to make learning the ethnoculture fun. For example, it bought Christmas presents and 'two hundred and fifty stockings' for the pupils. As the school year drew to a close, the committee presented the children with Turkish delight and other candy treats. In 1935, the committee decided to 'buy three hundred packages of candy for the pupils.' In 1939, it tried to generate a commitment to academic excellence by its decision 'to give a prize to the pupils who are distinctive in the first, second, third and fourth grades.'[23]

Executive committees did everything in their power to encourage the students' sense of responsibility. Students were expected to attend the school regularly. Some children saw it as an additional and unnecessary burden, cutting into play and leisure time: 'My father kept me up till midnight to learn things, especially poetry.' Such youngsters attended class sporadically, only long enough to pick up a bit of Bulgarian reading and writing. The committee for 1929 wrote to the parents of students with poor attendance records, urging them to bring their children regularly in order to prepare them for the upcoming annual examinations. The church also demanded good conduct on the part of all students. The committee for 1926 appointed Elia Stoyanoff and Delo Tashunoff to visit 'the fathers of the pupils who do not keep order in the school.' An apparently flustered committee in 1932 was moved by the students' spirited and rambunctious behaviour to give a little gift to the most quiet pupil at the end of the academic year.[24] Nurturing ethnic persistence and encouraging Macedonian national identity were no easy task for men who knew that they wished the next generation to honour their parents' way but had little pedagogical or cultural experience to call on in organizing a smooth-running institution.

By 1924, the church was seriously considering the request of Junction-area 'compatriots' for a local Bulgarian-language school; members of the executive committee took up the idea and began making preparations. The school was held in a small house on St Clair Avenue West, near Gunn's and Swift Canadian slaughterhouses. By 1925, the church also responded favourably to a request from the people of Niagara Street for a school. Arrangements were made to conduct it in a local hall. For the West End schools, the church had blackboards brought from the church office and secured textbooks and written material from *Naroden Glas*. It supplied the lumber, and Macedonian men made pews and benches, particularly for the school on Niagara Street. It appears that by 1929 classes were being held in both places on Monday, Wednesday, and Saturday evenings. That same year saw fewer pupils attending the Junction school, and the executive committee talked about closing it, 'seeing that not too many children are attending,' in favour of concentrating all energies and resources towards 'the benefit of the central school [conducted at the church] in which many more are attending.' The committee decided, however, to keep the school after a successful campaign against absenteeism. Pupils were expected to bring five dollars from their parents as a fee and guarantee of attendance.[25]

ATHLETICS

Boys and young men had an additional ethnic agency through which to identify with Macedonian folkways and share time and develop fellow-feeling with other Macedonians. That route was membership in the athletic and cultural society Balkanski Unak. The organization had met before 1917 at such East End locations as River and Queen streets and Sherbourne and Dundas streets. On 11 November 1917, Balkanski Unak had entered into a working relationship with SS Cyril and Methody Church. Acknowledging the society's important work and position within the youthful immigrant community, the church's executive committee made the second, or upper floor of the church building available rent free to the organization and its members. Balkanski Unak agreed to assume half the renovation costs and to pay utility costs. It, like the Society Prosveta, was invited to seat a watchful representative on the church's executive committee. Balkanski Unak also participated in the affairs of the parish in other ways – in 1926, its representatives helped plan celebrations for SS Cyril and Methody Day (24 May).[26]

    By 1920, Balkanski Unak had asked for permission to take over two rooms of the lower floor of the church building, principally for athletics. Instead of paying rent, the society was once again willing to undertake renovations. The executive committee granted the request, insisting that the society first submit a sketch and full explanation of the proposed building changes. At the committee's request, the society appointed an overseer – H. Matesoff, vice-president of the committee – to ensure that no 'catastrophic deed with the building' happened during construction. Balkanski Unak, under the direction of physician Dr Toma Dimitroff, was first and foremost an athletic society, similar to the more well-known turnverein of the Germans or the sokols of the Czechs. Athletic activity consisted of exercise sessions and gymnastic and weight-training drills; competitive team sports were not permitted. The society hosted lectures and evenings of entertainment. The church's executive committee in 1923 gave the society the contents of its library – an interesting collection of religious books, plays, and dramas.[27]

Following the departure of Dr Dimitroff to the United States in the late 1920s, Balkanski Unak entered a period of decline. In the early 1930s, there appeared a newly organized church athletic society for men and women – Macedonian Unak. Under church activist and committee member Lazar Evanoff, the group was to break new ground in terms of activities and membership. Evanoff set up such competitive sports as basketball. Whether afraid of broken windows or aware that the emphasis on basketball, baseball, and hockey over gymnastics represented a subtle form of acculturation, the executive committee in 1933 demanded that the group stop playing basketball, in favour of less potentially destructive 'sport games.' Women were allowed to participate in Macedonian Unak. Mary Evanoff, the daughter of its first instructor, ran a similar program for the young women of the community.[28]

A 'NATIONAL HOME'

The success of ethnocommunity events brought to the fore 'the need to have a hall and stage.' In 1922, a proposal to reconstruct and modify the second floor of the church house was rejected as too costly. In 1923, a proposal to construct a parish hall in the lower floor or the basement of the church building failed to pass.[29] Following a favourable recommendation by a sub-committee on building a parish hall, the 1927 executive committee decided to raise the question at a special meeting of the general membership. The committee offered 'strictly defined questions':

1   Do you agree with the policy of the committee with reference to the hall in question?
2   Do you agree that a hall should be built in the present place?
3   Do you agree to the purchase of the two adjacent houses next to the church?
4   Do you agree to the plan of the hall?
5   Do you agree with the method of collecting initial funds through soliciting $25.00 or more in the form of personal loans?
6   If you agree with the above mentioned questions and points, the church committee asks you to elect a new twelve member committee in undertaking the construction and collection of money. Together with the Church Committee it shall be known as the 'Construction Committee.'

The questions brought on considerable debate and dialogue. Church members accepted the recommendation to build a hall and elect a construction committee. They also elected a sub-committee – Dimitar Hadjieff, Naum Nakeff, and Lambro Tenekeff – to 'enter into contract with the owners of the adjacent houses on Eastern Avenue for their purchase.' Members 'loaned money to the church to the general amount of $2,000 which was to guarantee the beginning of construction.'

Lotteries, donations, and additional loans helped pay for the parish hall. Individuals donated sizeable amounts – for example: E. Stoyanoff, $200; L. Tenekeff, $200; D. Evanoff, $100; H. Tipeff, $100; and F.S. Tomev, $50. More money was raised by borrowing from church members. L. Andreev, who owned and operated a bus line between Hamilton and Toronto, extended $8,000 in loans.[30]

The hall opened in 1928 with a performance of the play *Makedonska Krvava Svadba* (Macedonian Bloody Wedding). Over the entrance was inscribed in old Slavonic letters 'Macedono-Bulgarian Parish Hall, SS. Cyril and Methody.' The inscription 'through culture and education to prosperity and patriotism' was placed above the curtain on the stage. The parish hall soon became the centre for social and cultural activity for both the immigrants and the Canadian-born: 'Dramas, concerts, socials, talks, lectures, national gatherings, horo, gymnastic exercises and games, teaching the youth Bulgarian reading and writing, acquainting the youth with the history of our people, with our national and cultural heritage, with our faith and the history of our Holy Church, public and membership meetings all took place there.'[31]

The parish hall generated its own income. In 1931, village associations and political organizations paid rental fees of fifteen dollars for concert nights and ten dollars for membership meetings. By 1935, groups were required to pay a flat rental fee of twenty dollars per session. By 1932, individuals were also required to pay parish hall membership fees of a dollar a month. The hall 'was our pleasure, our everything,' informants answered happily, recalling the Sunday vecherinki. They paid 'a quarter or ten cents or twenty cents or whatever you want to throw on the tray to get in the place.' Macedonians enjoyed these entertainment evenings of music and dancing. The festivities drew people from the West End settlements as well. A group of sixteen to eighteen youngsters from the Junction made their way to the church each Sunday on foot or by streetcar.[32]

Building the new parish hall was the real and symbolic culmination of the effort to create institutions to sustain Macedonian identity in Toronto. The new 'National Home' symbolized the dual loyalties of Macedonians – their long-standing commitment to the old country and their newfound obligation to Canada.

9

The Church and Ethnicity

SS Cyril and Methody Church had emerged in 1910 as a community and Macedonian national institution, both incorporating and often transcending traditional village loyalties. In the settler period following the First World War, this occasionally parochial but egalitarian and democratic organization permitted and encouraged community and national ideals. It had close contact with the new Macedonian Political Organization (MPO, founded in 1921) and fiercely independent, and finally explosive relations with the Bulgarian Orthodox Holy Synod.

CHURCH GOVERNANCE

Supervision of the church's business affairs was scrupulous and democratic. From 1920 on, the church's executive committee, elected annually, dutifully printed the financial report for the past year and distributed copies 'to all immigrants here in the city' and members outside Toronto. Each month, the controller's commission, composed of three elected church members, carefully scrutinized the parish's income, expenses, and receipt books. Aware that financial misdeeds – or rumours of them – could create an atmosphere in which 'nobody would face towards the Church,' the commission made recommendations and suggestions for improvement. In 1917, for instance, it proposed that income be immediately deposited in the bank, as opposed to being carried about by the church secretary, or placed in the church's treasury. From 1920, all cheques required the signatures of the president, secretary, and treasurer of the executive committee.

Suspected cases of financial wrongdoing by individual members of the executive committee were also thoroughly investigated and acted on. The church secretary for 1923 was held accountable for irregularities in that year's parish records and receipt books. He was informed that he would be subject to court action if he proved incapable of exonerating himself. In 1940, the church recruited a City of Toronto auditor to examine the records and conduct of a former church secretary. The investigations confirmed the absence of $153 in membership fees. The former officer was suspended and barred from attending all church meetings for two years. The church and its committee emerged through these careful fiscal practices and vigorous fundraising as an independent community organization. It depended on the whole community, not on the Bulgarian exarchate or on the energy and power of the various village brotherhoods and societies alone. Through the 1920s and 1930s, SS Cyril and Methody was the central institution of the Macedonian community.[1]

The church tried to lessen the influence of village loyalties by taking control of its financial destiny, replacing tithing by village with a central church committee and collectors. In the period 1924–32, the senior collector received between 5 and 30 per cent of the proceeds as salary and expenses. Appointment of district collectors eased his workload. In 1920, for instance, he was aided by Nikola Georgiev in the Niagara Street district and by Stavro Gemandoff in the Junction. Unlike their counterparts who collected the village-based tithe, parish collectors could canvass all the Macedonian settlement areas. They operated effectively beyond the village network, reaching those immigrants who did not, either by choice or by lack of opportunity, belong to village benevolent societies.[2]

There was also a fee for church membership – in 1921, fifty cents a month. By 1927, men and women paid annual fees of four and two dollars, respectively. There were also charges for performance of specific rites and practices. In 1923, a wedding cost twelve dollars, baptism seven dollars, and burial ten dollars. By 1924, community pressure brought about a change in fees: baptism went, 'regretfully for the cause and the church income,' from seven to six dollars – competitive with the rates of the Canadian Protestant churches; burial fees for children dropped to five dollars. Macedonians had taken some sacraments from the Anglican church at Trinity and King Street East before 1911; in their popular theology, they seem to have accepted the sacerdotal quality of the Anglican clergy, especially when the price was right, while not straying from their Orthodox faith.

The church raised funds through celebration of religious holy days, group entertainments, and socials. The twenty-fifth anniversary of the church, on 24 May (patron saints' day) 1935, raised $1,500 during the banquet festivities. At such occasions, lucky draws proved popular and were an effective means of raising money. First prize at one was a new Canadian refrigerator, but the second and third prizes were embroidered Macedonian blouses.

The church always attempted to pay back loans promptly and with interest. In 1931, for example, D. Evanoff received an interest payment of ten dollars for his $1,000 loan. More often than not, however, members were asked to be generous and patient while waiting to be reimbursed. In 1930, committee members regretfully informed Nicola Bitove that he would have to wait for payment of his $100 loan as the 'parish is not in a condition to pay loans.' In 1935, A. Metoff, N. Nakeff, A. Novachkoff, and H. Traikoff were asked to forgo interest payments on their loans to the church.[3]

The house at 95 Trinity Street, next to the church, generated income for the church through rental of extra space in the priest's quarters. A member of the Macedonian community, Atanas Geleff, rented the second-floor space for twelve dollars a month after Archimandrite Theophilact failed to take up the appointed accommodations. By 1920, Geleff was asked to pay twenty dollars a month, in line with rent increases in the city. In 1940, the committee sought to rent out the space 'to a reliable person of our nationality,' after Reverend Vasil Mihailoff stated that he could not 'live there by his own reasons'; it was prepared to rent to other nationalities if it were unable to attract 'our people.' The church committee attempted also to lower expenses. The desire to save on the coal being used in the parish hall prompted a decision to relocate the Bulgarian-language school. So classes were conducted in the church, either in the old school-room, on the upper floor, or in the office and committee room. In 1932, the church purchased and installed gas and water meters; subsequent billings, however, indicated higher costs than those obtained on the old flat-rate system.

The church came to depend on volunteer skilled labour from its members to maintain the building and develop projects. Most members performed repair and maintenance work free of charge, with the church paying for materials. In 1920, Lambro Fileff volunteered to repair the building's walls, which had cracked during heavy rains; the church supplied sand and lime. In 1935, Sido Doncheff, a painter and decorator by trade, volunteered to paint the structure free of charge. At different times, members agreed to perform repair and maintenance work for a fee or some form of financial compensation. In 1932, for example, N. Nakeff agreed to make repairs to the altar on all three sides for fifty cents an hour.

Members also ran the buffet or refreshment stand at various events. While they had to pay a rental fee to use the buffet, they could keep the profits. In 1935, the executive committee announced that the buffet was available for $100 a year. It was only in 1939 that the buffet ceased to be a franchise and was run directly by the committee.

Finally, members also could be caretakers, cleaning the church building, including the school-rooms and the parish hall, especially the washroom facilities, about which there had long been 'much complaints.' The caretaker was expected also to clean the sidewalk, start the coal stoves of the Bulgarian-language school when necessary, open the doors to the hall on Sundays before the conclusion of services, and light and replace candles during services. In 1918, the caretaker received a salary of eight dollars per month, and in 1923, fifteen dollars a month plus fifty cents per baptism. In 1930, caretaker Traian Tipeff agreed with the church committee to perform his duties for rent-free use (and profits) of the buffet.[4]

The heavy representation of merchants and businessmen on church committees suggests a structure of 'notability,' but at no time was that structure based on class or income alone. Macedonian labourers and workingmen sought and attained church office. Men such as Lazo Evanoff, a sheet-metal labourer at Kemp's, and Karsto Mladenoff, who cleaned hides and drums at Clarke's tannery, also sat on committees. Evanoff directed Macedonian Unak and was church president for 1928, 1939, 1940, 1941, and 1942. Men who had demonstrated their religious and patriotic zeal or had shown oratorical flair – often more useful than literary skills in moving their co-nationals – had a good chance to be chosen. A man could sometimes retain his standing in the church even after a financial fall. Hadji Peroff's declaration of bankruptcy as a banker and steamship agent in 1917 in no way dampened his prestige within the church; in 1938, he was fêted as its first honorary member. Indeed, Peroff had seen fit after his bankruptcy to ask for and receive the post of caretaker, at eight dollars a month.[5]

Geography, I suspect, came also to affect the composition of the executive committee. Proximity to Trinity Street helps account for the East Enders' usual majority. Evan Repatseff, church president for 1937, managed a variety store at Sydenham and Sackville streets, right in the heart of the East End community. Hadji Peroff's business and agency at 18 Eastern

Avenue were only minutes and steps away from the church. East Enders dominated the committee in 1917:

EAST END		WEST END	
George Dineff	352 King E	N. Evanoff	573 Wellington W
D. Evanoff	408 King E	K. Naumoff	731 Clarens
G. Ganoff	405 King E	D.C. Tashoff	290 Royce
S. Kiproff	–	T. Yoteff	179 Keele[6]
K. Koneff	–		
D. Krieff	364 King E		
M. Mihailoff	360 King E		
H.D. Peroff	122 Parliament		
A. Stoyacheff	16 Wilkins		
D. Stoyanoff	405 King E		

The committee also sought to help shape and protect the immigrant community. Since its inception in 1893, the Internal Macedonian Revolutionary Organization (IMRO), an Old World political movement, had complemented its political activities with family and social reforms. IMRO, for example, advised village women not to waste their energies on intricate embroidery. Needlework designs were to be kept simple. Following the example of IMRO, the church committee became involved in the structure and workings of the Macedonian family. In 1923, Pavel Vasileff appeared before the committee to ask for help with his marital problems: 'Complaining that his wife, Anka, left him without any cause and [he] begs the church committee to do something and call her to advise her to come back to him.' Ever mindful of the reputation of the collectivity and subscribing to the notion of 'let's settle it among ourselves, not in the civil courts,' the group set up a commission, composed of the priest, Reverend Velik Karajoff, and Georgi Dineff, Naum Phillips, Grigor Stoyanoff, Kuzo Temelkeff, and Elia Vasileff, to deal with this and similar cases.

Acting on such matters of substance, which went beyond either religion or nationalism, the executive assumed an important position within the immigrant community. Membership was a mark not just of piety but of concern for the welfare of one's fellow Macedonians, or the national cause, or both. Patriotic young men coveted only one position – a seat on the MPO's local (Pravda) or central committee. Long and dedicated service was not reserved for notables – rather, it made people notables. In 1937, members of the church committee, the Ladies' Auxiliary, and the committee of Pravda planned a pilgrimage to the grave of

Lambro Tenekeff, a highly popular church president and Pravda committee member. The pomp and ceremony accorded his memory testify to the position that such men came to occupy.

Not all Macedonian men were able or willing to cope with committee duties. In 1920, church secretary K. Koinev asked his colleagues to appoint an assistant, as he was 'too busy' with his own affairs. Despite deep interest in church affairs and ethnic group politics, one East End butcher studiously avoided running for office because he feared that he would alienate his Greek and Serbian customers.[7]

ADJUSTING TO NORTH AMERICA

The signs of transition from the values of the Old World village to those of a Canadian ethnic group were sometimes subtle, unnoticed by outsiders. The church's executive committee monitored, formally and informally, the spread of various North American influences and practices. Noting 'that all are not able to attend church especially the businessmen,' the committee in 1920 approved services to start at 9 a.m., an hour later than had been traditional in Macedonian villages, so as to facilitate attendance by those, especially shopkeepers, who had worked to 11 p.m. or midnight on Saturday. Orthodox services and village ways had long prescribed only male voices for the liturgy, but by 1927 the community had a mixed-voice choir. Founded by Mr B. Beneff, the choir performed around the city at church socials and festivals, such as Music Day at the Canadian National Exhibition. Thus Canadians who went to hear traditional Macedonian music were listening to what was already an ethnic adaptation to North America. With Beneff's departure to Bulgaria in 1934, the choir was dissolved until its revival in 1941.[8]

The linguistic preference of younger Macedonians and the practicality of a common language for dealing with the larger Canadian community, led the committee to increase the use and presence of English. Membership booklets, baptism certificates, and picnic circulars, by the late 1920s, were issued in both Bulgarian and English. The committee approved in 1930 the motion to 'put a sign in the hall in Bulgarian and English so people getting into [the hall] keep order.' Remarkably, it invited Protestant missionaries to conduct English-language classes and asked them to remain during most of the 1930s, but it asked only Protestant teachers of English who promised not to proselytize or who did so without offending. Hence it denied the 1935 request of 'stubborn' and zealous Jehovah's Witnesses to use the premises of the Niagara Street Bulgarian-language school.[9]

SS Cyril and Methody further attempted to solidify its respectability within Toronto 'the Good' by playing the role of Christian neighbour to all East End residents, regardless of ethnic origin. It laid wreaths – 'not to cost more than ten dollars' – in honour of the Unknown Soldier at City Hall. It donated, whenever possible, proceeds of nightly entertainments to the Red Cross. In 1935, members of the Toronto press were invited to attend a patron saints' day celebration and informed of its meaning and importance. The church committee and the MPO sent telegrams of congratulations to King George VI on the day of his coronation in May 1937; church circulars appeared bearing his portrait.[10]

As it became more aware of the pastoral ways of the local evangelical ministers, the church's executive committee pushed the clergy, often content with the role of ritual leader, towards more pastoral activity. Lengthy debate produced a 1927 by-law – 'a priest must wear a vestment according to the priests living in Canada, namely a black shirt, with a white collar, ordinary vest and black coat' – but marking the priest off by his dress was not the same as keeping track of him. In the old country, villagers usually had an idea of his whereabouts. Given the width and breadth of Toronto, the committee felt that the priest had to abandon the informality of the village and adopt a regular schedule of office hours in order to accommodate parishioners scattered across the city. By 1923, the priest was required to be at the church office between 10 a.m. and 12 noon each day, leaving a note indicating his whereabouts if he had to leave. By 1935, the office had a sign, in both English and Bulgarian, stating that the priest was in the office 'every Monday, Wednesday and Saturday between the hours of 10 am and 1 pm' and from '6 to 8 pm each evening.'[11]

Priests and committees also disagreed over duties. Drawing from the Protestant example, the church committee expected the priest to be a leader and recruiter of the congregation. The 1935 committee had no qualms about leaving the collecting of membership fees to Reverend Haralampi Elieff; he saw the task as beneath his dignity as an Orthodox clergyman and argued that the committee, as a representative body of the membership, should fulfil this responsibility. He finally brought a curt end to debate when he stated that the committee 'could take this question before the [Canadian] Parliament' for resolution but he would not change.[12]

The question arose next as to whether the priest's occupation was a full- or part-time job. Shortly after he came to the church in 1931, Elieff had started up a wholesale coffee business. By 1937, church and committee members began to ask, 'Is he a coffee man or a priest?'

Demands for him to liquidate his business soon arose. 'Born in a village,' but having 'grown up in a city,' he argued that it was not unnatural for a village priest to work at things that were not religious in nature. Standing on tradition, the members disagreed. Parishioner Lambro Fileff took the floor at a general meeting on 6 June 1937 and said: 'I have not seen a priest to be occupied in business, but I have seen that our priests in the village, in their part time, they cultivate the land only or other chores around the house. This priest does not respect us people.'

The community had been proud of its generous financial and living provisions for priests, and that fact added to its dismay. Elieff received a salary of sixty-five dollars a month, living quarters rent-free, and 'religious taxes' – fees for baptisms, burials, and weddings. Macedonian Canadians believed that their priest should therefore dedicate himself, like his Protestant counterparts, fully to his religious tasks. Elieff promised to sell his business but later reneged. His failure to comply with the wishes of the church community led the committee in 1937 to reduce his salary to forty dollars a month and to withdraw his right to the religious taxes. The financial restrictions were too much for Elieff, and he submitted his resignation on 1 August 1937. The affair firmly established the tradition of a full-time priesthood.[13]

THE ROLE OF THE CHURCH

As a national institution and centre of ethnic identity, SS Cyril and Methody took an active and regulatory interest in its members' actions towards the church and towards other Canadians. The executive committee decided in 1923 'that some one who ridiculed that church, they should be corrected.' The by-laws of 1927 gave permanent form and substance to such concerns; according to article 11, a member 'who with his actions' had hampered 'the progress of our nationalist church interest' first stood to receive two warnings from the committee about his conduct. Failure to correct conduct and attitude could lead to permanent 'excommunication from the membership list.' The committee did not look kindly on those who 'brought shame' upon the Macedonian community. In 1932, member and former president Naum Phillips took the church to court to recover a loan. Arguing that he had 'defamed our church by taking her to Court before the local authorities,' the executive committee got the membership to suspend Phillips until he corrected his conduct. Similarly, in 1940, when member A.K. Tenekeff sent a writ through his lawyer to recover his loan, the committee described his actions as a 'shame, [a] wrong doing, and unchristian.' He received a two-year suspension.[14]

As much as it tried, SS Cyril and Methody simply could not be the church for all Macedonians at all times. Unhappiness with the clergyman of the day often prompted a rash of temporary defections or preferences for the visiting Russian priests. Discontent with Velik Karajoff in 1924 propelled unhappy parishioners to ask for Russian priests to perform baptisms and weddings.[15]

The church also had to contend with the activities of groups of long-standing outsiders: 'About the end of 1918, a sizeable group of church members were discontent ... This group was the first one to leave the Church for good.' The Progressives, as the members of the Macedonian political left came to be called, were the first to abandon SS. Cyril and Methody. Macedonian Protestants likewise operated outside the church's regular sphere of control.[16]

In times of great need or unusual circumstances, all parties demonstrated an ability to bend, to cooperate for the moment. Reverend Andoff, a Baptist preacher and missionary, attended a meeting at SS Cyril and Methody on 10 December 1918, called to discuss and draft a community appeal to members of the League of Nations asking for the 'freedom' of Macedonia. The good reverend suffered a fall in the church basement. He threatened a lawsuit as a result of injuries, and the executive committee decided, by twenty to ten, to settle outside court, eventually paying damages of $746. In 1921, the Progressives sought and received charitable support from the membership and the Presbyterian minister and missionary, Reverend Atanasoff, in their efforts to combat hunger and starvation in Russia.[17]

The church thus stood for ethnic and political homogeneity within the Macedonian entity almost as much as it did for religious orthodoxy. Macedonians were expected to demonstrate a common national and religious loyalty. Village loyalties and their potential for factionalism were supposed to be left outside the door. Church officials, however, still had to contend with occasional flare-ups of village sentiment. After the general membership failed in 1921 and 1931 to elect as priest a candidate from Tersie, several Tersiani withdrew temporarily; in 1931, the new priest, Reverend Elieff, visited the homes of the discontented members and sprinkled holy water as part of the Epiphany celebrations while ingratiating himself to one and all.[18]

For SS Cyril and Methody to remain the centre of ethnic identity, it had to come to grips with the geographical and mental gap between its East End base and the Junction and Niagara Street areas, where distance and streetcar fares caused many families to forgo religious and cultural events at the church. Church officials and priests attempted to take the community religious experience to the West End. David Nakoff, priest from 1921 to 1923, conducted special Easter services for West End residents at a home on Portland Avenue.

The executive committee kept a sharp eye as well on the political beliefs and activities of the ethnocultural groups that rented its spaces. In 1929, it denied members of the Bulgarian Society use of the Bulgarian-language school and the parish hall: 'We do not know their aim and they have not a Constitution.' And it turned down the request of Serbians to rent the hall but allowed the Croatians to do so for three dollars a night. Croatians and Macedonians both objected to the politics of the Serbian-dominated Yugoslav monarchy.[19]

THE CHURCH AND THE MPO

The political ambience in which the Canadian Macedonians operated was complex. The equal prominence given in the MPO's 1936 almanac to photographs of the revolutionary Ivan Mihailoff and of Ontario's premier, Mitchell F. Hepburn, suggests ambiguities and subtleties that few historians have observed. Some sense of the group's political mentality may emerge from a look at the relationship between the MPO and the church. Oral sources have used one metaphor in describing that relationship: if the church and the MPO were a coin, then the MPO would be the head side; most remembered, inaccurately, membership in both bodies as being synonymous.[20]

The written sources, in contrast, note fissures, strains, and obvious disagreements between the MPO's most virulent partisans and some parish elders and officials. The MPO spoke proudly of the 'Bulgarian character of the Slavs of Macedonia' in its 1936 almanac. One suspects that this proclamation did not sit easily with men who had once turned down a teacher candidate for the Bulgarian-language school because he was Bulgarian, not Macedonian. When the committee of the MPO's Toronto local, Pravda (Macedonian for 'Justice'), approved the Serbian request to rent the parish hall in 1930, an incensed executive committee made it clear that it did 'not approve their act. We wrote a letter to the MPO this month in case there is a controversy.'

The MPO was destined, never the less, to occupy an important and visible position within the life of the church through Pravda and its Ladies' and Youth sections. In 1922, Pravda asked for use of the church office for its regular meetings. The executive committee granted the request after the MPO agreed to pay one dollar per week in rent. After completion of the parish hall in 1928, Pravda negotiated to use it instead, obtaining a twenty-five–year lease for regular use at a token rent of one dollar per annum. In 1930, the MPO was granted a twenty-five–year extension in return for advance payment of twenty-five dollars.[21]

As a major tenant, the MPO came to exercise considerable control over the parish hall and the church. In 1937, MPO Pravda, its Ladies' and Youth sections, and the church committee decided that the space could be rented only to individuals and groups on 'good terms with the church and the Organization.' Interested and acceptable parties were to apply to the MPO 'two weeks in advance.' Trayan Tirpoff, who sought the post of caretaker, remembered being told to apply by letter to both Pravda and the church's building committee. The MPO increasingly identified with and infiltrated the church committee. At no time was the general membership consulted on the matter. The memory culture suggests that failure to consult the members was a result of the committee's sloppiness or sheer ignorance of the reporting and accounting procedures as outlined in the by-laws of 1927.[22]

Through the efforts of the Ladies' and Youth sections, the MPO created and helped to organize much of SS Cyril and Methody's social and religious life. It arranged vecherinki, or entertainment evenings, church benefit concerts, and picnics. Often at these events, the MPO Justice Orchestra, an eight-piece ensemble, offered both horos and the 'latest Modern Pieces.' The MPO likewise participated in all the major religious, group, and Canadian holiday celebrations. In 1920, the MPO asked to 'bedeck' the church 'with greens' in preparation for SS Cyril and Methody Day. Under MPO sponsorship, Macedonians turned out in enthusiastic crowds for Ilinden Day, Dominion Day, and (in 1934) City of Toronto Centennial celebrations. The MPO, however, ran events that centred on its own political purposes. It twice held its annual convention in Toronto; in 1929 and 1936, Macedonians from all over North America assembled in the city over the Labour Day weekend to attend a host of meetings, speeches, and dances at the parish hall.[23]

The MPO also had strong financial ties with the church. While most income from the parish hall went to the church's treasury, the MPO received the income for February and May. February's income went to the MPO's weekly, *Makedonska tribuna* (Macedonian Tribune), while May's supported its governing central committee in Indianapolis. The church also patronized the MPO's publishing and communication facilities – in 1935, for example, arranging to have the *Tribune* print a supply of baptismal certificates in both Bulgarian and English. The *Tribune* also printed up and prepared for distribution the church's pokani (invitations), circulars, and appeals and accepted advertising from the church.[24]

On 14 April 1942, the church's executive committee, MPO Pravda, the Ladies' Section, and the Youth Section decided that Pravda was to 'discontinue its political activities temporarily for the duration' of the war. As a result, the Ladies' and Youth sections were temporarily joined to the church. One five-member committee was elected to direct and organize the cultural activities of the church and community, and another 'to determine the opportune time to revive the political organization.' The decision proved of great significance to both the church and the MPO. The church gained the opportunity to complete its powers and to enhance its social and cultural responsibilities unencumbered by the nationalist political weight of the MPO. More important, both the church and the MPO were now placed squarely on the road to institutional separation.[25]

RELATIONS WITH THE BULGARIAN EXARCHATE

Despite strong commitment to their nationalist ideals and the MPO and much ambiguity about their identity vis-á-vis Bulgarian institutions, Macedonians in Toronto had of necessity formed links with the Bulgarian state and, of course, with the exarch in Sofia. They dealt with the Bulgarian legation in Washington, DC – there was no such legation or equivalent representative body in Canada – and the Holy Synod, through its spiritual representative, Dr K. Tsenoff. As priest, philosopher, and theologian, Tsenoff headed the synod's North American mission. While Macedonians were prepared to seek advice, assistance, and literary, liturgical, and cultural materials from these sources, they adamantly maintained full control of their religious destiny and, for the most part, sought a separate and free Macedonia.[26]

Through the executive committee of SS Cyril and Methody, Toronto's Macedonians developed the ability to make independent decisions that depended little on Old World politics or institutions. For example, in the key work of selecting and annually confirming a parish priest, executive committees set their own criteria in terms that satisfied the immigrant community.[27] Priests ideally had to be men of good education and sound Macedonian independentist principles, keenly aware and appreciative of the nationalist movement and its goals and objectives. Even the first priest, Archimandrite Theophilact (1911–21), originally from the Bulgarian village of Vrachesh, became a Toronto Macedonian in sentiment, anxious not to identify with Bulgaria. His successor was Reverend David Nakoff (1921–3), whose family had a long tradition of activism in the Macedonian revolutionary effort; Nakoff regaled students of the Bulgarian-language school with popular nationalist and patriotic songs. Reverend Vasil Mihailoff (1938–40) also fulfilled the prescribed patriotic requirements, for his father had been a prominent comitadji (nationalist guerrilla).[28]

The executive committee also controlled each search for a priest. It designed and ran job advertisements in the group's publications and newspapers. While Macedonians had warmly welcomed the Bulgarian consul to the United States, Mr Panaretoff, on his visit to Toronto in 1915, they were not willing to accept any meddling or political influence. In 1921, the church committee formally announced Theophilact's resignation in *Naroden Glas*, an American-based and widely distributed Bulgarian-language newspaper, along with a call for interested candidates.

When the Bulgarian legation in Washington took it upon itself, without the knowledge or consent of church officials in Toronto, to advertise for a successor to Theophilact, it received not thanks but a severe reprimand. An angry executive committee sternly informed it that 'this was not needed' and that the ad 'brought us into disharmony.'[29]

Concerned about possible complaints from the congregation or Canadian immigration officials, committees screened even candidates recommended by the Holy Synod and sought members' opinions. In 1923, Reverend Velik Karajoff presented authorizations and references from the metropolitan of Sofia, the ministries of Foreign Affairs and Religious Affairs, and the British legation in Sofia, which had tended to his passport and visa requirements. The committee presented choices to the membership at large. Parishioners cast secret ballots for the candidate of their choice. At a special membership meeting in 1931, Reverend Haralampi Elieff was elected priest over his rival, Andon Evanoff, by 109 votes to 9.

In keeping with their traditions of lay initiative and local community power, the Macedonians of Toronto removed priests or accepted resignations prior to informing the Holy Synod that they were doing so. When a priest sought to be relieved of his duties or simply resigned, he first took the matter up with the executive committee, which had the power to accept the resignation. The committee in turn informed the Holy Synod. The committee wrote to the Holy Synod about Theophilact's resignation in 1921 in order that it 'be known to them that he is no longer a priest and that his resignation was accepted by the committee.'

The executive committee could demand a priest's resignation. David Nakoff's failure to appear to officiate at a Russian funeral and to respond to a call to baptize a dying infant prompted the church committee in 1923 to seek his resignation – his 'inattentive relations with the Christians' had 'provoked a high indignation amid our parishioners.' The 1925 committee pressured Nakoff's successor, Velik Karajoff, to resign after it was discovered that he had not 'entered baptism and wedding fees into the church treasury.'[30]

The representative of the Holy Synod in New York was simply notified after the fact on a range of religious and church administrative matters. Church committees sent the Holy Synod copies of protocols and texts containing the proceedings and decisions rendered at executive and general membership meetings. Dr Tsenoff and the synod were expected only to give their customary rubber stamp of approval to the actions of the good Orthodox Christians of Toronto.

Macedonians in North America had long wanted a ritual head for their church. Citing poverty of resources – especially after the disasters of the Balkan and First World wars – the Holy Synod had turned down the immigrants' repeated pleas for a bishop. Macedonians made do with the assistance of the Russian religious hierarchy in North America. They often called on Russian bishops and metropolitans for major religious celebrations and activities. SS Cyril and Methody's executive committee invited the Russian bishop of Detroit to conduct its patron saint's day services for 1925. Russian priests, such as Reverend Jaroshurski of Welland, Ontario, came to serve when Macedonian priests were unavailable. Indeed, following the resignation of Velik Karajoff in 1925, Russians served for almost two years until Sotir Nikoloff was elected priest in 1927.[31]

In 1938, the Holy Synod finally mustered enough resources to send Andrey Velichki as 'ruling bishop of the newly organized Bulgarian Diocese of North America.' Dr Tsenoff was named his assistant. Greeted warmly at first, Bishop Andrey soon confronted a powerful wave of suspicion and anger from Macedonians in Toronto. These people were committed to the Bulgarian Orthodox faith and to Macedonian as their language but not to Bulgaria or its irredentist aspirations towards their homeland. Bishop Andrey broke down a subtle distinction that had held the community together since the Patriarchists had drifted away to the Greek church. He generated considerable hostility with his remark, 'We are all Bulgarians,' and with such actions as ceremoniously affixing a Bulgarian flag on his staff before addressing the congregation of SS Cyril and Methody. Through the MPO, Macedonians in Europe also provoked hostility against the bishop when they made known their view that he would be a destructive force in the immigrant community, an agent of a government that had recently harshly repressed Macedonian political activists and their brotherhoods in Bulgaria.[32]

Local church officials had forced the bishop to remove the flag. More important, they and the political leadership cultivated Canadian support against his actions. The mayor of Toronto, Ralph C. Day, had informed Macedonians of his concern and support:

It was with a very great deal of interest that I learned of an incident which recently occurred in your Church when a service was being conducted by a Bishop from Bulgaria. I understand that, when the Bishop brought out a Bulgarian flag, the Trustees of your Church and Society met and informed the Bishop that you were Canadian citizens and British subjects, and that the only flag that would be permitted would be the British flag.

May I most heartily commend this outward evidence of your loyalty to your adopted Country, and the Empire of which it forms a part. The grand old Union Jack, while but a piece of bunting, is nevertheless the symbol and a constant reminder of the freedom and justice which we enjoy in the British Empire.

It is encouraging to know that the Macedonian people of this City are embued with the ideals of their Canadian citizenship. I congratulate you on your display of loyalty to the flag under which we are all so proud to live.[33]

More than just being budding subjects of the British Empire, members of the community were intensely patriotic, proudly Macedonian, standing against all who impinged on their identity and sense of community. But they wisely did not try to explain that to the city fathers.

Macedonian parishioners also expressed their irritation in a more formal and official manner. Congregations in both the United States and Canada supported a motion not to recognize the bishop's legitimacy. Either as political back-pedalling or from personal sentiment, Dr Tsenoff expressed his sympathy for the Macedonian cause. The Toronto church's 1939 executive committee rejected all attempts at conciliation and informed the bishop of its intention to 'stand perseveringly to the old attitude.'

In trying to maintain their ethnic identity while under the religious jurisdiction of Bulgarian officials, Macedonian communities throughout North America established friendly and close working relations with each other. In 1939, for example, St Clement's Church in Detroit sent a telegram of congratulations to SS Cyril and Methody on patron saints' day. That same year, Macedonian churches in Toronto, Detroit, and Steelton, Pennsylvania, arranged to exchange priests for Christmas and Easter celebrations.

The failure of one Evan Repatseff to win and hold the office of church president at SS Cyril and Methody during 1939 and 1940 prompted Reverend Vasil Mihailoff, who had succeeded Elieff as priest, to resign in anger over the defeat of his friend. The 1940 committee, in the emergency, called on Elieff to return. Elieff initially took the post on a temporary basis. Throughout this period of clerical uncertainty, Bishop Andrey advised and officially helped the church. Thus Canadian Macedonians came, perhaps unwillingly, to depend more on the bishop and the Holy Synod for help appointing priests, compromising their own local tradition of lay initiative. The majority, but not all, of the community was coming to accept episcopal direction and Bulgarian influence.

On 24 November 1940, Bishop Andrey travelled to Toronto to celebrate the holy liturgy and to perform the marriage ceremony of the daughter of church president Lazo Evanoff. An 'irresponsible group' of approximately forty men and women, some already expelled as church members, greeted him with 'all kinds of vulgar words' and volleys of spoiled and stewed tomatoes. Pursued along King Street, the bishop finally found refuge in a Macedonian restaurant at 366 King East. Macedonian Canadians took their theological politics seriously.

The church's executive committee viewed the actions of the protestors as an 'infringement upon the prestige of our Holy Church.' It demanded the full and unconditional excommunication of all members who had demonstrated; membership was to be denied for ever to any outsiders involved. Reverend Mihailoff, 'whom we believe was the "main instigator" of the protest,' was also to receive permanent excommunication. These events led to foundation of a second community church; the undercurrent behind the split called for Macedonian ethnicism and less emphasis on things Bulgarian, except in matters of language. Whoever controlled the church, or churches, went some way to controlling the community.

CONCLUSION

SS Cyril and Methody Church stood, until the split and the creation of a new church in the early 1940s, as the centre of Macedonian ethnicity in Toronto. It grew and survived in the face of a variety of competing forces. Village loyalties were met and subserved by the rise of Macedonian fellow-feeling. Most members felt that the Bulgarian Holy Synod and its influences were being effectively countered by Macedonian commitments and lay initiatives of the parish committee. Within the church, men and women strove for old political and religious aspirations while they also coped with the evolving new identity Macedonian Canadian. The church was a manifold institution – social, political, cultural, and religious. The small contextual changes that, as we have seen, took place within its many activities and folkways during the 1920s and 1930s reveal the evolution of Macedonian ethnicity within North American society.

10

The MPO: Balkan Dreams, Canadian Reality

The failure to free Macedonia and the signing of the peace treaties of 1919, heedless of the nation's claims, demanded a systematic response from expatriates. The community in North America responded by creating the Macedonian Political (later Patriotic) Organization (MPO) in 1921. Article 2 of the MPO's *Constitution and By-laws* stated the hallowed aims: 'To fight and work in a legal manner for the establishment of Macedonia as an independent republic within her geographical boundaries.' The MPO called for independence and was lukewarm about federating Slavic peoples in the Balkans. Facing the reality of its nation's participation in such a federation, however, the MPO also lobbied to protect human and cultural rights for Macedonians in Greece, Bulgaria, and the newly formed Kingdom of Yugoslavia.[1]

In Toronto, MPO's local, Pravda, came very much into its own between its inception in 1922 and the year 1940. During this time of growth and development, it stood beside, and in some sense within, the structure of SS Cyril and Methody Church as a centre of Macedonian nationalism and ethnic identity. The political preoccupations and emblematics of Macedonians in Toronto demonstrate graphically the situation. Fierce commitment to the liberation of their homeland went hand in hand with participation in Ontario and local politics. The almanac for the MPO's 1936 convention in Toronto contained photographs of Ivan Mihailoff, head of the MPO, Mitchell F. Hepburn, Liberal premier of Ontario, and Arthur W. Roebuck, the province's attorney general.[2]

In this chapter, I use the MPO and its publications to explore the attitudes of Macedonian immigrants to Canada in the 1920s and 1930s. Such a study may help avoid the one-dimensional understanding of ethnic politics that comes from looking at newcomers simply as emigrants or immigrants and not as both. Macedonians were people clearly operating between two worlds – that of the old country and the new. This divided consciousness helps explain the political climate of the village and homeland before migration and afterwards, people's perception of themselves in the old country and in Canada, and their ideology and symbols of national identity. Investigating the MPO is a first step toward a more nuanced understanding of Macedonian-Canadian politics and identity. If development of a church was the central ethnic manifestation of the community before the First World War, development of the MPO became the central effort of the 1920s and 1930s.

ORIGINS OF THE MPO

The MPO was founded in Fort Wayne, Indiana, in 1921. It set up headquarters in Indianapolis. Macedonians throughout North America and Australia participated in the life of the MPO through their local organizations. Chapters were founded in Melbourne and Shepparton, Australia, as well as in North America. In the United States, Macedonians founded MPO locals in the Midwest and the Northeast – one in Missouri (at St Louis), one in Illinois (Granite City), ten in Ohio, three in Michigan, and four in each of New York and Pennsylvania. Chapters emerged as well on the west coast, in Los Angeles and San Francisco.[3]

In Canada, MPO interest and activities were created in the Ontario cities of Kitchener, Toronto, and Windsor. The Toronto chapter, which first took the name Macedonian Brotherhood, was founded on 1 May 1922. Members of the immigrant community, with the organizational assistance of Srebren pope Petroff – a gifted speaker and a nationalist – met at the Bull's Head Hotel and appointed John Grudeff, a young Macedonian Protestant and law student, as temporary first president.

A second meeting took place on 1 July 1922 at SS Cyril and Methody Church. Srebren pope Petroff once again presided. Those in attendance considered and voted upon suggested names for the brotherhood. The name Pravda ('Justice') won over 'Fatherland' or 'Liberty' by fifteen votes to six and five, respectively. The organization was known as the Macedonian Brotherhood Pravda until 1925, when it became the Macedonian Political Organization Pravda. Lambro Sotiroff, active in SS Cyril and Methody parish and respected for his oratorical ability, became president.

Membership in Toronto and North America mirrored immigration patterns. The *1937 Annual Convention Almanac* – unfortunately the only annual to attempt to list the village and/or district of origin of each member or sympathizer who pledged faith or purchased space in the book – showed the community, or certainly the most militantly Macedonian part of it, to be drawn from Aegean Macedonia (now in Greece). These members were mostly village folk from places such as Armensko, Buf, Gabresh, and Tersie in the districts of Kostur and Lerin. Immigrants from western Macedonian centres including Bitola, Prespa, Prilep, and Skopje were few in number.

Emigrants to Toronto from villages that supported a Macedonian national revolution were advised by representatives of the Internal Macedonian Revolutionary Organization (IMRO) to take up membership in the MPO when they arrived in Canada: 'When you go there, work for the MPO. I'd like you to be in the right organization, right people, right place.' Men who had, for reasons of language and culture, chosen to identify themselves as Bulgarians from Macedonia or Macedonian Bulgarians were welcomed into the MPO; Bulgarian nationals were encouraged to join as well. Toronto Pravda and SS Cyril and Methody Church shared the same block of immigrant support, but the MPO tried to predict and accommodate all varieties of self-identity, accepting Protestants and free thinkers as long as they were Macedonian nationalists. The MPO's written materials speak variously of Macedonians, Macedonian Slavs, and Bulgarians from Macedonia.[4]

With Greece as the avowed enemy, the organization did not, as a rule, attract Macedonian Patriarchists. It also failed to bring in the Progressives, members of the political left. In Toronto, most Progressives denounced Pravda because it was first and foremost a nationalist body. They saw nationalism as akin to fascism but thought communism properly internationalist in scope. The Progressives also objected to the MPO's ties with SS Cyril and Methody Church.

MEMBERS' RIGHTS AND DUTIES

In this chapter, we are concerned less with the political thought of the MPO and more with how membership activity shaped the immigrant community into a polity. The MPO described itself as the instrument of Macedonian nationality in North America. Its constitution and by-laws opened membership to any Macedonian 'of age' who believed in the cause and was willing to abide by the decisions and orders of the organization.

The local branches and their by-laws set down and enforced the specifics of membership. According to the local Toronto by-laws – similar to those of other branches and printed in 1930 – any Macedonian who was 'over 16 years of age' and backed the MPO's stated aims could gain entry. A new member could cast his first vote one month after being accepted. At the age of twenty-one or over, members became eligible to run for committee office. The memory culture recalls that Toronto Pravda created a youth section for men between sixteen and twenty-five. This extended apprenticeship displeased many young men, who lobbied for lowering the age of entry into the adult group. Pravda, however, remained firm in its requirements; the youth section was deemed especially appropriate for bachelors, even those in their mid-twenties. Pravda reflected the community's understanding of sojourners as men arrested in their social growth.

MPO membership was portable, accommodating the tendency among Macedonian migrants in North America to move from one area and job to another within a common national diaspora. Article 64 of the local by-laws stated: 'A member who changes his abode [residence] rightly becomes a member of the Organization where he goes to live. In such a case, he takes a letter from the committee of the former Organization to the new Organization.' Members who had moved to an area that did not have an organization were invited to retain membership in their old locals.

Local organizations were expected to call a regular membership meeting 'at least once in two months.' All members had the right to speak to issues raised. Each was permitted to speak twice on a question; additional remarks were made only with approval of the general membership body. Issues were decided by majority vote; half the number of regular members plus one constituted both a quorum and a majority. A special meeting could be called if the executive committee thought it necessary, or if one-third of the members requested it in writing. Executive committees could even call for a public meeting, subject to approval of the central committee, which reviewed the choice of speaker and the issue at hand.

Beyond avowing nationalist Macedonian goals, members had duties and obligations. They were expected to pay their dues on time. Those who failed to make payment within a five-month period were deemed to have 'left the Organization.' Mavericks or traitors to the cause who carried on with 'activities against our constitutional deeds' were a matter of great concern to their compatriots and to the local executive committee. The offending member was first 'reminded' of his duties by the president. Failure to correct his ways brought a second reprimand, this time from the executive committee. A persistent and hardened case was then subject to a public 'chiding' by the executive committee at a general membership meeting. The last straw came in the form of expulsion proceedings. The committee drew up its report on the offender's activities and presented it to the membership, which then decided on the verdict; a member could be expelled for a term or life.[5]

The MPO's sensitivity to the role of women grew quickly; women had long participated in the Old World nationalist struggle. A few, such as Mara Buneva, gained notoriety as nationalist fighters and assassins. In the old country, women acted as messengers and gun-runners who moved through the night with their supplies to the mountain retreats of the comitadjiis. Legends grew of female bravery, especially the ability to keep silent about the revolutionary effort before all manner of inquisitors. In North America, women played a part in Macedonian national politics through membership in the various 'ladies' sections.

The first Ladies' Section of the MPO in North America was founded in Toronto on 13 March 1927. The Toronto community had received many women in the immediate post-war years, as US immigration laws slowed arrival of women and family reconstitution. Toronto members took pride in this pioneering role and, as a result, felt obliged to take a leadership role in MPO conventions. 'As the founders of ... Ladies' Sections we ask every Macedonian woman to join us in the struggle for [a] *Free* and *Independent Macedonia*.' Membership fees for women were initially set at ten cents a month or one dollar and twenty cents per annum. By the 1930s, they increased to three dollars per annum as dues. Payment was not taken lightly: 'Ten cents meant an awful lot to us. You could buy an ice cream cone for five cents. [There] wasn't that much money around, and we had to save that just to pay our dues. I was very proud just to be in it.'

The Ladies' Section was at the forefront of the church and community's social life. Tea parties, dances, vecherinki, and a host of religious and political celebrations were all organized and orchestrated in the SS Cyril and Methody's parish hall, not by a parish women's association but by the Ladies' Section of Toronto's MPO Pravda.[6]

ORGANIZATION

The executive committee of Pravda consisted of five officers elected annually. A three-man election bureau had been established by the general membership as an independent body, free from the grasp and control of MPO's central committee in the United States. An annually appointed five-man entertainment commission planned and executed a variety of social activities, including picnics and concerts. The executive committee, whose approval was needed for all ventures, made necessary funds available to the commission, which, in turn, was obliged to provide frequent and up-to-date accounts of income and expenditure. The committee was also expected to operate and maintain an MPO library. It appointed a librarian and provided money for bookshelves and binding. The library's holdings, available to members on loan, included MPO books and Pravda's records, as well as works on 'educational' or 'true Macedonian' subjects.

The executive committee was itself subject to scrutiny and approval. It was expected to account for its decisions and actions before the membership at each and every meeting. An elected board of control monitored its financial activities and was, for example, empowered to audit the committee's financial records once every six months. Thus in politics as in religion, Toronto's Macedonian community showed how fiercely it defended local and democratic rights from centralizing institutions and potentially unresponsive leaders.[7]

The executive ranks of Pravda were both a reflection and a result of the unique relationship between the political organization and the nationalist church. Many community leaders exercised power in both organizations. Lambro Sotiroff, for example, first president of Pravda in 1922, was president of both the Parish Hall and Church Construction committees. Lambro Tenekeff – a man who, in the words of his business partner, attained 'the name not only of a fervent and devoted Macedonian but also of a wise and brave leader of the Macedonian population in Toronto' – served, at different times, as president of both the church's executive committee and Pravda.[8]

The diaspora-wide Union of Macedonian Political Organizations of the United States and Canada was governed from Indianapolis by a central committee – president, vice-president, secretary, treasury, and counsellor – elected from and by the delegates at an annual convention. The committee had a working life of one year; members were obliged to submit their resignations each year at the first meeting of the annual convention. The central committee was dominated by Macedonian Americans, despite the size and importance of Toronto's Macedonian community. Consider the officers for 1937: 'P.G. Shaneff, President, Indianapolis, Ind. Dr. T. Anastasoff, Vice-President, Detroit, Mich. Kosta

Popoff, Vice-President, McKeesport, Pa. Tashe Popcheff, Treasurer, Indianapolis, Ind. Carl Chaleff, Counsellor, Indianapolis, Ind. Luben Dimitroff, Counsellor, Indianapolis, Ind. Peter Atzeff, Secretary, Indianapolis, Ind.'[9] Although some Torontonians coveted membership in the central committee (it was, according to the memory culture, much more prestigious than a post on the church executive committee), travel to Indianapolis and stringent US immigration rules made high office expensive and difficult for Macedonian Canadians and few attained it.

The central committee was the sole representative body of the Union of MPOs. It alone chose the organization's representatives and sent them worldwide, to wherever the cause had need of protection or promotion. The committee was collectively responsible to the organization for its decisions and actions. It was obliged to outline, explain, or even defend its actions before the delegates at each and every annual convention. It derived its operating funds from a variety of sources, including voluntary donations, contributions, and subscriptions. It expected to receive 50 per cent of the total monthly income of every local branch. Each member was also expected to 'pay to the treasury of the Central Committee one day's wages which are remitted through the local organization to which he belongs.'

Few immigrants, however, in the opinion of many Macedonians, could afford to honour the secular tithe. The practice, according to the memory culture, was neither popular nor widespread. Pravda in Toronto had established strong financial ties with SS Cyril and Methody Church; the parish hall's income for May was earmarked as support for Indianapolis. The central committee, in turn, was required to keep the funds in a 'first class bank' and to credit the money to the local. Funds could be deposited and withdrawn only under the name of the president and the secretary of the central committee.

Despite such measures, however, the committee's overall financial decisions and activities did not escape scrutiny. The annual convention elected three members to a board of control, which monitored financial accounts. Financial checks and monitoring system aside, the decision of men in Toronto – mostly labourers and small shopkeepers – to send hard-earned money to Indianapolis bespoke trust, the simple power of loyalty and patriotism.[10]

THE *MACEDONIAN TRIBUNE*

The MPO's major literary vehicle for group communication and for dialogue was its weekly newspaper, the *Macedonian Tribune* (Makedonska tribuna), published, beginning in 1927, in Indianapolis in its own printing shop. The paper attempted to inform readers about social, political, and economic developments in the Balkans and their impact upon the 'Macedonian question.' It also allowed the MPO to state its case and cajole and remind members and sympathizers of their heroic duties as well as their moral and financial obligations to the cause.

The newspaper was funded and supported through subscriptions – two or three dollars a year in the 1920s and 1930s – donations, printing, book publishing, and sale of advertising space. While this last affected mainly those in the ethnoculture, Preston G. Woolf, one of the paper's national advertising representatives, tried to entice non-Macedonian businessmen: 'Would you like to find a new and virgin market of 50,000 people, before which you could place your advertising message? Such a field exists today among the Macedonian people of the United States and Canada. They can be reached only through their official newspaper, *The Macedonian Tribune.*'[11] SS Cyril and Methody Church in Toronto transferred the parish hall's income for February to the MPO and its newspaper. It did so through the purchase of books, including Bulgarian-language school texts, from the MPO and through its use of the *Tribune*'s printing facilities. The parish paid the *Tribune* to print invitations, notices, and programs.

The *Tribune* helped immigrants develop deeper awareness of their compatriots' activities and happenings in other immigrant centres. Each community, including Toronto, had its own member-correspondent, who recorded items of local and international immigrant interest. Toronto's was appointed by his compatriots at a Pravda meeting. He was required to report only 'verified deeds' so as not to mislead or embarrass the editorial staff and the immigrant community at large. The general membership could suspend him for violations of Pravda's or the MPO's rules. The *Tribune* thus maintained both a valuable news service in the field and rigorous control over submissions; correspondents could not submit their work to other newspapers and publications. And so the journal came to play a significant role in the community. By its Macedonian ethnicity, if not its purity of language, it dislodged the older Bulgarian newspaper, *Naroden Glas*, from its lofty position as the community's literary centrepiece.[12]

ANNUAL CONVENTIONS

The annual convention was the MPO's other social link and communications tool; it was also an instrument through which to attempt to maintain political orthodoxy and nationalist fervour. Conventions were held early each September over the Labour/Labor Day holiday. The location changed each year, and local organizations took on a mountain of hospitality duties. Cleveland, for example, hosted the eleventh annual conclave in 1932, and the Toronto chapter, Pravda, the fifteenth, in 1936. Elected delegates represented local organizations. Locals with more than seven members were entitled to send one or more delegates – one delegate for every thirty members. The branches and their delegates had to have their credentials accepted by the central committee, based on their ability to demonstrate friendship and 'sympathy with the ideas of the Macedonian movement' and to prove that all concerned had 'paid all dues two months before the convention.' Toronto's Pravda elected its delegates by secret ballot and then, agenda in hand, briefed and instructed them on issues to be discussed. Delegates were bound and expected to uphold the views of their locals.[13]

Each convention spawned celebration, socialization, and group inter-action. It was a point in the ethnic liturgical year as much as a political gathering. The Toronto convention of 1936 was a community-wide event. Given the cost of hotels – rooms at the Royal York started at four dollars per day by 1937 – most of the delegates stayed with local Macedonians. Recalling the laughter and fellow-feeling generated by his house guests, one informant stated that he 'used to have twenty people at my house [who slept] all over, like the old country.' Even people not involved in the convention offered lodging to out-of-town acquain-tances. Thus in 1936 a barber, not active in the MPO, and his wife who lived in the Junction eagerly awaited a delegate who was a friend and fellow-barber from Michigan.[14]

Parades and celebratory marches helped launch each convention. The MPO's magazine, *Macedonia*, described the opening of the 1932 gathering:

On the morning of the 4th of September this multitude [two thousand individuals – guests, delegates, and members] gathered before the [Cleveland] City Hall, whence, after being photographed, it started the manifestation to the strains of the large 'Russo Band' which played 'Star Spangled Banner' and the Macedonian National March. The manifestation was headed by an automobile decorated with flowers. Seated in the automobile were several Macedonian girls arrayed in their national costumes, and holding a large placard bearing the inscription 'Macedonia for the Macedonians.' Following this the manifestants marched bearing American and Macedonian flags. Many placards were on display ... In perfect harmony and discipline the manifestation stopped before the Moose Hall, where the opening of the convention took place.

A participant in 1936 in Toronto recalled the opening exercises: 'From Trinity [Street] we used to walk to City Hall, all dressed up in Macedonian clothes. [We laid] wreaths at the Cenotaph ... The English people loved MPO parades. [It was] like Christmas. The whole of King Street was ours.'[15]

Banquets, celebrations, and entertainments dominated the evening sessions. The 1937 convention in Indianapolis, for example, featured two dances, two plays, *The Moralist* and *A Woman's Mind*, and two musical concerts, performed by the host organization, MPO Damien Grueff, and the Ladies' Section. Each convention reflected evolving local attitudes. Delegates elected a committee from among themselves to conduct the transactions and affairs of the convention sessions.[16]

These gatherings could re-establish and reaffirm collective political goals. Thus the 1932 convention stated that 'its supreme duty' was 'to redouble its efforts for the conquest of the rights of its oppressed fellow-countrymen in Macedonia.' It offered moral, spiritual, and financial support to those back in the homeland: 'And to those of our brothers, who, in Summer heat or icy Winter, weapons in hand, incessantly cross the sacred Macedonian land, bearing in the depths of their heart the revolutionary lore of Macedonia, the convention sends its most heartfelt greetings ... To them we wish a granite solidarity, an indomitable fighting spirit, and a never abating courage in this glorious struggle.' The statement also expressed solidarity with all other Macedonian legal political organizations around the world and with the Croatian people and their cause. The convention also called for enforcement of League of Nations' treaties protecting minorities. Acknowledging Britain's leadership in establishing provisions for protection of minority rights, it argued that his majesty's government and its representatives now had a special responsibility to see that these stipulations were upheld and 'made effective.' Macedonians also pressed for a plebiscite to decide the true nationality of the subject Macedonians – 'to determine whether they are Serbs or Bulgars or just Macedonians.'[17]

Conventions were the time and place for a review of the MPO's procedures and even its constitution. Delegates could change the constitution and by-laws – articles could be added or deleted. The outgoing central committee presented and defended its record – the only occasion when local organizations could take issue with its decisions and actions.

In 1932, the departing committee and its report met with delegates' approval. Conventions also elected the incoming central committee, which took office immediately.[18]

RELATIONS WITH OTHERS

Macedonians generally, and the MPO especially, understood the value of having the goodwill of other North Americans. They succeeded in recruiting a few able supporters and propagandists from outside their own community. 'I have good reason to know [the adversity of Macedonians], the Yugoslav police having very kindly provided me with abundant demonstration during the brief period I spent in their hands in 1929!' wrote John Bakeless, an American journalist and sympathizer. He warned Macedonians that they could expect little sympathy over the state of affairs in their homeland from a typical North American: 'it's so strange, so dreadful that even when he is told about it, he only half believes.'[19]

Macedonians had long tried to explain their identity and their problem to their neighbours. Nedelkoff's *English-Bulgarian and Bulgarian-English Letters* (1911) offered a description and translation of a Macedonian's account, cast as a letter to an American acquaintance, of life under the 'enlightened' Young Turks: 'This talk of reforms, constitution, parliament ... etc., is a joke and a mockery on progress and civilization but must be endured until either the Christian people, composing the bulk of the population, arise against Turkish misrule, or, some European Power ... should smash up the rocking remnants of the once mighty empire of the Ottomans.'

The MPO tried, more systematically, to explain its view of Balkan history. In 1927, it began to wage its campaign with literary weapons carefully crafted not to offend and to play on North American sensibilities. The Pro Macedonia Series of pamphlets included *The Macedonian Slavs: Their National Character and Struggles*. In 1932, the MPO's publishing wing started producing a monthly periodical, *Macedonia: A Magazine Devoted to the Macedonian Movement for Liberty and Independence*. The inaugural edition told all first-time readers: 'In an effort to enlighten the friends of freedom in the Balkans, we have taken the liberty of presenting to them the first number of the monthly "Macedonia," hoping that it will receive their kind attention and enlist their sympathy in the colossal struggle of a nation, which has proven by dint of its self-sacrifice, that it is entitled to the right to liberty and independence. The acknowledgement of the receipt of the current issue of this magazine, as well as encouragement along the lines of its program, will be appreciated.'[20]

At first glance, *Macedonia* appeared to be little more than a collection of the speeches and writings of the 'friends of Macedonia' – sympathetic New World scholars and European advocates. As a scholar, Herbert Adams Gibbons had written a book on fourteenth-century Macedonia and the foundations of the Ottoman Empire; as a journalist, he covered the Balkan Wars for the *New York Herald*. And so he wrote commentary for *Macedonia* on Balkan affairs.[21]

The magazine also attempted to prime its readers' knowledge with articles on the physical and human setting of Macedonia. The editor of the *Macedonian Tribune*, Luben Dimitroff, contributed a detailed account of life in one of the heartland districts, Pirin, and a series of articles described the situation and plight of the Jews in Macedonia.[22] The magazine tried to show the homeland's ethnic diversity while maintaining that all minorities would be safer under Macedonian rule. It produced thorough and unsparing accounts of life under the twin oppressors Yugoslavia and Greece, which were portrayed as perpetrating cultural genocide through denationalization programs. Colonel Leon Lamouche, a French student of Macedonian affairs and a former member of the International Commission for the Reorganization of the Ottoman Police Force, wrote sympathetically of those Macedonians who 'felt themselves to be Bulgarians' who were suffocating under Greek rule.[23]

Ethnic identity aside, Macedonians also wanted to be known by their neighbours on this continent as a civilized, if politically committed, people. 'The Tourists Paradise, an Englishman's Impressions of Macedonia under Bulgarian Domination,' turned stereotype into pun: 'The people in Macedonia are all brigands, but of the right type. That they try to kill a stranger entering their territory is true, not by bullets but by kindness.'[24] The suffering of villagers and comitadjiis at the hands of oppressive officialdom was asserted in *Macedonia*'s monthly list of martyrs. The entries were simple and graphic: martyrdom for the cause of independence was a theme of Macedonian ethnicity in the diaspora. A typical entry read: 'None Andoff of Village Raychani, 21 years [of age], Murdered in a most barbarous way at the locality, Suha Vodenitsa, near the village Spanchevo, county of Cochansco. The Serbians pulled out his eyes and cut off his ears.'[25]

The periodical also used fiction to promote the national cause. America's best Macedonian writer, *Chicago Daily News* journalist Stoyan

Christowe, depicted the homeland's problems in very human terms through his serialized account of the life of a young village boy, Paul Dragor.[26] The magazine and Macedonians generally tried to show a congruence between the American struggle for liberty and their own cause: 'The American people, who have won their freedom and democracy with the blood of their best sons are known as the traditional sympathizers of downtrodden nations. True to their pacific nature, they cannot be indifferent to the fate of Macedonia.'[27] For Canadian Macedonians, educated in a British dominion, there must have been irony in the *Macedonian Tribune*'s use of a revolutionary quotation from Patrick Henry on its masthead. The MPO warned Anglo-Americans of the repercussions of inaction or of failure to bring about Macedonia's freedom and autonomy. Following a visit to the Balkan peninsula, the French writer Albert Lantoine berated *Macedonia*'s readers: 'We are willing to concern ourselves with this Balkan question. We pretend to believe it settled. But it isn't. Before the war – long before – alert minds, well acquainted with conditions in Macedonia endeavored to sound the alarm, proclaiming: "This is the spark that will enkindle the next conflagration." We don't believe them. Let us go on being the ostrich and hiding our heads in the sand so as not to see the danger.'[28]

The power of the ethnic press to persuade the host society was supplemented by the immigrants' own efforts to establish good personal and working relationships with influential citizens and elected officials. In 1932, the president of the MPO's central committee, P.G. Shaneff, proudly informed the convention delegates 'that at this juncture our cause is very much advanced. The connections which the Central Committee has made with prominent social workers and men of political prominence are noteworthy, a fact which is greatly encouraging to us in our struggle against the tyrants of Macedonia.'[29]

Toronto's leadership worked assiduously to build political connections with the host society. Whether to raise support for an independent homeland or to get a liquor licence or zoning changes, Macedonians cultivated the city's politicians. It was a tactic so successful that it suggests, despite protestations of unrelenting enmity, that they had learned this way of dealing with authorities back in the Ottoman Empire. Allan Lamport, alderman and later mayor, was a 'good friend [of the community] before he was Mayor [and] after that [his election]. Everybody [Macedonians] vote for him at that time.' The MPP for St David's riding, Wilfrid Heighington, was a 'tried and true friend of the Macedonian People in Ontario.' Such politicians were guaranteed delivery of a large bloc of ethnic votes.[30]

What did the Macedonians get beyond lip service for their cause and the small 'ward heeling' favours that any group seeks? In the 1930s, at a time when their reputation in the world was badly compromised by IMRO assassins working with and for other revisionist movements, Toronto's press and public did not fault the local community or turn on its cause. The murder of King Alexander I of Yugoslavia and the French foreign minister, Louis Barthou, in 1934 gave the *Toronto Star* a chance to identify Macedonian extremism with political terrorism, but the paper did not. It had no reason to turn on Macedonians, and doing so would not sell more papers: 'Paradoxically, police had in their hands the body of the assassin, but they did not know who he was. His Czechoslovakian passport was definitely proved to have been forged. His name was a fake. Martyr to a grim purpose he had succeeded in death in covering up his trail. Tattooed initials found on his body linked him to the dread "IMRO," the independent Macedonian revolutionary organization, but detectives thought this, too, might have been a "red herring" to throw police off the trail of his co-conspirators.' The paper concerned itself more with possible Italian fascist involvement, identified the murders as the product of Croatian violence, and made little of the Macedonian identity of the trigger man.[31]

If Macedonians in Toronto secretly approved of acts that might lead to the freeing of the homeland, they were usually discreet in their manifestations of Old World struggle in Canada. The emerging alliance between IMRO and the avowedly fascist Croatian Ustashi presented problems for those in Toronto who wished loyalty to the British Empire and to Macedonia to be compatible. IMRO's long-time chieftain, Ivan Mihailoff, had made available to the Croatians the services of some of his political operatives – read 'assassins.' Vladimir (Vlado) Gheroghieff Tchernosemsky, the future killer of the Yugoslav king, was one of them. It would not do for Anglo-Canadians to come to think of Macedonians as political terrorists. Nonetheless, feelings of brotherhood and solidarity with Croatians against a common Serbian oppressor did surface in the New World.

The president of the Croatian Peasant Party in America appeared at the MPO's 1932 convention and reminded the audience of the importance of strengthening 'the common Macedono-Croat front, against the dictatorship of Belgrade.' The Croatian Home Defenders of the United States demonstrated support for the Macedonians and their cause with a full-page ad in the *16th Annual Convention Almanac* (1937), which stated: '... wish you success in your cause, and hope that the spirits of your martyrs lead you through the convention. Long Live Macedonia! Long Live Vancho Mihailoff!'[32] Partially in response to this incipient North American alliance of dissidents, pro-Yugoslav or anti-fascist elements began to take note of the Macedonian community. For example, fourteen members of the Yugoslav Benefit Society Blue Adriatic drew up a petition for the attention of the Yugoslav consulate. The document called for Canadian government authorities to 'prevent' members of Toronto's MPO Pravda 'from further insulting our nation' during their meetings.

In the summer of 1928, A.V. Seferovitch, who held a post in Canada that seemed to sum up all of Macedonia's oppressors – he was 'Consul for the Serbs, Croats, and Slovenes and Acting Consul for Greece' – responded to the petition's request and initiated a round of correspondence with O.D. Skelton, Canada's under-secretary of state for external affairs, concerning the political activities of Toronto's Macedonian community. The consul described Pravda as being a New World appendage of IMRO, a 'nest breeding revolution' in Macedonia. Whether he believed the MPO to be an IMRO front or saw this as the best tactic with which to approach Canadian authorities is unclear. He wrote that it was an organization to be feared, since it had 'developed its activities greatly' and provided arms and funds 'for the *Komitadjis* to kill mercilessly our officials and attack peaceable inhabitants in Southern Serbia.' More important, he wrote, the continued subversive existence of Pravda seemed assured, since Toronto's Macedonian colony was large and close to the United States. He depicted a never-ending stream of revolutionaries passing through a Canadian city.

The consul and his petitioners were especially upset by the MPO's blatant display of patriotic zeal and anti-Serbian and anti-Greek sentiment. There had been public display of the photograph of the heroine assassin Mara Buneva and 'hateful songs'; furthermore, 'theatrical tragedies with Serbian officers as villains and murderers have been performed, and speeches delivered on the same occasions with wild shouts of "down with the Jugoslav Government and the King and down with the Hellenic Republic!" and other insulting expressions.' Such events had to be curbed if not eliminated by Canadian authorities, claimed the consul, if good relations between states were to be maintained and tragedy avoided.

The diplomat suggested a course of action: Canadian officials should examine the identity and resident status of some of the officers and participants of Pravda. One of them, L.A. Basheff, was identified as a leader and 'paid agitator' and was accused of having entered Canada illegally under the assumed name Doleff. The consul asked for deportation proceedings against him. Nicholas Shonteff, a Toronto court interpreter and commissioner of oaths, and a past president of Pravda and staunch activist, was described as a police informer, and, if the Macedonian political left were to be believed, a spy who supported the Yugoslav cause. The Yugoslavs of Toronto had raised the following question for their consul's consideration: 'How can he be a good interpreter if he is a member of the revolutionary organization and employs Basheff as a clerk in his office.' The consul urged Skelton and his staff to act against Pravda 'to prevent eventual serious conflicts and clashes which might occur.'

The consul wanted Pravda to conduct its proceedings entirely in English so that it might better be monitored by the authorities. He claimed that such action was both timely and not without precedent. In May 1928, Toronto's police commissioners had put the Macedonian Progressives' club, Hristo Botev, on 'six months probation and forbade it to hold meetings in any language other than English,' after public disturbances involving its members and Pravda's.

Skelton, later at the centre of wartime dealings with Canada's ethnic groups, acknowledged receipt of the consul's letter with thanks for the information contained therein. He sent copies of the letter and its attachments to Colonel Sarnes, commissioner of the Royal Canadian Mounted Police, for further study and recommendations. In his reply to Skelton, Assistant Commissioner A.W. Duffus of the RCMP characterized Pravda as a 'more or less religious' society 'apparently anti-Serbian,' and the Progressives' club as 'communistic' and an obvious opponent of MPO Pravda. Promising to have the matter looked into further, he concluded: 'As regards action, I hardly know what to do. The Communists of course contravene Canadian laws, but they are of very little importance compared with the Ukrainian, French and Jewish revolutionists, and it has not been our policy to do more than watch their people. As for the racial quarrels, the situation seems to me still less susceptible of action.' The best way to proceed on such a low-priority item was, according to the RCMP, to sit and watch, acting only if the situation deteriorated. Skelton, noting that 'the information brought forward by Capt. Seferovitch was wholly an old story to you,' thanked the force, saying, 'It is extremely difficult to ascertain the truth in these Balkan wrangles.' MPO Pravda had no direct confrontation with Canadian authorities.[33]

A SEA CHANGE

Whatever the MPO's relationship to the sporadic war of liberation in Macedonia, its role changed when IMRO used political terrorism against Yugoslavia and Greece to keep its cause front and centre after being crippled by its former Bulgarian allies. The Macedonian revolutionaries under Mihailoff had appointed 'school teachers, municipal clerks, tax collectors ... mayors of towns and villages' in the Petrich district of Bulgaria. By the mid-1930s, the Bulgarian government forcefully 'regained' control of the region, arresting or exiling a number of comitadjiis. Mihailoff had to flee the country for the safety of Turkey. The government also seized the assets and holdings of IMRO, including cash, food, artillery, and garment supplies.[34]

These events had a double impact on Macedonian identity in North America. First, the burden of maintaining both nationalism and ethnicity fell increasingly on legal entities such as the MPO. Men now hoped that lobbies and petitions could do what the gun and the sword could not. As one old MPO member put it: '[We were] working to free Macedonia from three countries: Yugoslavia, Bulgaria [and] Greece. We can never fight [and win] with guns.'[35] Second, a less easily defined malaise emerged within the New World's Macedonian identity itself. At a time when acculturation was taking its toll, those loyal to the homeland's culture found that they had to rethink the Bulgarian component of their identity. If the Bulgarian regime betrayed IMRO, could they in good faith continue to describe themselves as the Bulgarians of Macedonia, call their language Bulgarian, and deal with the Bulgarian Orthodox church? We saw in chapter 9 the growing tensions with the Holy Synod in this very period.

The MPO also began to realize that its obligations lay as much with North American reality as with Balkan dreams. The community was large, permanently settled, but threatened with ethnocultural decline. Pravda's 15th Annual Convention Almanac (1936) began: 'The Macedonian Political Organization "Justice" considers it its first and imperative duty to emphasize the sincere attachment of the Macedonians living in Canada toward their adopted country, where they are able to find a welcome refuge from the persecution and tyranny of the foreign subjugators in their own native land. A haven which is similar to that extended to their brothers and sisters in the United States.' The organization sought to elevate the immigrants' 'social consciousness' both in terms of Macedonian culture and as good Canadian citizens. Macedonians in Toronto made public and symbolic display of their newfound loyalty at every possible opportunity. Pravda, in conjunction with SS Cyril and Methody Church, conducted its meetings, Dominion Day parades, and Macedonian memorial marches under the twin banners of the MPO and the Union Jack.[36]

THE EVENTS OF 1940

After eighteen years of activity on behalf of the ethnic group, something happened to Toronto's MPO Pravda that offers a valuable insight into the relationship of Toronto's Macedonians to one another and to the Macedonian cause in the United States and the Balkans. The changes that occurred in Pravda's relations with the international MPO represent shifts in Macedonian-Canadian self-perception.

It all began with the 1940 election to Pravda's executive committee of men who had shown disloyalty to the international body. A counter-group emerged loyal to Indianapolis and committed to traditional MPO discipline. The memory culture offers two possible explanations. Some informants spoke of long-standing jealousy and hostility between Pravda's new president and one of the leaders who remained loyal to the central committee. Others argue that the new officers were deemed unacceptable because of their conduct at the previous annual convention. There they had challenged headquarters over its financial activities and had raised questions about the MPO's relationship with IMRO. Did the central committee provide a pension for the widow of the Macedonian assassin of the Yugoslav king? Raising these questions, which had not been authorized by Pravda's general membership, was embarrassing. The questions also reflected Canadian Macedonians' efforts to distance themselves from images of terrorism and to appear to support Great Britain's allies.

Concerns about the international organization's dispersal of funds had often been raised in Toronto. Suspicion and rumours of wrongdoing had arisen occasionally, but people usually kept their doubts to themselves. To do otherwise could very well have seemed disloyal, and Macedonian-ness exerted powerful social coercion on them all. The outbreak at the 1939 convention and the subsequent election of those who had questioned the central committee demanded some response from the international body and those loyal to it in Toronto, especially since the MPO had always maintained that it did not support terrorist acts in the Balkans. The Toronto loyalists wrote to Indianapolis seeking a new election and the turning out of the dissident executive; headquarters agreed. The second election was held, but the dissident committee, which obviously represented the majority view in Toronto, was returned once more, with an even larger majority. The loyalists were unable to turn out the dissidents and so asked the MPO to dispatch representatives to Canada in an effort to put Pravda back together again.

The efforts of the representatives proved fruitless. The two meetings that they called at SS Cyril and Methody Church accomplished nothing; the men were booed and hissed by the Pravda majority. And so with thoughts of reconciliation and peace gone from their minds, they huddled in the store of an MPO loyalist and made some decisions – swift and harsh. They ordered the expulsion of eighteen members of Pravda, including the twice–duly elected executive. The arbitrary move stunned the entire membership. The representatives had simply announced the expulsions as a fait accompli, without stating the grounds for the decision and, most important, without seeking members' approval. Most Toronto Macedonians saw the action as high-handed and illegal, and so the situation deteriorated further. There is no doubt that an emerging Toronto and Canadian consciousness of being dictated to by smaller, old-fashioned US communities also fuelled the flames.

As the governing body of the MPO, the central committee now felt that it had to act quickly to force the errant Toronto unit back into line. It stepped outside the arena of the ethnoculture and took Pravda, still operating under the dissidents, to the Canadian courts in an effort to strip it of its charter. Pravda won in the courts. The central committee's representatives had to desist, returning to Indianapolis to wait for the upcoming annual convention, at which time they quite legally expelled the entire Pravda local from the MPO. Indianapolis then encouraged the loyalist rump to form a new local, Victory. Members and supporters of Pravda, who were in the majority, resurrected the old organization and refused to leave the field to the new local. The constitution and by-laws of the MPO stated that there could be only one local per city. Article IV of section III of the 1928 edition read, 'More than one Macedonian Political Organization in one city cannot exist.'

The new local Victory, and only Victory, was allowed to represent Toronto at subsequent annual conventions. This practice was spiteful and self-defeating for maintenance of both the ethnic group in Toronto and the Macedonian national idea in the world. Eventually relations were restored with Pravda. Both it and Victory became Toronto's representatives. Thus the note following article V of section II in the 1956 edition of the by-laws reads: 'More than one Macedonian Patriotic

Organization [as the body came to be known later] in one city cannot exist, with the exception of the already approved two MPO in Toronto, Canada.'

Although the concession, in turn, stood as eloquent testimony to Toronto's importance within the diaspora, in many ways it came too late. Pravda's difficulties had taken their toll on the membership ranks. The controversy had led members to withdraw from the MPO and immigrant public life in general and had accelerated acculturation and community disintegration in Toronto. As a result MPO members who clung to mental images of a Macedonian diaspora throughout the world, of a free and whole Macedonia, and who read and followed the dictates of the MPO's newspaper from Indianapolis, were no longer the majority in Toronto's community but rather a small, dedicated rump group.[37]

CONCLUSION

The MPO and its Toronto chapter, Pravda, proved powerful expressions of Macedonian identity through the 1920s and 1930s. The pictures of Macedonian revolutionaries and Canadian politicians juxtaposed in the MPO's annual almanacs revealed both the immigrants' attitudes and their position between two worlds. Political propagandists and their kinfolk still in the villages tied them to the Macedonian national idea. At the same time, generational attrition and acculturation in North America and changing politics in the Balkans – as well as a slowly developing distinction between American and Canadian Macedonian identities – were causing individuals and institutions in Toronto's Macedonian community to change their emphasis from the Old World to the New, as witnessed in the dramatic events in Pravda about 1940, which paralleled similar upheavals at SS Cyril and Methody Church. Men and women were becoming Macedonians, plain and simple, at the same time that they were becoming Canadian.

11

Evolving Definitions

Who were the Macedonians of Toronto in the period before 1940? What was their sense of identity? How did they see the social and cultural processes that were changing them from Old World villagers? How had their sense of being Macedonian evolved in reaction to Turkish or Greek overlords and then in the face of the Anglo-Celtic society in Toronto? Both the boundaries and the substance of Macedonian ethnicity in Canada are best understood as process, not as cultural baggage from the Old World or as simply an artefact made by circumstance in the New. The social and geographical processes of migration and settlement – the early years of sojourning and the various formal and informal group institutions established within sojourner/settler life by Macedonians in Toronto – both created a Macedonian ethnicity and made people who were products of it.

Everyday life affected ethnic identity in terms of individual, family, and household. If we now have an idea of who the Macedonians thought they were in the sojourner and settler phases, we must ask how consciously they held this identity and whether they tried and succeeded in keeping it. They made complex decisions each day about relationships to fellow villagers, other Macedonians, and other Torontonians – immigrant and native. Cultural and social pre-conditioning affected such choices, but that is not to say that they came carelessly. These people – who established boarding-houses and the codes of behaviour that went with them, who as sojourners shunned English-language classes but as settlers went to night school, who built village-based mutual and fraternal organizations and a national parish – were not passive victims of acculturation any more than they were diehard sojourners, wanting only to return home. Encounters with the larger Canadian society made Macedonians, as thinking and reflective people, modify, abandon, or assert with even more resolve many of their folk-ways and mores.

CARETAKERS' ATTITUDES

How the 'caretakers' viewed the Macedonians is a valid subject of inquiry, but precisely because Macedonian Canadians have been so fugitive in the traditional sources and in danger of disappearing from our history as articulate actors, I have tried here to re-create the world of a people looking inwards and then out. This book examines how Macedonians perceived and responded to the Canadians around them rather than the reverse.

While the Anglo-Protestant churches and schools tried to capture the minds and souls of the immigrants and their families, doctors and nurses cared about their physical health and well-being. Public health nurses were the most visible 'caretakers' in the immigrant neighbour-hood. The work of the nursing service in the crowded East End was made easier by the appointment of 'ethnic language' nurses. In 1914 'a young Italian nurse,' Miss Matilda Simoni, was the first such person to join the staff. In 1920, a young Macedonian nurse, Miss Parashka Stamenova, also signed on. Stamenova taught both English and infant care to Macedonian mothers. 'She would,' in the opinion of one respondent, 'assist in the life of things.' She also made regular health inspections of children in neighbourhood public schools. Usually suspicious, Macedonian youngsters submitted, along with the rest of their classmates, to Stamenova's routine examination of hair, teeth, and eyes. In the West End, Macedonian students at Niagara Street Public School were ably tended to by Nurse Fraser, who had done Red Cross work in the Balkans during the First World War. The students were awed by her knowledge and understanding of Macedonia and its way of life: 'She know how they [the villagers] lived. She told us about Florina.'[1]

Stamenova became a vital link with the strange ways of the city for Macedonian mothers and their children. For the group as a whole, Stamenova and, of course, Dr Mallin (formerly Archimandrite Theophi-lact) led the movement from Old World cures to the acceptance of modern medicine. When Stamenova escorted a mother and her sick child to hospital in the aftermath of a winter storm, and when Mallin paid the cost of X-rays and treatment, they acquainted their compatriots with new possibilities, opportunities for life and survival that did not exist in the village. It was part of the acculturation process.[2]

Macedonians, of course, were quick to appreciate anything that modern medicine could do for them. They were also bitter and quick to realize that access to such treatment depended on cash. The care of a good doctor and a proper hospital stay cost money. In the first years of settlement, the limits of family income led to heart-breaking decisions about seeking medical help. Macedonians often had to move uncomfortably within a complex set of choices and beliefs – among Old World cures, modern medicine, and the usual effort to save money. Remembering the death by pneumonia of a strapping baby brother, a woman respondent angrily concluded that her mother should have abandoned her frugal ways, and even been willing to violate a sharing-of-expenses agreement with her boarders, in order to call a doctor at the first sign of trouble. Sometimes, it seems, Old World cures were called on as a last resort by poor people who had come to know better.[3]

Illness took its toll of the Macedonian young in Canada at a higher rate than those outside the immigrant quarters. Macedonian infants and children died of such diseases as pneumonia, diphtheria, typhoid, and infant diarrhoea. SS Cyril and Methody's burial records tell us, for example, of a two-and-a-half-year-old victim of diphtheria and a six-month-old baby who died of 'terminal diarrhea acid.' Adults likewise succumbed to the prevailing respiratory diseases, such as tuberculosis and pneumonia. The great influenza epidemic of 1919–20 also claimed its share of Macedonian victims: 'The combana [bell] at SS. Cyril and Methody was banging every day as Macedonians died.' Funeral services were held a day or two after death; interment was usually at Toronto's Necropolis Cemetery. Macedonians depended on the services of Anglo-Canadian funeral directors; whether from lack of capital or other prohibitions, Macedonians simply did not enter the funeral business.[4]

Macedonian dealings with Toronto's various 'caretakers' formed an important part of the acculturation process. The encounter between immigrant and 'caretaker' was a lesson from which Macedonians, used to dealing carefully with officials of other ethnicities in the homeland, learned.

The simple working of neighbourhood, the response and reaction of native Canadians to the Macedonian presence, and the places where they let their feelings be known (such as streets and schoolyards) also affected the group's acculturation. Former sojourners all recall endless rounds of verbal and physical abuse, having epithets such as 'Dago' and 'Wop' thrown at them, along with stones and tomatoes. In time, such prejudice caused strains between parents and offspring. Motivated by embarrassment or even anger, children frequently sought to sit apart from 'their foreign parents' on the streetcar or in other public places. At school, the young people were themselves subject to abuse. Some respondents remember being called 'Macedonian Wops' or 'greaseballs' by classmates. The hostility was also expressed in racial terms – they were often reminded that they were not 'White' Anglo-Saxons.[5]

Part of the process of assimilation was apparently learning to take one's place in the pecking order. While Macedonian youngsters were themselves abused, they participated in attacks against Jewish and Black students. Outside the school, some Macedonians joined Protestant gangs in numerous street fights against the Catholic students of nearby separate schools. They scrapped and brawled but rarely joined the ranks of the officially delinquent. In the East End particularly, Macedonians noted but did not share their Anglo-Canadian working-class school-mates' penchant for early and frequent run-ins with the police. Adults in the community exhibit pride in the record of the group's good conduct; they point to how few Macedonians have ever been convicted of criminal activities in Canada. Dr Mallin attributed their civil behaviour to lessons learned under Turkish rule. The good physician is remembered to have said, perhaps with tongue in cheek: 'We hated the Turks but they gave us character, made us respect and obey the law.'[6]

THE TORONTO CRUCIBLE

It was their ambition and goals that governed the Macedonians' perceptions of themselves. Their basic sense of decency and good conduct as well as their ideas on the purpose of the settlement and uses of the neighbourhood dictated their behaviour. The East End experience of the group can teach us much about the psychology of immigrant life.[7] The sojourners who decided to stay and rear families moved beyond their village identities when they became Macedonians together in Canada. They also took the first step in creating a Macedonian-Canadian community when they started legal procedures to become citizens. The naturalization process, given the dealings with officialdom and the paper work, was an important confrontation with modernity. For the first time, Macedonians did not dissemble or practise evasion in the face of government. They registered marriages, births, and deaths.[8] It was not possible for many, except the most politicized, to see that Canadianization might in the end lead to a total extirpation of Macedonian-ness that neither Turkish swords nor Greek denial of their existence had been able to accomplish.

Their children and even some of the adults were 'at home' in Canada. They were Macedonian and Canadian in a way that the first sojourners and the MPO could not comprehend. Their Macedonian-ness was broad-based in its origins. It was nurtured in kitchens and living-rooms and by participation in the youth programs sponsored by nationalist/group and village/fraternal organizations. Village loyalties, ethnic nationalism, and Toronto neighbourhoods were touchstones of Macedonian-Canadian ethnicity. Yet lines of internal division that had ferocity of meaning to the immigrant generation were easily crossed in a haze of Macedonian-Canadian nostalgia by their children. Thus the offspring of church-goers joined the picnics of the hated Progressives after the Second World War.[9]

Settlers expanded and enhanced their Macedonian-ness through dating and marriage within the group. Few parents felt that, given the size of the available pool of candidates, village endogamy was possible (inter-village unions were not unknown in the old country). Immigrants from Zhelevo and Oshchima, for example, formed a number of such alliances, which tended, however, to link young people from villages proximate to one another in the old country. The growth of a larger Macedonian identity – a response to the reality and demands of New World life – made these 'mixed marriages' perfectly acceptable.

It is difficult to prove going back through the layers of the memory culture, but by the mid-1920s most parents probably cared more that their offspring marry Macedonians than that they be mated with a fellow villager. The community at large organized and held picnics, SS Cyril and Methody Youth Nights, and weekly dances for all the eligible young men and women. Economic and occupational status began to be the chief measurement of a match. For example, when a butcher's daughter married her father's apprentice delivery boy, despite a 'battle royal'; her parents said 'he's not for you, he's working for us. [Her grandmother said] he's not for you, he doesn't have any money.'[10]

Sons and daughters in the first generation varied in the amount of social freedom and in dating privileges. Though expected to marry a good Macedonian girl, many boys were first quietly and practically permitted to date Anglo-Canadians and others. Young women were expected to date only approved suitors; some were even chaperoned on these outings. One respondent remembered her father's insistence that younger brothers accompany her on dates. Some girls balked at these restrictions; one woman remembered having had a couple of forbidden dates with 'Canadian boys': 'I went even without their [her parents'] consent – let's put it that way.' Many were shocked, envious, and even titillated by the social freedoms enjoyed by others. One respondent, perhaps laundering the language and including a bit too much retrospection, recalled the words of a French-Canadian girlfriend: 'I go out with boys and I have intercourse but I go to church and confess my sins.'[11]

It was the universal opinion of all people interviewed that the vast majority of young Macedonians married within the group. Their wedding celebrations differed from the spartan nuptials of their parents; printed invitations, orchestras, and caterers were required. Macedonians had entered that branch of the food service industry and so could serve the reception needs of the community.[12]

It was not just that the logic of settlement and mutual dependence forged a Macedonian-Canadian identity which either subsumed village loyalties or made them part of a consistent continuum of identity. The ethnicity that emerged was less brittle than the political ethnicism of the MPO; its contours were generally defined by loyalty to the Orthodox church and the Bulgarian Holy Synod. But it went beyond that to embrace both Protestant and Progressive families who had shared the Macedonian immigrant experience in one or another of Toronto's three settlement areas. Macedonian-ness, in a more ecumenical form, was instilled in the second and third generations as well.

If natural social reasons – to do with marriage and neighbourhood ties, ease of communication, and work and leisure networks – explain the evolution and substance of a Macedonian-Canadian ethnoculture, then continuing external prejudice against working-class and small-shop-keeping southeastern European immigrants in Toronto formed a boundary and helped Macedonian Canadians to reflect on who they were. Anti-Macedonianism, or at least hostility to non–Anglo-Celts, did not go away when young people left behind their parents' accents and alien clothing. That which was Canadian about them above and beyond birthright was acquired, earned, even fought for in the schools, work-places, streets, and recreation centres. In the armed forces during the Second World War, young Macedonian Canadians still felt uncertainty about their place in Canada: 'I remember when I got my corporal stripes. First of all, I could see the dislike, why I [a foreigner] should get them and others didn't get them. I could see it.'[13]

What becomes clear is the larger Macedonian identity; its maintenance or persistence was only incidentally the product of the work of the various nationalist and ethno-religious institutions and their leadership. Rather, a 'shared social history,' to use Michael Novak's phrase, in which such institutions and emblems were merely familiar elements, led to a two- or three-generation experience of being a people, firmly based in Toronto, but linked by networks of sentiment and communication to the old country and to Macedonians elsewhere.

SS Cyril and Methody Church, the MPO, and its publication, the *Macedonian Tribune*, all kept alive and reminded the sojourners-turned-settlers and their families of their Old World ties and obligations. The organizations and their leaders called for and got committed and generous support from the immigrant community at large. They also confronted the group's New World loyalty to Canada. That dualism of loyalty was part of the unreflective 'shared social history,' and no priest fresh from Bulgaria or MPO ideologue dared to do other than encourage it.

DOUBLE LOYALTIES

Dr Mallin's address at the dedication in 1927 of SS Cyril and Methody's parish hall was an eloquent statement of concern for both Canada and the old country. It is a moving and precocious statement of a pluralist yet responsible place for ethnicity in a North American city:

We the Macedono-Bulgarians, residing in Toronto, Canada, having involuntarily left our fatherland due to oppression and persecution, but, who are however true to our race, language, church and traditions, united around our national church, SS Cyril and Methody, have decided to build this parish hall to serve as a meeting place from which we can derive learning and moral benefit, and wherein our children will be with one another in order to curtail their dispersion into the various ends of this large city, and to get together from time to time in their own place and to know that they are from one race, and that they have one common national ideal, even though in Canada, and which they should not forget. A Macedono-Bulgarian can be a worthy citizen of Canada and at the same time may be a true son of his fatherland, and his freedom, prosperity, and good fortune may do great things so long as this wish is entertained in his heart.[14]

The sojourners and settlers who came from the Macedonian villages to Toronto in the first four decades of this century formed a unique ethno-culture. It obviously grew from the fragments of literary culture, religion, and folkways that they brought with them, but it was a process, a new way of defining and being themselves that had barely emerged when the attrition of acculturation set in. Some who listened to Mallin's speech that day could still argue for hours over whether they should be called Macedonians, or Macedono-Bulgarians, or Macedonian Canadians. All understood ethnicity as process enough to know that they were not yet, and would never be, unhyphenated Canadians and that they were no longer villagers – Zhelevtsi, the men of Lerin, or Buf, and so on. They had learned to increase their vocabularies, to listen to each other's dialects with tolerance. Sadly, they learned that ability and openness at just about the time their children were proving unwilling or unable to communicate to one another in Macedonian.

The problem of definition – of seeing those villages of origin through the veils of foreign domination of their politics, religion, and education – as much as North American acculturation thwarts the maintenance of Macedonian identity. Just as Macedonians in Toronto today have changed, so, too, has their homeland. It has witnessed much – the Second World War, codification of the Macedonian language (1944), emergence of the Macedonian republic within Yugoslavia (1944), and, so recently, the collapse of communism and the disintegration of federal Yugoslavia. Macedonians in Toronto today, if they look beyond their own resources for help in ethnocultural persistence, must make difficult choices concerning cultural policies towards minorities in Bulgaria, Greece, and the former Yugoslavia and about the continuing relevance of the MPO (since 1952, the Macedonian Patriotic Organization).

The problem of ethnic continuity disrupts families from all the Macedonian villages of northern Greece. Consider the case of Gina Petroff, one of those brides sent to Toronto after the First World War from the village of Bobista. Her nephews arrived in Toronto well after the Second World War. They were born and raised in her village of origin. As young men, they fulfilled their military obligations in the Greek army. In Toronto, they opened a restaurant and took wives. Gina attended the weddings, which were held in the Greek Orthodox church. She could not understand the priest but knew the ritual structure. Greek became the working language of her nephews' Canadian households. They spoke Macedonian to their aunt out of courtesy, but also as the only way to communicate with her. They identified themselves as Greek Macedonians, something that Gina continued to find a contradiction in terms. The New World ethnicity created by Gina Petroff and her generation has been superseded by an Old World national identity.

A RANGE OF POSSIBILITIES

The broad spectrum of possibilities today runs from a grecophone identity, in which Macedonia is simply a region of origin, through various independent cultural and political positions, and dependence on what was until recently the Macedonian republic in Yugoslavia; to the old battle of whether Macedonians are simply the Slavic natives of Bulgaria's irredenta. The idea of being Macedonian in Canada has again become as much a matter of perception, volition, and generation as it was in the late nineteenth and early twentieth centuries. The shared social history of three generations of Macedonians in Canada, and the rich and complex ethnoculture that they elaborated, may be inaccessible to the next generation of scholars. The perspective of these new researchers may be skewed either by acculturation in North America or by the changes of sentiment, ethnic identity, and precepts that make those who now come from those same villages of origin peculiarly likely to misinterpret the Macedono-Canadian past.

This study is, because of the nature of the sources, as much anthropology as history. Macedonians have struggled to acquire the definitive badge of a historic people – a polity of their own, or a free homeland. Serious history of the group, here and in the Balkans, is a prerequisite for an understanding of who Macedonians were, are, and may or may not continue to be. This book, I hope, may suggest the possibility of such study, free of ideology and unsponsored by any of those states and organizations that have reason either to encourage or to repress Macedonian-ness in the Balkans and in North America. It attempts to honour, with a truthful historical reconstruction, the world that the sojourners and settlers built, and it paints a picture in some part of the complexity of their mental world and their ethnoculture.

Toronto was and is the largest Macedonian settlement outside the Balkans, and it would not do if the history of the immigrants here were left to the obscurity that affects so much Balkan history. It would not do if Canadians of all ethnic backgrounds were left unaware of the thousands of humble village men and women who lived articulate and aware lives here, who were actors in their own dramas, making collectively and individually the choices that made them a North American ethnic group.

Chronology 1885–1993

1885
Thousands of eastern and southern Europeans, including a few Macedonians, began to arrive in Toronto in search of economic opportunity.

1893
The Internal Macedonian Revolutionary Organization (IMRO) was founded in Macedonia.

1903
Illinden Uprising: Macedonians waged a short-lived and unsuccessful armed struggle against the Ottoman Empire.
The majority of Macedonians who migrated from Aegean Macedonia (northern Greece) began to arrive and settled initially in Cabbagetown, in the city's East End.

1905–12
West Toronto Junction became the centre of Toronto's meatpacking industry. Macedonian slaughterhouse workers moved to the new housing and job sites.

1907
Many Macedonians sojourners found themselves without jobs during the recession.
The Oshchima Benefit Society St Nicholas was founded.

The Zhelevo Benevolence Brotherhood was founded; it was short-lived.

1908
Reverend John Kolesnikoff surveyed the opportunities for Baptist missionary work among Macedonians in Toronto.

1910
An internal group census tallied the presence of 1,090 Macedonians in Toronto.
SS Cyril and Methody Church was founded in Cabbagetown, at the corner of Trinity Street and Eastern Avenue. The Hieromonak, later Archimandrite, Theophilact accepted the position of parish priest.

1911
The Russian metropolitan of New York and other church dignitaries consecrated SS Cyril and Methody Church.
The muckraking weekly review *Jack Canuck* attacked the highly visible presence of Macedonians in Toronto's sheet-metal industries.
The Banitsa Benevolent Society Hope was founded.

1912–1913
Balkan Wars led to Treaty of Bucharest (1913), which devided Macedonia among Greece, Bulgaria, and Serbia.The confused and unhappy situation in the old country convinced many sojourners to become permanent settlers in Toronto.
The creation of the Municipal Abattoir helps to bring Macedonians to the Niagara Street district.

1914–1918
As subjects of the Ottoman Empire or Bulgaria, many Macedonians were sometimes treated in Canada as enemy aliens. A few Macedonians, in turn, decided to serve in the Canadian forces overseas during the First World War.

1915
The first Bulgarian-language school was formed in Toronto by the educational and cultural society Prosveta.
The men's athletic and cultural society, Balkanski Unak, was founded.

1918
The political left (Progressives) ended their participation in the parish life of SS Cyril and Methody and created their own club on Ontario Street.

1921
Archimandrite Theophilact resigned as parish priest of SS Cyril and Methody to pursue a medical career as Dr Demetrius Mallin.
The Macedonian Political (later Patriotic) Organization (MPO) was founded in Fort Wayne, Indiana.
The Zhelevo Benevolence Brotherhood was refounded.

1922
The Toronto chapter of the MPO was founded and took the name 'Macedonian Brotherhood.'   It became known as the Macedonian Political Organization Pravda (Justice) in 1925.

1923
The educational and cultural society Prosveta was dissolved. SS Cyril and Methody Church assumed control of the Bulgarian-language school.

1927
The first Ladies' Section of the MPO in North America was founded in Toronto. The MPO began publishing the weekly *Macedonian Tribune*.

1928
SS Cyril and Methody Church built a parish hall.

1939–1945
Toronto's MPO Pravda discontinued its political activities for the duration of the Second World War. The MPO Ladies' and Youth sections were placed under the church's control.

1940
Approximately twelve hundred families resided in Toronto – the largest Macedonian community in Canada and probably in North America.
Macedonians began moving out of the three original settlement areas. Municipal, provincial, and federal politicians had become aware of Macedonians as a new bloc of voters to be wooed.

1941

St George's Macedono-Bulgarian Eastern Orthodox Church is built on Regent Street in Cabbagetown.

The Macedonian and Bulgarian political left (Progressives) banded together to form Branch 619 of the Independent Mutual Benefit Federation (IMBF).

1942

The First Annual Macedonian Open Golf Tournament was held.

1944

Macedonia became one of the six republics of the new Yugoslav federation. The Macedonian language was codified.

Property at Sackville and Dundas streets was purchased as the new site of SS Cyril and Methody Church.

1947–1948

The exodus of Macedonians from Aegean Macedonia continued in the aftermath of the Second World War and the Greek Civil War. The 1950s witnessed the arrival of about 2,000 Macedonian refugee children (decata begalci) in Canada.

1949

Dr Demetrius Mallin died on 30 April.

The new SS Cyril and Methody Church was consecrated.

1953

Construction of a new parish hall for SS Cyril and Methody began. The hall was completed in 1954.

1956

Reverend Jordan Dimoff was appointed as the first trilingual (English/Macedonian/Bulgarian) parish priest of SS Cyril and Methody Church.

1958

The radio program 'Macedonian Hour,' hosted by Helen 'Elinka' Petroff, was a community favourite.

1959
The social, cultural, and educational organization United Macedonians of Canada was founded.

1960
Peter Vasil was elected president of the SS Cyril and Methody Church's executive committee – the first Canadian-born (Toronto) person to hold that office.
Immigration from Vardar (formerly Yugoslav) Macedonia, which began after 1945, gained momentum in the 1960s and continues to the present.

1964
St Clement of Ohrid Macedonian Orthodox Church was founded in Toronto.

1975
The Canadian Macedonian Academic Society was formed.

1977
Macedonia Magazine first appeared in the mid-1970s.
'Voice of Macedonia' radio program began.

1979
Canadian Macedonian Place was built; it is a senior citizens' centre and home for the aged.
St Ilia Macedonian Orthodox Church was formed in Mississauga, Ontario. A temporary church was built in 1980; the congregation hoped to build a permanent church and hall in 1994.
The Association of Refugee Children from Aegean Macedonia (ARCAM) was founded.
The Canadian Macedonian Restaurant Co-op was formed.

1982
The Association of Veterans from Macedonia–Toronto Inc. was formed as part of the Royal Canadian Legion, Branch 617. It became an independent organization in 1991.

1984
The Canadian Macedonian Hockey League (CMHL) was formed.

The monthly newspaper, *Makedonija*, first appeared.
The Canadian Macedonian Anglers and Hunters Club was formed.
'Makedonski Svet' radio program began.

1985

The Canadian Macedonian Soccer League was formed.
TV program 'Macedonian Nation' went on the air.

1986

The Macedonian Canadian Human Rights Committee (MCHRC) was founded in Scarborough, Ontario.

1987

The organization Macedonian Canadian Community for Cambridge, Kitchener, Waterloo, and Guelph was formed.
The Literary Society Miladinov Brothers was established.

1989

The Association of Macedonian Students at the University of Toronto (AMSUT) was formed.

1990

The Canadian Macedonian Federation was founded.
The Canadian Macedonian Historical Society was founded.
The Macedonian Canadian Health Professionals Association was formed under the name Macedonian Canadian Medical Society. In 1992, it changed to its present name in order to broaden membership.
'Macedonin Heritage' began airing on TV.

1991

The republic of Macedonia declared independence from Yugoslavia.

1992

The First Annual Macedonian Independence Day Parade was held on 22 November.
St Dimitria of Solun Macedonian Orthodox Church was founded in Markham, Ontario.
The Canadian Macedonian Business and Professional Association (CMBPA) was formed.

The Macedonian Association of Canadian Youth (MACY) was established.
The Ryerson Association of Macedonian Students was started.

1993
The General Assembly of the United Nations admitted the independent republic of Macedonia as its 181st member.
The monthly newspaper *Macedonian Canadian News* first appeared.

Notes

A note may include references to one or more paragraphs.

EPIGRAPH (p. vii)

1   Quoted in Frederic W.L. Kovacs *The Untamed Balkans* (New York 1941) 55.

PREFACE

1   Robert F. Harney and Harold M. Troper *Immigrants: A Portrait of the Urban Experience, 1890–1930* (Toronto: Van Nostrand Reinhold 1975); see also Robert F. Harney ed. *Gathering Place: Peoples and Neighbourhoods of Toronto, 1834–1945* (Toronto: Multicultural History Society of Ontario 1985).
2   Hugh Garner *Cabbagetown*, first published 1950 (Toronto: McGraw-Hill Ryerson 1968); Michael Ondaatje *In the Skin of a Lion* (Toronto: McClelland and Stewart 1987).

CHAPTER ONE: Village Life

1   For an introduction to the problems in studying Macedonia as a nation, see H.N. Brailsford *Macedonia: Its Races and Their Future* (London: Methuen 1906; reprinted New York: Arno Press and The New York Times 1971) and E. Barker *Macedonia: Its Place in Balkan Politics* (London 1950). I have written more extensively about the process of emigration in 'The Macedonian Community in Toronto to 1930' (MA thesis, University of Toronto, 1976) and in 'Macedonians: From Village to City' *Canadian Ethnic Studies* 9 (1977) 29–41; see also R.F. Harney 'Primary Sources: A Note on Sources in Urban and Immigrant History' *Canadian Ethnic Studies* 9 (1977) 60–76, for a detailed account of the migration route from Macedonia to Canada.

2 F.S. Tomev 'Memoirs,' Macedonian Collection, Multicultural History Society of Ontario (MHSO), Toronto, 1979; Stoyan Christowe *The Eagle and the Stork: An American Memoir* (New York: Harper's Magazine Press 1976) 88.

3 F.S. Tomev *A Short History of Zhelevo Village Macedonia* (Toronto: Zhelevo Brotherhood 1971) 9; interviews with Mr Dono Evans, 2 Aug. 1975; with Mrs Hope Paliare, 15 July 1975; with Mr Vasil Dimitroff, 26 Aug. 1976; with Mrs F.S. Tomev, 13 Feb. 1976; with Mr Stoyan Duke, 21 April 1977; with Mr Bill Stefoff, 17 Dec. 1975. Interview with Mrs Gina Petroff by R.F. Harney, 21 Jan. 1977, MHSO; Brailsford *Macedonia* 50; SS Cyril and Methody (SS CM) *National Calendar, 1916*.

4 Brailsford *Macedonia* 50.

5 Interviews with Mr Bill Stefoff, 17 Dec. 1975; with Mr Jimmy German, 14 March 1979; with Mrs F.S. Tomev, 13 Feb. 1976; with Mr Dono Evans, 2 Aug. 1975; with Mrs Robert Pappas, 23 Jan. 1976; and with Mrs Sophie Pandoff, 30 March 1977; Tomev *Short History* 7–9.

6 Tomev *Short History* 7–9; see Tomev's work for a full account of acquisition of territory by means of boycott, sabotage, and outright purchase; interviews with Mrs Gina Petroff, 21 Jan. 1977; and with Mr Dono Evans, 2 Aug. 1975.

7 Tomev *Short History* 9; interviews with Mr Dono Evans, 2 Aug. 1975; with Mrs Hope Paliare, 15 July 1975; with Mr Vasil Dimitroff, 26 Aug. 1976, with Mrs F.S. Tomev, 13 Feb. 1976; with Mr Stoyan Duke, 21 April 1977; and with Mr Bill Stefoff, 17 Dec. 1975; interview with Mrs Gina Petroff by R.F. Harney, 21 Jan. 1977, MHSO; Brailsford *Macedonia* 50; SS Cyril and Methody *National Calendar*.

8 Tomev *Short History* 19–21; interviews with Mrs Gina Petroff by R.F. Harney, 15 Jan. 1977, MHSO; with Mrs Robert Pappas, 23 Jan. 1976.

9 Stoyan Christowe *Heroes and Assassins* (New York: Robert M. McBride and Co. 1935) 47–9, 67–75; Basil Balgor 'The IMRO and Immigrant Macedonian Societies' *Macedonia* 1 (Sept. 1932) 115.

10 Tomev *Short History* 45–49; Macedonian Political Organization (MPO) *15th Annual Convention Almanac* (Indianapolis, Ind., 1936) 34–5; Christowe *The Eagle and the Stork* 47–8.

11 SS CM *50th Anniversary Almanac, 1910–1960* (Toronto 1960) 27; Christowe *The Eagle and the Stork* 75 (Christowe did not identify his village of origin in the book; as a contributor of fiction to the magazine, *Macedonia*, his birthplace was listed as the village of Konomladi). Interviews with Mr Mike Tallin, 25 Aug. 1975; with Mr Blazo Markoff, 9 Dec. 1975; with Mr Methody Sarbinoff (Mike Phillips), 7 May 1977; interview with Mrs Gina Petroff by R.F. Harney, 21 Jan. 1977, MHSO.

12 The Ilinden veteran Nako G. Grozdanoff went on to open a butcher shop in Toronto. Proud of his patriotic activities, he identified himself as an Ilindentz in his advertisements in the MPO's *15th Annual Convention Almanac* 29; interview with Mrs Robert Pappas, 23 Jan. 1976; SS

CM *50th Anniversary Almanac* 35; SS CM *National Calendar, 1916.*

13   SS CM *National Calendar, 1916.* Of the 1,090 Macedonians in Toronto in 1910, 514 came from villages in the province of Kostur (Castoria), and 332 came from Lerin (Florina); see SS CM *50th Anniversary Almanac* 24.

14   Harney and Troper *Immigrants* 147–8; MPO *The Macedonian Slavs: Their National Character and Struggles* Pro Macedonia Series (Indianapolis, Ind., 1927) Preface, 2–3.

CHAPTER TWO: A Temporary Stay

1   Interview with Mrs Gina Petroff, 29 June 1975; SS CM *National Calendar, 1916*; internal census of 1910 cited in SS CM *50th Anniversary Almanac, 1910–1960* (Toronto 1960) 31–5.

Immigration began from Bitola, Prespa, Prilep, and Skopje, in Vardar Macedonia, after 1945, gained momentum in the 1960s, and still continues; immigration from northern Greece resumed after the end of the Greek Civil War in 1948. In the Canadian census of 1991, which provided for self-declaration of ethnic origin, 21,035 respondents indicated that they were fully or partly of Macedonian origin; 17,050 of these people lived in Toronto. Community spokespersons believe that there are actually 100–150,000 Macedonians in Metropolitan Toronto, which is thus the largest Macedonian settlement outside the Balkans.

2   Tomev *Short History* 75; SS CM *50th Anniversary Almanac* 35.

3   F.S. Tomev 'Rough Notes,' in 'Memoirs,' MHSO; see Christowe, *The Eagle and the Stork* for a fine description of the impact of village returnees; interviews with Mr Robert Pappas, 7 June 1977; and with Mr Anastas Petroff, 6 Dec. 1975; interview with Mrs Gina Petroff by R.F. Harney, 21 Jan. 1977, MHSO.

4   John S. MacDonald and Leatrice D. MacDonald 'Chain Migration, Ethnic Neighbourhood Formation, and Social Network' in Charles Tilly ed. *An Urban World* (Boston: Little, Brown 1974) 226–36; interview with Mr Blazo Markoff, 9 Dec. 1975; Tomev 'Memoirs.'

5   Tomev 'Memoirs'; interview with Mr Dono Evans, 2 Aug. 1975; memorandum of an unrecorded conversation with Mr Chris Mitanis, 10 Oct. 1975.

6   A.C. Yovcheff *Various Bulgarian-American Letters* (hereinafter *Letters*) (n.p. 1917) 97, 155; C. Nedelkoff *English-Bulgarian and Bulgarian-English Letters* (hereinafter *Letters*) (Granite City, Ill.: Elia K. Mircheff and Co. 1911) 28–9, 115; D.G. Malincheff/J. Theophilact *First Bulgarian-English Pocket Dictionary* (Toronto, 1913) 390–410; memorandum of an unrecorded conversation with Mr F.S. Tomev, 5 Feb. 1981.

7   Tomev *Short History* 79, 25. Interviews with Mr Vasil Trenton, 19 July 1978, and with Mr Dono Evans, 2 Aug. 1975. Tomev 'Memoirs'; memorandum of my unrecorded conversation with Mrs Gina Petroff, 10 Oct. 1981.

8   Tax Assessment Rolls, 1915–20, Ward 2 Division 1, Ward 7 Division 1.
    Unless otherwise indicated, information on the Macedonians of
    Toronto is obtained from *Might's City Directory,* an annual publication,
    1903–40, and City of Toronto Tax Assessment Rolls 1903–43, on
    deposit at the City of Toronto Archives and Central Records.
9   Re all three areas: Tax Assessment Rolls 1910–27, Ward 2 Divisions 1
    and 2, Ward 5 Division 1, Ward 7 Division 1.
10 Re young labourers: interviews with Mr Methody Sarbinoff (Mike
    Phillips), 7 May 1977, and Mr Dono Evans, 2 Aug. 1975; SS CM *50th
    Anniversary Almanac* 24; interviews with Mr Vasil Trenton, 19 July
    1978, and with Mr Anastas Petroff, 6 Dec. 1975; Christowe *The Eagle
    and the Stork* 147.
11 Re rent and landlords: City of Toronto, Tax Assessment Rolls, 1903–43,
    Ward 2 Divisions 1 and 2, Ward 5 Division 1, Ward 7 Division 1;
    memorandum of an unrecorded conversation with Mr F.S. Tomev, 5
    Feb. 1981; Christowe *The Eagle and the Stork* 146; Tax Assessment Rolls
    1919, Ward 7 Division 1.
12 Re Health Department and MOH: Toronto Department of Health
    *Report of the Medical Health Officer Dealing with the Recent Investigation of
    Slum Conditions in Toronto, Embodying Recommendations for the
    Amelioration of the Same* (Toronto 1911) 2, 8, 12; interviews with Mr
    Tony Phillips, 22 July 1975; and with Mr Nicholas S. Temelcoff, 8 July
    1975.
13 *Might's City Directory* (annual), 1903–14; interview with Mrs F.S.
    Tomev, 13 Feb. 1976.
14 Christowe *The Eagle and the Stork* 185, 212.
15 Plates of 1910 maps revised to 1923 in *Goad's Insurance Atlas* (Toronto:
    Charles E. Goad 1923) (on deposit at the City of Toronto Archives): the
    Niagara-Wellington District, 1923, plate 17: Ward 5, plate 18: Ward 4,
    plate 19: Wards 4 and 5; the Junction District, 1923, plate 63: Ward 7,
    plate 64: Ward 7, plate 65: Wards 6 and 7; the East End District, 1923,
    plate 28: Wards 1 and 2; this is the general consensus of all oral
    respondents.
16 Re development of settlement areas: Tax Assessment Rolls 1903–43,
    Ward 2 Division 1, Ward 5 Division 1, Ward 7 Division 1; *Might's City
    Directory* 1903–43 – for example, the suburban listing for Toronto
    Junction in the 1908 *City Directory* 73–106; interview with Mr Vasil
    Dimitroff, 26 Aug. 1976; memorandum of an unrecorded conversation
    with Mr F.S. Tomev, 5 Feb. 1981; Christopher Andreae re the great fire
    of 1904.
17 Gregory Clark 'The Homesick Dance in Toronto's Balkans' *Toronto Star
    Weekly* 31 March 1923.
18 Interview with Mrs F.S. Tomev, 13 Feb. 1976.
19 Yovcheff *Letters* 61–2, 84; Nedelkoff *Letters* 50, 66–7.

CHAPTER THREE: Seasoned Artisans

1   Interview with Mrs Gina Petroff, 21 Jan. 1977; see also Tomev *Short History* 87.
2   Interviews with Mr Spero Bassil Tupurkovski, 19 Nov. 1975; with Mr Dono Evans, 2 Aug. 1975; with Mrs Blazo Markoff, 9 Dec. 1975; and with Mrs Gina Petroff, 13 Oct. 1976.
3   Interview with Mrs Gina Petroff by R.F. Harney, 14 Feb. 1976, MHSO; interviews with Mr Dono Evans, 2 Aug. 1975; and with Mr Vasil Dimitroff, 26 Aug. 1976.
4   Interviews with Mrs Helen Petroff, 17 July 1975; and with Mrs Hope Paliare, 15 July 1975.
5   Tomev 'Memoirs'; also interview with Mrs Gina Petroff by R.F. Harney, 21 Jan. 1977, MHSO.
6   See Dincho N. Ralley's private document collection, especially the Membership Record Book for 1942 of Branch 619 of the Independent Mutual Benefit Federation (IMBF), MHSO; see also *Might's City Directory* 1903–40; interview with Mr Dono Evans, 2 Aug. 1975.
7   Ralley collection, especially Branch 619's Membership Record Book for 1942; interview with Mr Stoyan Duke, 21 April 1977; memorandum of an unrecorded conversation with Mr. Chris Mitanis, 10 Oct. 1975.
8   Interviews with Mr Dincho N. Ralley, 4 July 1975; and with Mrs E. Mallin and Mr John Grudeff, 1 Aug, 1975.
9   Upton Sinclair *The Jungle* (reprinted New York: New American Library 1960) 66. This monumental work offers an intimate and turbulent account of the experience of immigrant slaughterhouse workers in Chicago at the turn of the century. Tomev 'Memoirs'; and recent additions to the manuscript; Salom Rizk *Syrian Yankee* (Garden City, NY: Doubleday 1943) includes an account of a young man's short career in an abattoir.
10 Interviews with Mrs E. Mallin and Mr John Grudeff, 1 Aug. 1975; with Mr Louis Mladen, 24 Oct. 1976; with Mr Mike Tallin, 25 Aug 1975; and with Mr Tony Phillips, 22 July 1975.
11 Interview with Mr Nicholas S. Temelcoff, 8 July 1975. See also Ondaatje *In the Skin of a Lion*.
12 Interviews with Mr Mike Tallin, 25 Aug. 1975; with Mr Dono Evans, 2 Aug. 1975; and with Mr Ted Vangel, 24 Nov. 1975; memorandum of an unrecorded conversation with Mr Chris Mitanis, 10 Oct. 1975; Merrill Denison *Harvest Triumphant: The Story of Massey-Harris* (Toronto: Wm. Collins Sons 1949) 201; Tomev 'Memoirs'; see also Stephen A. Speisman's account of the difficulties encountered by Toronto's Jews over the issue of working on the Sabbath in *The Jews of Toronto: A History to 1937* (Toronto: McClelland and Stewart 1979) 278–9.
13 Tomev 'Memoirs'; interview with Mrs Gina Petroff by R.F. Harney, 21 Jan. 1977, MHSO; see also Christowe *The Eagle and the Stork*: chapter 11

includes an interesting account of the author as a young boy attempting to obtain compensation from his employer for an injury that he received while working at the railway terminal in St Louis, Missouri.

14   Interview with Mr Methody Sarbinoff (Mike Phillips), 7 May 1977.
15   Interviews with Mr Mike Tallin, 25 Aug. 1975; with Mr Dono Evans, 2 Aug. 1975; and with Mr Anastas Petroff, 6 Dec. 1975; Malincheff/Theophilact *Dictionary* 403–4; on phrasebooks and guidebooks generally, see *Polyphony* 3 no. 1 (winter 1981), especially L. Petroff 'An Everyday Book: The First Bulgarian-English Pocket Dictionary' 20–5.
16   Interview with Mr Anastas Petroff, 6 Dec. 1975; Tax Assessment Rolls 1919, Ward 2 Division 1; — Ward 7 division 1; interviews with Mr Dono Evans, 2 Aug. 1975, and with Mr Nicholas Temelcoff, 8 July 1975.
17   Re mobility of labourers: interview with Mr Nicholas Temelcoff, 8 July 1975; interview with Mike Tallin, 25 Aug. 1975; with Mr Anastas Petroff, 6 Dec. 1975; Tax Assessment Rolls Ward 2 Division I; — Ward 7 Division I; interview with Mr Dono Evans, 2 Aug. 1975.
18   On work in southern, western, and northern Ontario: John Grudeff 'Memoirs,' Macedonian Collection, MHSO, Toronto, 1975; interviews with Mr Stoyan Duke, 21 April 1977; with Mr Harry Luticoff, 25 May 1976; with Mr Dincho N. Ralley, 4 July 1975; with Mrs E. Mallin and Mr John Grudeff, 1 Aug. 1975.
19   Interview with Mr Methody Sarbinoff (Mike Phillips), 7 May 1977.
20   Malincheff/Theophilact *Dictionary* 365, 399; Yovcheff *Letters* 61–4.
21   'Without Money Nothing To Eat' *Toronto Daily News* 30 Nov. 1907; see also City Clerk of Toronto 'List of Bulgarian Immigrants Referred to in a Letter to the Honourable Minister of the Interior' Toronto, 7 Dec. 1907, National Archives of Canada (NA), Ottawa, RG 76, Vol. 483, File 745964.
22   Re city's response: 'Assistance for Starving Men by the House of Industry and Many Kind-Hearted Citizens' *Toronto Daily News* 2 Dec. 1907.
23   'Food, Fuel, Shelter for 100 Bulgarians' *Toronto Daily News* 9 Dec. 1907, and 'Dairy Building for Bulgarians' 4 Dec. 1907; see also telegram to the Honourable Frank Oliver, Minister of the Interior, from Mayor Coatsworth of Toronto, NA, RG 76, Vol. 483, File 745964.
24   See correspondence between the Assistant Superintendent of Immigration, E. Blake Robertson, and the Superintendent of Immigration, W.D. Scott, 5 Dec. 1907, and see also Blake's memorandum to the Immigration Department, Ottawa, 17 Dec., NA, RG 76, Vol. 483, File 745964.
25   See W.D. Scott's telegramme to Eastern Construction Co., 4 Nov. 1907, and the company's reply, 6 Dec. 1907, NA, RG 76, Vol. 483, File 745964; 'Bulgarians to be Deported' *Toronto Star* 6 Dec. 1907; see also correspondence from E. Blake Robertson to W.D. Scott, 23 Dec. 1907, NA, RG 76, Vol. 483, File 745964.

26   R. Rogers ed *Jack Canuck: A Weekly Review of What the Public Say, Do and Think* 1 (Toronto) 29 July 1911, 1; 20 April 1912, 17; 19 Aug. 1911, 15.

27   Harney and Troper *Immigrants* 52; see *Might's City Directory* 1903—40; interview with Mr Mike Tallin, 25 Aug. 1975.

28   Re padroni: Thomas Burgess *Greeks in America: An Account of Their Coming Progress, Customs, Living and Aspirations* (New York: Arno Press and New York Times 1970) 46; see also R.F. Harney 'The Padrone and the Immigrant' *Canadian Review of American Studies* 5 (Fall 1974) 101–18; interviews with Mr Dono Evans, 2 Aug. 1975 and with Mr Dincho N. Ralley, 4 July 1975.

29   Interviews with Mr Methody Sarbinoff (Mike Phillips), 7 May 1977; with Mrs E. Mallin and Mr John Grudeff, 1 Aug. 1975; and with Mr Tony Phillips, 22 July 1975; Malincheff/Theophilact *Dictionary*, see the advertisement; C.J. Cameron *Foreigners or Canadians?* (Toronto: Standard Publishing 1913) 46–7.

30   Malincheff/Theophilact *Dictionary* 404–7, 417–19.

31   Yovcheff *Letters* 32; and Nedelkoff *Letters* 52, 58–60.

CHAPTER FOUR: Village Societies, National Church

1   Zhelevo Benevolence Brotherhood *Constitution* (Toronto: B.A. Kaloyanov 192?), see article 3; on the use of rewards of mutual aid and benevolent societies see R.F. Harney 'Unique Features of Fraternal Records' in *Records of Ethnic Fraternal Benefit Associations in the United States: Essays and Inventories* (St Paul, Minn.: Immigration History Research Centre 1981); Zagoriskoto Benevolence Society Peace *Constitution* (Toronto n.d.) 1, see article 3; Gabresh Benevolence Society *By-laws* (Toronto n.d.) 2; Benefit Society Oshchima *50th Anniversary Almanac, 1907–1957* (Toronto 1957) 47.

2   Gabresh Society *By-Laws* 1, see article 2 and notation below it in the text of the constitution; Zagoriskoto Society *Constitution* 1, see article 2 and notation below it in the text of the constitution; Zhelevo Brotherhood *Constitution* 1, see article 2 and the notation it in the text of the constitution; Tomev *Short History* 95; Benefit Society Oshchima *50th Anniversary Almanac* 47.

3   Zhelevo Brotherhood *Constitution* 1, see article 1; Zagoriskoto Society *Constitution* 1, see article 1; Gabresh Society *By-laws* 1, see article 1; Benefit Society Oshchima *50th Anniversary Almanac* 47.

4   See Zhelevo Brotherhood *Constitution* 1, see articles 5, 21, see article 2; Gabresh Society, *By-Laws* 2, see article 2; on arrival of a name-day greeting card, the recipient was expected to express his thanks through a donation to the society; see also 3, article 11; Zagoriskoto Society *Constitution* 2, see article 5, and 3, see article 11; Banitsa Benevolence Society Hope *By-Laws* (Toronto 1954) 56.

Tomev *Short History* 91–5. The Zhelevo brotherhood soon stagnated under the incessant quarrelling of its disparate members. Only after the voluntary withdrawal of its Patriarchist members did it begin to operate successfully.

Zhelevo Brotherhood *Constitution* 2, 4, see articles 14, 15, and 28; in times of difficulty, a member could forgo payment of his dues for six months. The brotherhood thus reserved the right to act on the question of membership if an individual was unable to pay his fees; in the Zagoriskoto Society *Constitution* 4, 6–7, see article 14, 27–30 a three-month period of grace was extended to financially ailing members.

5   Zhelevo Brotherhood *Constitution* 2; Gabresh Society *By-laws* 3, see note below article 11 in the text; Zagoriskoto Society *Constitution* 3, see note below article 11 in the text, and see also article 24, which states that all members of the governing committee 'must be living continuously in Toronto' during their term of office, 6.

Election of the organizations' executive committees, by a secret ballot in most cases, was for one year; Zhelevo Brotherhood *Constitution* 3, see articles 20 and 25; Gabresh Society *By-laws* 2, see article 9; Zagoriskoto Society *Constitution* see articles 8, 9, 14, and 24; Zhelevo Brotherhood *Constitution* 3, see article 27.

6   Benefit Society Oshchima *50th Anniversary Almanac* 47; in 1934, the Oschchima Benefit Society St Nicholas changed its name to Benefit Society Oshchima, at which time Temoff's original constitution underwent its first revision. Banitsa Benevolent Society *By-laws* 25–8.

7   According to Tomev *Short History* 91, the Zhelevo brotherhood was re-founded 1 Oct. 1921. He contends it had been formed much earlier. 'We have definite information that in 1907 there was a Benevolent Brotherhood. However, as to when and how it stopped functioning, we have no exact information. It is definitely known that the first president of this brotherhood was Atanas Petrov Markovski, treasurer – Foto N. Markov.' Note spellings of Balkanski Unak used by Tomev and in SS CM *50th Anniversary Almanac*.

8   The following sources are used extensively: SS Cyril and Methody Church (SS CM) Protocols 1910–40; SS CM *National Calendar, 1916 including the Financial Report for 1914–1915* (Toronto 1916) and *50th Anniversary Almanac, 1910–1960* (Toronto 1960). Protocols no. 4, 28 March 1929; no. 8, 29 June 1930; no. 1, 28 Feb. 1937.

9   SS CM *National Calendar, 1916* 1; Brailsford *Macedonia* 61; SS CM *50th Anniversary Almanac* 27.

10   Re establishment of parish: SS CM *50th Anniversary Almanac* 8–9, 24, 29–31; see also Tomev 'Memoirs' and *Short History*; interviews with Mr Vasil Trenton, 19 July 1978, and with Mr Tony Phillips, 22 July 1975.

11   SS CM *50th Anniversary Almanac*.

12   Ibid 8–9, 31–5; SS CM *National Calendar, 1916* 15, 17–18; interview with Mr Dono Evans, 2 Aug. 1975.

13   On improvements to church: memorandum of an unrecorded conversation with Mr F.S. Tomev on 10 Dec. 1979; SS CM *50th Anniversary Almanac* 38; SS CM *National Calendar, 1916* 15, 17. Comparative studies of communities' donations by Toronto's Macedonians, both ethnic and Protestant, would be useful.

14   On purchase of new building and fundraising: SS CM *50th Anniversary Almanac* 40–1, 44–5; see also Protocols dated 3 May 1914 and 9 May 1916; no. 2, 21 Aug. 1921; no. –, 3 May 1914; no. 2, 17 Jan. 1932; interview with Mrs Robert Pappas, 23 Jan. 1976; SS CM, Protocols no. –, 20 June 1914; no. 6, following no. 5, 24 May 1918.

15   SS CM *50th Anniversary Almanac* 36–9; Protocol no. 2, March 1941; *50th Anniversary Almanac* 39, 48.

16   On women's role: interviews with Mrs Lennie Vasil, 2 Dec. 1975; with Mrs C. Lewis, 22 Sept. 1977; with Mrs Mara Kercheff, 25 Nov. 1975; and with Mrs Fanche T. Nicoloff, 15 Aug. 1975; memorandum of an unrecorded conversation with Mrs Gina Petroff, 18 Feb. 1980; SS CM *50th Anniversary Almanac* 41, 65, 68, 75. 'From Baba's Hope Chest: Macedonian Treasures in Canada' (Museum for Textiles, Toronto, 1995), produced by Angela Wood, assisted by museum staff and twelve volunteers, displayed costumes, rugs, and textiles made by Macedonian women.

17   Re school, Prosveta, and Balkanski Unak: SS CM *National Calendar, 1916* 16; *50th Anniversary Almanac*, 43, 55–8; Protocols no. 18, 19 July 1920; no. 9, 1 Sept. 1918.

18   SS CM *50th Anniversary Almanac* 24–5, 43, 69.

CHAPTER FIVE: Preachers, Teachers, Soldiers, War

1   R. Allen *The Social Passion: Religion and Social Reform in Canada, 1914–1928* (Toronto: University of Toronto Press 1971) 4; J.S. Woodsworth *The Strangers within Our Gates* first published 1908 (reprinted Toronto: University of Toronto Press 1972).

2   Re Baptist efforts: Baptist Home Mission Board *Strangers within the Gates* (Toronto n.d.) 6; C.J. Cameron *Foreigners or Canadians?* (Toronto: Standard Publishing 1913) 42–7, 56, 152; for more on Kolesnikoff, including pictures of him and his missions, see Harney and Troper *Immigrants* 62, 154–5; City of Toronto, Tax Assessment Rolls, 1910, Ward 2 Division 1; interview with Mr Dono Evans, 2 Aug. 1975.

3   On Presbyterian work: Grudeff 'Memoirs,' MHSO; interviews with Mr Mike Tallin, 25 Aug. 1975, and with Mrs E. Mallin and Mr John Grudeff, 1 Aug. 1975.

4   Task Force on Ethnic Minorities (Anglican Church of Canada) *Canadians by Choice: Changing Opportunities for Minority Groups* Bulletin 203 (Toronto June 1971); interviews with Mr Dincho N. Ralley, 4 July 1975, and with Mrs Helen Petroff, 17 July 1975.

5 Interviews with Professor B.P. Stoicheff, 28 Jan. 1976; with Mr Vasil
   Dimitroff, 26 Aug. 1976; and with Mr Dono Evans, 2 Aug. 1975; most
   of Macedonians rallied around their Eastern Orthodox institutions.
6 On Baptist efforts and Macedonian Protestants: interviews with Mr
   Nicholas S. Temelcoff, 8 July 1975, and with Mrs Dana Spero Nicoloff,
   29 Nov. 1975; see Cameron *Foreigners or Canadians?* and SS CM *50th
   Anniversary Almanac*; interviews with Mr Dono Evans, 2 Aug. 1975,
   and with Miss H. Stamenova, 6 May 1976; Grudeff, 'Memoirs.'
7 Grudeff 'Memoirs'; interview with Mrs E. Mallin and Mr John Grudeff,
   1 Aug. 1975; John Grudeff Family Collection of documents, MHSO.
   This is the general response of all Macedonians interviewed who
   attended such classes. In general, the educational opportunities were
   greater for the Presbyterians than for the Baptists. In both cases,
   association with Canadian Protestantism broke down barriers for the
   immigrant child in the public schools as well.
8 On public schools: Toronto Board of Education *Annual Report* (1913)
   468, 501; interviews with Mr Nicholas S. Temelcoff, 8 July 1976, and
   with Mr Anastas Petroff, 6 Dec. 1975; Toronto Board *Annual Report*
   (1909) 9; interview with Mr Vasil Dimitroff, 26 Aug. 1976.
9 Interview with Mr Dincho N. Ralley, 4 July 1975; Grudeff, 'Memoirs';
   interviews with Mrs E. Mallin and Mr John Grudeff, 1 Aug. 1975.
10 Interview with Mr Anastas Petroff, 6 Dec. 1975.
11 On women and English language: C. Evans *Basic English* pamphlet
   (Toronto: Women's Baptist Home Missionary Society n.d.) 1; interviews with Mrs Dana Spero Nicoloff, 29 Nov. 1975; Mrs Tina Vassil, 2
   Dec. 1975; and with Mrs Mara Kercheff, 25 Nov. 1975.
12 J.T.M. Anderson *The Education of the New Canadian* (Toronto: J.M. Dent
   and Sons 1918) 9; Harney and Troper *Immigrants* 109.
13 W.A. Craick 'Sackville Street School Aims to Teach Pupils How to
   Work, and Gets Jobs for Them' *Toronto Star Weekly* 13 April 1918.
14 On teachers and students: interviews with Mr Bill Stefoff, 17 Dec. 1975;
   with Mr Ted Vangel, 24 Nov. 1975; with Mrs J. German, 14 March
   1979; with Mr Robert Pappas, 7 June 1977; with Mrs Hope Paliare, 15
   July 1975; with Mr John Spero, 29 Nov. 1975; and with Mrs Sophie
   Pandoff, 30 March 1977.
15 Re situation from 1912 on: Malincheff/Theophilact *Dictionary* 427–8;
   see my article 'Macedonians in Toronto: From Encampment to Settlement' *Urban History Review* no. 2-78, 58–73, and 'An Everyday Book:
   The First Bulgarian-English Pocket Dictionary' *Polyphony* 3 (winter
   1981) 20–5; Tomev *Short History* 7–9; memorandum of my unrecorded
   conversation with Mr Chris Mitanis, 10 Oct. 1975; NA, RG 25, A2, vol.
   182: see correspondence between A. Monck Mason, Acting Consul
   General for Britain, and Lord Granville on, for example, the subject of
   Arger Mishailoff; interviews with Mrs F.S. Tomev, 13 Feb. 1976; with
   Mr Nicholas S. Temelcoff, 8 July 1975; and with Mr Tony Phillips, 22
   July 1975.

16   Re confusion over status in Canada: interviews with Mr Nicholas
      Temelcoff, 8 July 1976; with Mr Dincho N. Ralley, 4 July 1975; and
      with Mr Dono Evans, 2 Aug. 1975.
17   Interview with Mr Vasil Dimitroff, 26 Aug. 1976; memorandum of an
      unrecorded conversation with Mr F.S. Tomev, 5 Feb. 1981.
18   On beginning of transition: Christowe *The Eagle and the Stork* 232; inter-
      views with Mr Anastas Petroff, 6 Dec. 1975; with Mr Vasil Dimitroff,
      26 Aug. 1976; and with Mr Nicholas S. Temelcoff, 8 July 1975.
19   Emergence of the bachelor settler: interviews with Mr Tony Phillips,
      22 July 1975; with Mr Louis Mladen, 24 Oct. 1976; and with Mr Sto-
      yan Duke, 21 April 1977; memorandum of my unrecorded conversa-
      tion with Mr F.S. Tomev, 9 Jan. 1981; Tomev 'Memoirs'; Grudeff
      'Memoirs.'
20   'Uneasy truce'; Tax Assessment Rolls 1919, Ward 7 Division 1; *Jack
      Canuck: A Weekly Review of What the Public Say, Do and Think* I 22 June
      1912, 7, on deposit at the City of Toronto Archives; interviews with Mr
      Dincho N. Ralley, 14 July 1975; and with Mrs Lennie Vasil, 2 Dec.
      1975.

CHAPTER SIX: Settler Households

1   Interview with Mr Vasil Dimitroff, 26 Aug. 1976.
2   On family reunification: interviews with Mr Bill Stefoff, 17 Dec. 1975;
     with Mrs Blazo Markoff, 9 Dec. 1975; with Mrs F.S. Tomev, 13 Feb.
     1976; with Mrs Gina Petroff, 13 Dec. 1975; with Mr Ted Vangel, 24
     Nov. 1975; and with Mrs Lennie Vasil, 2 Dec. 1975.
3   Tomev *Short History*; interviews with Mrs Gina Petroff, 27 Oct. 1976;
     and with Mrs Tina Vasil, 2 Dec. 1975.
4   Interview with Mrs Gina Petroff by R.F. Harney, 15 Jan. 1977, MHSO;
     memorandum of an unrecorded conversation with Mrs Gina Petroff, 9
     Dec. 1979.
5   Interview with Mrs Gina Petroff by R.F. Harney, 15 Jan. 1977, MHSO;
     interviews with Mrs Fanche Nicoloff, 15 Aug. 1975; with Mrs Tina
     Vasil, 2 Dec. 1975; and with Mrs Robert Pappas, 23 Jan. 1976.
6   Go-betweens: interview with Mrs Gina Petroff, 27 Oct. 1976; interview
     with Mrs Gina Petroff by R.F. Harney, 15 Jan. 1977, MHSO; interview
     with Mr Vasil Trenton, 19 July 1978; see also the Trenton Family
     Collection of documents on deposit at the MHSO; R.F. Harney 'Pri-
     mary Sources' *Canadian Ethnic Studies* 9 (1977) 60–76.
7   Arrival and marriage: interviews with Mrs C. Lewis, 22 Sept. 1977;
     with Mrs Gina Petroff, 13 Dec. 1975; with Mrs Gina Petroff, 29 June
     1975; Tomev *Short History* 109–23, 134; SS CM, Marriage Registers,
     1930; Christ the Saviour (Russian) Orthodox Cathedral, Marriage
     Register, 1922–26.
8   Interviews with Mrs Mara Kercheff, 25 Nov. 1975; with Mr Vasil

Trenton, 19 July 1978; and with Mrs Gina Petroff, 13 Dec. 1975.

9   Variations on selection and marriage process: SS CM, Marriage Registers, 1915, 1923, 1924, 1929, 1930; Christ the Saviour, Marriage Registers, 1922–26; interview with Mr Louis Mladen, 24 Oct. 1976.

10 Women and boarding-houses: interviews with Mrs Sophie Pandoff, 30 March 1977; and with Mr Louis Mladen, 24 Oct. 1976.

11 Borders' accommodation: interviews with Mrs Helen Petroff, 17 July 1975; and with Professor B.P. Stoicheff, 28 Jan. 1976; memorandum of an unrecorded conversation with Mrs Gina Petroff, 12 Feb. 1981.

12 Interviews with Mr Louis Mladen, 24 Oct. 1976; and with Mrs Gina Petroff, 29 June 1975; memorandum of an unrecorded conversation with Mrs Gina Petroff, 10 Feb. 1981.

13 On boarding-houses as businesses: interviews with Mrs Hope Paliare, 15 July 1975; with Mrs Gina Petroff, 12 Oct. 1976; with Mrs Helen Petroff, 17 July 1975; with Mrs Gina Petroff, 12 Oct. 1976; and with Mrs Gina Petroff, 13 Oct. 1976; R.F. Harney 'Boarding and Belonging: Thoughts on Sojourner Institutions' *Urban History Review* no. 2-78, 8-37.

14 Interviews with Mrs Gina Petroff, 21 Jan. 1977, and 29 June 1975; memoranda of unrecorded conversations with Mrs Gina Petroff on 12 Feb. and 1 Aug. 1980.

15 Harney 'Boarding and Belonging' 22; interview with Mr Louis Mladen, 24 Oct. 1976.

16 Macedonian Political Organization (MPO) *16th Annual Convention Almanac* (Indianapolis, Ind., 1937) 25.

17 On women's perception of Toronto: interviews with Mrs Helen Petroff, 17 July 1975; with Mrs Dana Spero Nicoloff, 29 Nov. 1975; with Mrs Lennie Vasil, 2 Dec. 1975; with Mrs Tina Vasil, 2 Dec. 1975; with Mr Stoyan Duke, 21 April 1977; and with Mrs Sophie Pandoff, 30 March 1977; MPO *16th Annual Convention Almanac* 25.

18 On comparisons with other women: interview with Mrs Dana Spero Nicoloff, 29 Nov. 1975; Hugh Garner *Cabbagetown* (reprinted Toronto: Simon and Schuster 1975) 274; interviews with Mrs Fanche Nicoloff, 15 Aug. 1975; and with Mrs Lennie Vasil, 2 Dec. 1975.

19 Re children: interviews with Mrs Anastas Petroff, 6 Dec. 1975; with Mr Louis Mladen, 24 Oct. 1976; with Mrs S. Florinoff, 23 Feb. 1977; with Professor B.P. Stoicheff, 28 Jan. 1976; with Mrs Sophie Pandoff, 30 March 1976; and with Mr Ted Vangel, 24 Nov. 1975.

20 Re older children: interviews with Mrs Dana Spero Nicoloff, 29 Nov. 1975; with Mrs Lennie Vasil, 2 Dec. 1975; with Mrs Tina Vasil, 2 Dec. 1975; with Mr Stoyan Duke, 21 April 1977; and with Mrs Sophie Pandoff, 30 March 1977; see MPO *16th Annual Convention Almanac* 25.

21 Malincheff/Theophilact *Dictionary* 400.

22 Re economic difficulties and attitudes to housing: interviews with Mr John Spero, 29 Nov. 1975; and with Mr Vasil Trenton, 19 July 1978; memoranda of unrecorded conversations with Mrs Gina Petroff, 12

Feb. 1981, and with Mr F.S. Tomev, 5 Feb. 1981.

23   Sharing rental accommodations: interviews with Mrs Helen Petroff, 17 July 1975; with Mrs Gina Petroff, 29 June 1975; and with Mr Tony Phillips 22 July 1975; Tax Assessment Rolls 1919, Ward 7 Division 1.

24   Re property acquisition: Tax Assessment Rolls, 1921, Ward 2 Division 1; 1916, Ward 2 Division 1; 1927, Ward 7 Division 1; interviews with Mrs Sophie Pandoff, 30 March 1977; and with Mrs Gina Petroff, 21 Jan. 1977; memorandum of an unrecorded conversation with Mrs Gina Petroff, 12 Feb. 1981.

25   Interviews with Mrs Hope Paliare, 15 July 1975; with Mr Tony Phillips, 22 July 1975; with Mrs Gina Petroff, 21 Jan. 1977; and with Mrs Mara Kercheff, 25 Nov. 1977; Tax Assessment Rolls, 1931, Ward 5 Division 1; 1927, Ward 7 Division 1.

26   Re other groups and expansion of settlements: interviews with Mrs Dana Spero Nicoloff, 29 Nov. 1975; with Mrs Blazo Markoff, 9 Dec. 1975; and with Mr Mike Tallin, 25 Aug. 1975; Tax Assessment Rolls, 1903–43, especially for Ward 2 Division 1.

CHAPTER SEVEN: Cooperation and Competition

1   Interviews with Mrs Robert Pappas, 23 Jan. 1976; and with Mr Mike Tallin, 25 Aug. 1975; in MPO *15th Annual Convention Almanac*, see the following advertisements: Nicola Bittoff (Bitove) and son, Louis Meat Market, 1122 Queen St. E., 13; A. Stavroff, Louis Meat Market, 1598 Queen St. E., 78; A. Kizoff, Louis Meat Market, 437 Parliament St., 54; Dimitar Foteff, Louis Meat Market, 786 Broadview Ave., 82; see also interview with Mrs Sophie Pandoff, 30 March 1977.

2   Interviews with Mr Methody Sarbinoff (Mike Phillips) 7 May 1977; and with Mr Robert Pappas, 22 June 1977.

3   Interview with Mr Louis Mladen, 24 Oct. 1976; see also '50 Years of Serving the Horsey Set Hasn't Dimmed Brother's Enthusiasm' *Toronto Daily Star* 26 Feb. 1979.

4   Interview with Mrs Gina Petroff by R.F. Harney, 15 Jan. 1977, MHSO; see also R.F. Harney 'The Odyssey of a Macedonian Woman Immigrant' *Canadian Ethnic Studies* 9 (1977) 69–76; interview with Mrs D.K. Thomas, 25 Feb. 1978.

5   As note 4.

6   City of Toronto, Tax Assessment Rolls, 1913; interview with Mrs Helen Petroff, 17 July 1975.

7   Interviews with Mr Tony Phillips, 22 July 1975; and with Mr Robert Pappas, 22 June 1977.

8   Interviews with Mr Vasil Trenton, 19 July 1978; and with Mr Robert Pappas, 22 June 1977.

9   Yovcheff *Various Bulgarian-American Letters* 179, 181–2; Nedelkoff *English-Bulgarian and Bulgarian-English Letters* 17–19, 23–4.

10   Malincheff/Theophilact *The First Bulgarian-English Pocket Dictionary*, advertisement.

11   Interviews with Mr Jimmy German, 14 March 1979; with Mr Dono Evans, 2 Aug. 1975; and with Mrs Sophie Pandoff, 30 March 1977; see also Yovcheff *Letters* 88–91: the book taught men how to make a request and possible replies for a loan in writing.

12   Interview with Mr Stoyan Duke, 21 April 1977.

13   On enterprise in the West End: *Might's City Directory* annual, 1915–40; memorandum of my unrecorded conversation with Mr F.S. Tomev, 25 Feb. 1981; interview with Mrs Gina Petroff by R.F. Harney, 21 Jan. 1977, MHSO; memorandum of my unrecorded conversation with Mrs Gina Petroff, 12 Feb. 1981; R.F. Harney 'Boarding and Belonging: Thoughts on Sojourner Institutions' *Urban History Review* no. 2-78, 8-37.

14   Tomev 'Memoirs.'

15   MPO *15th Annual Convention Almanac* 15, 91.

16   Interviews with Mrs Gina Petroff, 21 Jan. 1977; and with Mr John Spero, 29 Nov. 1975.

17   On women's changing situation in the homeland: Lillian Petroff 'Macedonians: From Village to City' *Canadian Ethnic Studies* 9 (1977) 29–41 and 'The Macedonian Community in Toronto to 1930: Women and Emigration' *Canadian Women's History Series* 5 (Toronto: Department of History and Philosophy of Education, Ontario Institute for Studies in Education, 1977); interviews with Mrs Mara Kercheff, 25 Nov. 1976; and with Mr and Mrs Bill Stefoff, 17 Dec. 1975; Tomev *Short History* 9.

18   Interviews with Mrs Gina Petroff, 21 Jan. 1976; with Mrs Helen Petroff, 17 July 1975; with Mrs Hope Paliare, 15 July 1975; with Mrs Fanche Nicoloff, 15 Aug. 1976; and with Mrs D.K. Thomas, 25 Feb. 1978.

19   G. Leslie 'Domestic Service in Canada, 1880–1920' in J. Acton, P. Goldsmith, and B. Shepard eds *Women at Work: Ontario 1850–1930* (Toronto: Canadian Women's Educational Press 1974) 87.

20   On children's role: interviews with Mr Ted Vangel, 24 Nov. 1975; with Professor B.P. Stoicheff, 28 Jan. 1976; with Mrs Sophie Pandoff, 30 March 1977; with Mr Robert Pappas, 7 June and 22 June 1977; and with Mr Louis Mladen, 24 Oct. 1976; W.A. Craick 'Sackville Street School Aims to Teach Pupils How to Work, and Gets Jobs for Them' *Toronto Star Weekly* 13 April 1918.

21   Interviews with Miss H. Stamenova, 6 May 1976; with Mrs Sophie Florinoff, 23 Feb. 1977, and with Mrs D.K. Thomas, 25 Feb. 1978. Macedonian women generally quit their factory jobs after marriage and therefore did not have a long and sustained presence in the world of industry. As a result, they did not become involved in such things as labour unions.

22   Interviews with Mr Ted Vangel, 24 Nov. 1975; with Professor B.P. Stoicheff, 28 Jan. 1976; and with Mrs Lennie Vasil, 2 Dec. 1975. MPO *15th Annual Convention Almanac* 36: see the advertisement for the La

Paloma Restaurants, 19 Richmond St. E. and 386 Yonge St. in Toronto; see also 73 for the advertisement for Nick Kusitaseff, a Windsor, Ontario, restaurateur who owned Capital Bar BQ, Marigold Bar BQ, Original Lunch, and Tasty Lunch.

23   Interviews with Mr Louis Mladen, 24 Oct. 1976; with Mr Robert Pappas, 22 June 1977; with Miss H. Stamenova, 6 May 1976; see also my article 'Macedonians: From Village to City' 29–41; see Zada Keefer ed 'The History of Public Health Nursing in Toronto' Jan. 1945, on deposit at the City of Toronto Archives; Grudeff 'Memoirs.'

24   Interview with Dr. E. Temelcoff, 21 Nov. 1975.

25   *Might's City Directory* 1920–40.

26   Interviews with Mrs Robert Pappas, 23 Jan. 1976; and with Mrs Tina Vasil, 2 Dec. 1975.

27   Interviews with Mrs D.K. Thomas, 25 Feb. 1978; and with Mr Anastas Petroff, 6 Dec. 1975; MPO *16th Annual Convention Almanac* (1937) 55, 67, 99, 103, and 105.

28   On usefulness of almanacs: MPO *15th Annual Convention Almanac* (1936); interview with Mrs Sophie Pandoff, 30 March 1977.

29   MPO *15th Annual Convention Almanac* 64, 143.

30   Ibid 24, 65, 71, 80, 84, 94, and 117. Toronto Dairies Ltd employed Boris Petroff as a company representative. Chris Lamboff represented of the National Showcase Co. Ltd. The White Way Linen Supply Co. employed Boris Stefoff as its representative to the Macedonian community.

31   Interview with Mr Dincho N. Ralley, 4 July 1975; MPO *15th Convention Almanac* 118; this is the general opinion of all oral history sources consulted.

32   US and non-Macedonian advertisers: MPO *15th Annual Convention Almanac* 126, 135, 170, 172, 185–86, and 189.

33   Interviews with Mr Vasil Dimitroff, 8 July 1975; with Mr Nicholas S. Temelcoff, 8 July 1975; and with Mr Dincho N. Ralley, 4 July 1975.

34   See SS CM, Minutes and Proceedings for 1929. The church records contain only a vague and inconclusive account of said misdeeds. See Protocol no. 7, 15 May 1929; Protocol no. 8, 13 June 1929; Protocol no. 11, 20 June 1929; Protocol no. 11, 30 July 1929; and Protocol no. 13, 22 Sept. 1929.

35   Malincheff/Theophilact *Dictionary*, see advertisements; MPO *15th Annual Convention Almanac* 74.

CHAPTER EIGHT: Community Life

1   On Macedonian neighbourhoods: interviews with Mr Louis Mladen, 24 Oct. 1976; with Mrs Sophie Florinoff, 23 Feb. 1977; with Mr Bill Stefoff, 17 Dec. 1975; and with Mrs Helen Petroff, 17 July 1975. See the advertisements of nationalist entrepreneurs in the MPO's publications *15th Annual Convention Almanac* (*15th Almanac*)(Indianapolis, Ind., 1936) and

16th Annual Convention Almanac (16th Almanac) (Indianapolis, Ind.,
1937).

2   The Niagara Street area: interviews with Mr Vasil Trenton, 19 July
1978; and with Mr Nicholas S. Temelcoff, 8 July 1975; memorandum of
an unrecorded conversation with Mr Chris Mitanis, 10 Oct. 1975.

3   On Exarchists and Patriarchists: memorandum of an unrecorded
conversation with Mr F.S. Tomev, 5 Feb. 1981; see also his *Short History* and his 'Memoirs.'

4   On the East End: unlike the Tersiani, the people of Zhelevo were
successful in their priestly demands and Haralampi Elieff was elected
priest in 1931; see my MA thesis, 'The Macedonian Community in
Toronto to 1930' (University of Toronto 1976); interview with Mr Spero
Bassil Tupurkovski, 19 Nov. 1975; also membership records of Branch
619, IMBF, Dincho N. Ralley private document collection, MHSO.

5   Re stereotypes and ethnic identity: memorandum of an unrecorded
conversation with Mr F.S. Tomev, 25 Feb. 1981.

6   For hinterland: MPO *16th Almanac* – for example, 55, 67, 103, and 105.
SS CM, Baptismal Registers, 1922; Marriage Registers, 1924 and 1928;
memorandum of an unrecorded conversation with Mrs Gina Petroff,
10 Nov. 1981.

7   MPO *15th Almanac* 15, 91.

8   Interviews with Mrs Lennie Vasil, 2 Dec. 1975; and with Mrs Helen
Petroff, 17 July 1975.

9   Re outsiders' attention: interviews with Mr Anastas Petroff, 6 Dec.
1975; and with Mr Vasil Dimitroff, 26 Aug. 1976.

10 On Macedonians' subtle presence: see Tomev *Short History* 97–9 and
'Rough Notes,' 1979, Macedonian Collection, MHSO; Spero Bassil
Tupurkovski ed *Brief History of the Canadian Macedonian Immigrants*
(Toronto: Macedonian Canadian Senior Citizens Clubs 1980).

11 Social gatherings: interviews with Mrs Sophie Pandoff, 30 March 1977;
with Mrs Tina Vasil, 2 Dec. 1975; with Mrs D.K. Thomas, 25 Feb. 1978;
and with Mrs Gina Petroff, 29 June 1975.

12 As note 11.

13 SS CM *50th Anniversary Almanac* 51; Protocols no. 8, 29 June 1930; no.
8, 18 June 1933.

14 Memorandum of an unrecorded conversation with Mrs Gina Petroff, 9
Feb. 1980; SS CM, Protocols no. 8, 29 June 1930; no. 8, 18 June 1933.

15 SS CM, Protocols no. 8, 29 June 1930; no. 8, 18 June 1933.

16 SS CM, Protocols no. 4, 28 March 1926; no. 4, 2 April 1922; no. 6, 17
April 1929; interview with Mr Louis Mladen, 24 Oct. 1976.

17 SS CM, Protocols no. 7, May 1930; no. 4, 17 May 1925; no. 7, 16 May
1926.

18 Relations with Prosveta: SS CM, Protocol no. 16, 28 Dec. 1922. The
matter does not appear in subsequent protocol accounts, and so I am
unable to outline the solution.

19 SS CM, Protocol no. 22, 30 Sept. 1923; *50th Anniversary Almanac* 47.

20 SS CM, Protocols no. 7, 13 Sept. 1925; no. 2, 2 Feb. 1926; no. 10, 9 Sept. 1926; interview with Mrs Blazo Markoff, 9 Dec. 1975; SS CM, Protocols no. 16, 6 Sept. 1932; no. 4, 3 March 1935; no. 9, 29 May 1935; no. 1, 27 Jan. 1935; no. 2, 2 Feb. 1926; no. 10, 11 Oct. 1925; no. 14, n.d., but follows no. 13, 22 Sept. 1929.

21 SS CM, Protocols no. 10, n.d.; no. 3–9, n.d.; no. 2, 14 March 1937; no. 14, 22 Sept. 1935; no. 17, 22 Sept. 1931; no. 7, 13 Sept. 1925.

22 SS CM, Protocols no. 7, 13 Sept. 1925; no. 13, 22 Sept. 1929; no. 22, 13 Nov. 1932; no. 7, 13 Sept. 1925; no. 8, 20 June 1926; memorandum of an unrecorded conversation with Mr F.S. Tomev, 10 Dec. 1979; SS CM, Protocol no. 1, 27 Feb. 1929.

23 Interview with Mrs Robert, Pappas, 23 Jan. 1976; SS CM, Protocols no. 17, 4 Dec. 1929; no. 7, 15 May 1929; no. 9, 29 May 1935; no. 12, 21 June 1939.

24 Interviews with Mrs Robert Pappas, 23 Jan. 1976; with Mr Bill Stefoff, 17 Dec. 1975; and with Mr Ted Vangel, 24 Nov. 1975; SS CM, Protocols no. 9, 12 June 1929; no. 4, 28 March 1926; no. 5, 7 March 1932.

25 SS CM, Protocols no. 10, 11 Oct. 1925; no. 1, 6 Jan. 1924; no. 2, 2 Feb. 1926; memorandum of an unrecorded conversation with Mrs Gina Petroff on 22 Feb. 1980; SS CM, Protocols no. 13, 22 Sept. 1929; no. 16, 28 Nov. 1926; no. 1, 27 Feb. 1929; interviews with Mr Louis Mladen, 24 Oct. 1976; with Mr Nicholas S. Temelcoff, 8 July 1975; and with Mr Dono Evans, 2 Aug. 1975; SS CM *50th Anniversary Almanac* 42–3.

26 SS CM, Protocol no. 6, 11 Nov. 1917; see also no. 18, 19 July 1920, which states that the Balkanski Unak representative to the executive committee, Mr N. Elieff, was to be succeeded by Mr V. Tsvetkoff.

27 SS CM, Protocols no. 5, 4 April 1926; no. 16, 23 May 1920; no. 18, 19 July 1920; interviews with Mr Louis Mladen, 24 Oct. 1976; with Mr Nicholas S. Temelcoff, 8 July 1975; and with Mrs Sophie Florinoff, 23 Feb. 1977; SS CM, Protocol no. 7, 25 March 1923.

28 SS CM, Protocol no. 1, 9 Jan. 1933; memorandum of an unrecorded conversation with Mr F.S. Tomev, 10 Dec. 1979.

29 SS CM *50th Anniversary Almanac* 48; SS CM, Protocols no. 14, 19 Nov. 1922; no. 18, 24 Jan. 1923.

30 SS CM *50th Anniversary Almanac* 49–52. Elected to the Constitution Committee were: (President) Lambro Sotiroff, (Secretary) Gligor Stoyanoff, (Treasurer) Milenko Yoleff, Karsto Brumaroff, Lambro Fileff, Elia Lambroff, Peter Saroff, Nikola Shonteff, Lambro Tenekeff, Tase Terpkoff, and Simo Velianoff; Protocols no. 5, 7 March 1932; no. 6, 18 April 1933; no. 15, 30 Nov. 1930; no. 2, 18 Jan. 1931.

31 SS CM *50th Anniversary Almanac* 53–54.

32 SS CM, Protocols no. 3, 1931; no. 15, 13 Oct. 1935; no. 21, 19 Oct. 1932; interviews with Mr and Mrs Blazo Markoff, 9 Dec. 1975; with Mrs Sophie Florinoff, 23 Feb. 1977; and with Mr Robert Pappas, 7 June 1977.

CHAPTER NINE: The Church and Ethnicity

1   On business affairs: SS CM, Protocols no. 15, 3 May 1920; no. 4, 22 July 1917; no. 10, Feb. 29, 1920; no. 20, 8 June 1923; no. 15, 15 Sept. 1940; no. 18, 7 Oct. 1940.
2   SS CM, Protocols no. 5, 13 April 1924; no. 4, 28 March 1926; no. 2, 17 Jan. 1932; no. 19, 9 Oct. 1932; no. 18, 19 July 1920; no. 17, 13 June 1920; no. 11, 4 April 1920.
3   Fees, funds, and loans: SS CM *By-laws* (Indianapolis, Ind.: Macedonian Tribune, 1927) see article 7; Protocols no. 3 , 25 Feb. 1923; no. 2, 18 Feb. 1923; no. 5, 13 April 1924; no. 9, 29 May 1935; see also no. 3, 12 Feb. 1935, which records the Church committee's decision to place the Easter banquet proceeds in the church treasury for the use and benefit of the church; no. 6, date unclear but follows no. 5, 24 May 1918; no. 3, no date but follows no. 2, 18 Jan. 1931; no. 14, 11 Nov. 1930; no. 4, 3 March 1935.
4   On rental income and members' involvement: SS CM, Protocols no. 16, 23 May 1920; no. 4, 20 May 1940; no. 5, 29 May 1940; no. 11, 30 June 1940; no. 13, 14 Aug. 1940; no. 12, 26 Nov. 1933; no. 6, 31 March 1932; see also memorandum of an unrecorded conversation with Mr F.S. Tomev on 10 Dec. 1979.
5   Interviews with Mr Nicholas S. Temelcoff, 5 July 1975; with Mr Dono Evans, 2 Aug. 1975; and Mr Dincho N. Ralley, 4 July 1975; SS CM *50th Anniversary Almanac* 67; Protocol no. 4, 17 May 1918. Peroff was soon replaced by a man who had volunteered to do the job for free.
6   SS CM, Protocol no. –, 18 Feb. 1917.
7   Committee activities: SS CM, Protocol no. 20, 8 June 1923; memorandum of an unrecorded conversation with F.S. Tomev, 10 Dec. 1979; SS CM, Protocol no. 9, 1937; memorandum of an unrecorded conversation with F.S. Tomev, 13 Feb. 1980; SS CM, Protocol no. 10, 29 Feb. 1920; interview with Mrs Sophie Pandoff, 30 March 1977.
8   SS CM, Protocol no. 9, 25 Jan. 1920; additional notes to Tomev 'Memoirs.'
9   SS CM *50th Anniversary Almanac* 70; Protocols no. 11, 14 Sept. 1930; no. 5, 30 March 1930; no. 8, 29 June 1930; no. 5, 7 April 1935; no. 8, 29 May 1935; no. 2, 2 Feb. 1926.
10 SS CM, Protocols no. 21, 19 Oct. 1932; no. 14, 16 Aug. 1939; no. 4, 1937; no. 7, 5 May 1935.
11 SS CM, Protocols no. 13, 19 Nov. 1926; no. 3, 25 Feb. 1923; no. 10, 7 June 1935.
12 SS CM, Protocol no. 11, 4 Aug. 1935.
13 Re Elieff: SS CM, Protocols no. 8, 1937; no. – , 18 April 1937; no. 3, 1937; no. 4, 6 June 1937; no. 10, 1937.
14 SS CM, Protocols no. 3, 25 Feb. 1923; no. 8, 22 April 1932; no. 20, 16 Oct. 1932; no. 21, 19 Oct. 1932; no. 18, 7 Oct. 1940.

15 SS CM, Protocol no. 3, 28 Feb. 1924.
16 See the additional notes to Tomev 'Memoirs'; interview with Mr Spero Bassil Tupurkovski, 19 Nov. 1975.
17 SS CM, Protocols no. 5, 21 Sept. 1921, no. 8, 23 Oct. 1921; *50th Anniversary Almanac* 44; Protocol no. 5, 8 June 1919.
18 The priest from Tersie in the 1921 election was Reverend H. Bujoff. The candidate from Tersie in 1931 was Reverend Andon Evanoff. See SS CM *50th Anniversary Almanac* 45–6, 62–3; Protocols no. 3, 28 Aug. 1921; no. 4, 7 Sept. 1921; no. 2, 17 Jan. 1932.
19 On distances and other groups: SS CM, Protocols no. 4, 28 March 1926; no. 16, 12 Nov. 1929; no. 13, 3 Nov. 1930; no. 19, 9 Oct. 1932.
20 MPO *15th Almanac* 72, 75; MPO *A Brief Outline* (Indianapolis, Ind., n.d.); memorandum of an unrecorded conversation with F.S. Tomev, 13 Feb. 1980.
21 Written sources and MPO's role: MPO *15th Almanac* 18; memorandum of an unrecorded conversation with F.S. Tomev, 13 Feb. 1980; SS CM, Protocol no. 14, 22 Sept. 1935. This case also raises the issue of the sources' respective merits. Written materials (Protocols) state that the candidate was unacceptable because he was not Orthodox. Memory culture argues that he was not accepted because he was a Bulgarian. Protocol no. 13, 3 Nov. 1930; MPO *15th Almanac* 90–1; Protocol no. 13, 29 Oct. 1922; SS CM *50th Anniversary Almanac* 60–1.
22 SS CM, Protocols no. 2, 14 March 1937; no. 1, 19 Jan. 1930; *By-laws of the Macedono-Bulgarian Orthodox Parish, SS. Cyril and Methody Cathedral* (Toronto 1959) contains revisions and references to the original 1927 edition – see parts IX, 'Regular General Membership Meetings'; XV, Church Property; and XVI, 'General Provisions'; see also memorandum of an unrecorded conversation with F.S. Tomev, 16 Feb. 1980; Tomev 'Memoirs,' including additional notes, for an account of the members' general lack of awareness of the contents of the by-laws.
23 MPO *15th Almanac* 83; SS CM, Protocol no. 5, 10 April 1929; Protocol no. 7, 5 May 1920; SS CM *50th Anniversary Almanac* 55–6, 60–1, 66, 73.
24 SS CM, Protocols no. 5, 7 April 1935; no. 1, 19 Jan. 1930.
25 SS CM *50th Anniversary Almanac* 71–4.
26 Tomev 'Memoirs.'
27 Ibid.
28 See the additional notes to Tomev 'Memoirs'; interview with Mrs Robert Pappas, 23 Jan. 1976.
29 SS CM, Protocol no. 1, 7 Aug. 1921; *50th Anniversary Almanac* 40; Protocols no. – , 2 Sept. 1915; and no. 11, Dec. 1921.
30 On committee's role in selecting priests: SS CM, Protocol no. 9, 1 April 1923; see the additional notes to Tomev 'Memoirs'; SS CM, Protocols no. 1, 7 Aug. 1921; no. – , 1 April 1923; no. 2, 29 March 1925.
31 SS CM, Protocol no. 4, 17 May 1925; 1921 Marriage Register; *50th Anniversary Almanac* 52.

32 SS CM *50th Anniversary Almanac* 67; see notes, Tomev 'Memoirs.'
33 *Bishop Andrey and the Slavic Immigrants in America* (Indianapolis, Ind.: Macedonian Tribune 1938).

CHAPTER TEN: The MPO: Balkan Dreams, Canadian Reality

1 MPO *Constitution and of the Union of the Macedonian Political Organizations of the United States of America and Canada* (Indianapolis, Ind., 1926) see article 2, 21–2; *The Macedonian Slavs, Their National Character and Struggles* Pro Macedonia Series (Indianapolis, Ind., 1927) Preface, 2–3, 9–11; SS CM, Protocol no. 3, 31 Jan. 1922.
2 MPO *15th Annual Convention Almanac* (hereafter *15th Almanac*) (Indianapolis, Ind., 1936) 49, 51; see also the photograph of Wilfrid Heighington, KC, member for St David, Legislative Assembly of Ontario, 15. The following year, the organization held its annual convention in Indianapolis. Thus the 1937 almanac held photographs of both Macedonian freedom fighters, such as Todor Alexandroff, and a host of state and local politicians, including M. Clifford Townsend, governor of Indiana. See MPO *16th Annual Convention Almanac* (*16th Almanac*) (Indianapolis, Ind., 1937).
3 MPO *15th Almanac* 84–7; *16th Almanac* 75–80.
4 Re founding of MPO Pravda: 'Rough Notes' taken by F.S. Tomev at the meeting on 1 July 1922, F.S. Tomev Family Collection, MHSO; see MPO *16th Almanac*; SS CM *National Calendar, 1916* 17–18; interview with Mr Methody Sarbinoff (Mike Phillips) 7 May 1977.
5 Members' rights and duties: MPO *Constitution and By-laws*, see section 3 on the organization, articles 4–7; MPO (Toronto) *By-laws: For the Life of the Organization* (Indianapolis, Ind., 1930), see section 5, 'Members' Duties,' articles 57–68.
6 On role of women: interviews with Mrs Gina Petroff, 13 Oct. 1976; and with Mrs Robert Pappas, 23 Jan. 1976; MPO *16th Almanac* 14; interview with Mrs Sophie Florinoff, 23 Feb. 1977; see Ladies' Section membership cards, 1928, 1929, 1930, 1936, and 1937, in the Mr and Mrs Blazo Markoff Family Documents Collection, MHSO.
7 Re executive committee: see MPO *By-laws* section 1, 'Administration of the Organization,' articles 1–39.
8 SS CM *50th Anniversary Almanac* 58, 69; MPO *16th Almanac* 25.
9 MPO *16th Almanac* 179.
10 Re Central Committee: MPO *Constitution and By-laws*, see section 5, 'Central Committee,' which includes articles 15–18; section 6, 'Material Means,' including articles 19–24; and section 7, 'Board of Control,' including articles 23 and 24.
11 *Macedonia* 1 (Jan. 1932) unnumbered back page.
12 MPO (Toronto) *By-laws* section 4, 'Organizational Correspondence,' articles 69–72, 19–22.

13   MPO *Constitution and By-laws* 25-6, article 9; MPO (Local) *By-laws* 22, articles 73–7.

14   Interviews with Mr Methody Sarbinoff (Mike Phillips) 7 May 1977; and with Mrs Gina Petroff, 21 Jan. 1977; MPO *16th Almanac* 156.

15   'An Impressive Manifestation of Loyalty to Macedonia and Its Great Cause' *Macedonia* 1 (Oct. 1932) 125–31; interview with Mr Methody Sarbinoff (Mike Phillips) 7 May 1977.

16   MPO *16th Almanac* 182–3.

17   'An Impressive Manifestation' 129–30.

18   MPO *Constitution and By-laws* 26–7, article 10; Tomev 'Memoirs.'

19   John Bakeless 'America and Macedonia' *Macedonia* 1 (March 1932) 39–40. Bakeless was eyed with suspicion by the Yugoslav police during his travels through the Balkans. Despite the surveillance, he was able to obtain a rare interview with IMRO leader Mihailoff at his mountain retreat; see Bakeless's article, 'Interviewing Ivan Mihailoff' *Macedonia* 1 (June 1932) 91–2.

20   Neldelkoff *English-Bulgarian and Bulgarian-English Letters* 101–2; *Macedonia* 1 (Jan. 1932) 16.

21   Herbert Adams Gibbons 'Why the Cry of Peace, When There Is No Peace?' *Macedonia* 1 (May 1932) 73–4.

22   Luben Dimitroff 'Pirin' *Macedonia* 1 (Jan. 1932) 14–16; Dr Saul Mezan 'The Hebrews in Macedonia' ibid (Sept. 1932) 116–20; see also ibid (Oct. 1932) 59–61, 133–8; ibid (April 1932) 59–61; ibid (May 1932) 84–7; ibid (June 1932) 102–4.

23   Col. Leon Lamouche 'Reminiscences of Macedonia, 1904–1909' *Macedonia* 1 (Nov. 1932) 143–5.

24   'The Tourists' Paradise, An Englishman's Impressions of Macedonia under Bulgarian Domination' *Macedonia* 1 (Dec. 1932) 164–7.

25   See, for example, 'The Macedonian Martyrdom' *Macedonia* 1 (Dec. 1932) 173–4.

26   See Stoyan Christowe – for example, *Macedonia* 1 (1932) 51–3.

27   *Macedonia* 1 (Jan. 1932) 1.

28   Albert Lanotine 'The Macedonian Problem' *Macedonia* 1 (Dec. 1932) 159–64.

29   'Impressive Manifestation' 126–31.

30   Interview with Mr Methody Sarbinoff (Mike Phillips) 7 May 1977; MPO *15th Almanac* 15; *16th Almanac* 182.

31   'Two Held as Accomplices of Monarch's Assassin,' *Toronto Daily Star* 11 Oct 1934; see the articles in the *Toronto Daily Star* including: 'Assassin Mounts Running Board Shoots Down Monarch, Minister during Marseilles Procession' 9 Oct. 1934; 'The Assassination' 10 Oct. 1934; and 'Two Held as Accomplices of Monarch's Assassin' 11 Oct. 1934.

32   MPO *16th Almanac* 15.

33   Re consul, Skelton, and RCMP: 'The Macedonian Martyrdom' *Macedonia* 1 (Dec. 1932) 173–4.

34 Christowe *Heroes and Assassins* 276–81.
35 Interview with Mr Methody Sarbinoff (Mike Phillips) 7 May 1977.
36 MPO *Constitution and By-laws*.
37 Events of 1940: MPO *Constitution and By-laws* see section 3, 'Organization,' note under article 4, 29; *By-laws of the Macedonian Patriotic Organization of the United States and Canada* (Indianapolis, Ind., 1956), see section 3, 'Organization,' note under article 5, 24–5; Tomev 'Memoirs.'

CHAPTER ELEVEN: Evolving Definitions

1 Zada Keefer ed 'History of Public Heath Nursing in Toronto' Jan. 1945, on deposit at the City of Toronto Archives; interviews with Mr Louis Mladen, 24 Oct. 1976; with Mrs F.S. Tomev, 13 Feb. 1976; and with Mr John Spero, 29 Nov. 1975.
2 Interviews with Mr Vasil Dimitroff, 26 Aug. 1976; and with Mrs Lennie Vasil, 2 Dec. 1975.
3 Interview with Mrs Helen Petroff, 17 July 1975.
4 SS CM, Burial Records, 1918–1932; interview with Mr Vasil Dimitroff, 26 Aug. 1976.
5 Interview with Mr Bill Stefoff, 17 Dec. 1975.
6 Interview with Mr John Spero, 24 Nov. 1975.
7 Interviews with Mr Vasil Dimitroff, 26 Aug. 1976; with Mr Ted Vangel, 24 Nov. 1975; and with Professor B.P. Stoicheff, 28 Jan. 1976.
8 Interview with Mr Bill Stefoff, 17 Dec. 1975.
9 Interview with Mr Ted Vangel, 24 Nov. 1975.
10 Interview with Mrs Sophie Pandoff, 30 March 1977.
11 Ibid.
12 Interviews with Mrs Jean George, 11 Dec. 1975; and with Mr Robert Pappas, 7 June 1977.
13 Interview with Mr Louis Mladen, 24 Oct. 1976.
14 SS CM *50th Anniversary Almanac* 54–5.

Note on Sources

Much of this book is based on interviews with Macedonians in Toronto; I conducted all interviews not otherwise attributed. Other information on Toronto's Macedonians comes, unless I cite other sources, from *Might's City Directory*, an annual publication, 1903–40, and the City of Toronto's Tax Assessment Rolls, 1903–43, on deposit at the City of Toronto Archives and Central Records (CTA). *Goad's Insurance Atlas* (Toronto: Charles E. Goad 1923), also on deposit at the CTA, contains plates of all parts of the city as it then was, including the Macedonian settlement areas.

For Macedonian institutions in Toronto, principal sources, in addition to interviews, are as follows:

- for village-based Macedonian societies: printed constitutions and by-laws; some minutes and proceedings, formal or informal
- for SS Cyril and Methody Church (SS CM), later SS Cyril and Methody Macedono-Bulgarian Cathedral: *National Calendar, 1916, including the Financial Report for 1914–1915* (Toronto 1916); *By-laws of the Macedono-Bulgarian Orthodox Parish, SS. Cyril and Methody Cathedral* revised edition of 1927 original (Toronto 1959); *50th Anniversary Almanac, 1910–1960* (Toronto 1960); and on microfilm at the Multicultural History Society of Ontario (MHSO), Toronto: Burial Records, Marriage Registers, and Protocols (cited by number and date), 1910–40
- and for MPO Pravda, Toronto: MPO *Constitution and By-laws of the Union of the Macedonian Political Organizations of the United States of America and Canada* (Indianapolis, Ind., 1926); MPO (Toronto) *By-laws: For the Life of the Organization* (Indianapolis, Ind., 1930); and MPO *15th Annual Convention Almanac* (Indianapolis, Ind., 1936), printed for the MPO's 1936 general convention, which was held in Toronto.

On Macedonian life and history, I found particularly useful H.N. Brailsford *Macedonia: Its Races and Their Future* (London: Methuen 1906, reprinted New York: Arno Press and The New York Times 1971) and F.S. Tomev *A Short History of Zhelevo Village, Macedonia* (Toronto: Zhelevo Brotherhood 1971). Tomev's unpublished 'Memoirs,' housed in the Macedonian Collection of the MHSO, and Stoyan Christowe's *The Eagle and the Stork: An American Memoir* (New York: Harper's Magazine Press 1979) were most helpful concerning the Macedonian immigrant experience in North America.

Two major studies on immigration history were crucial in shaping my work – particularly the concept of distinct sojourner and settler phases: Robert F. Harney and Harold M. Troper *Immigrants: A Portrait of the Urban Experience, 1890–1930* (Toronto: Van Nostrand Reinhold 1975) and Robert F. Harney ed *Gathering Place: People and Neighbourhoods of Toronto, 1834–1945* (Toronto: Multicultural History Society of Ontario 1985).

Three guidebooks assisted Macedonian sojourners in coping with the New World and reveal much about the newcomers' lives, needs, and aspirations: C. Nedelkoff *English-Bulgarian and Bulgarian-English Letters* (Granite City, Ill., Elia K. Mircheff and Co. 1911); D.G. Malincheff (= J. Theophilact) *First Bulgarian-English Pocket Dictionary* (Toronto 1913); and A.C. Yovcheff *Various Bulgarian-American Letters* (n.p. 1917). These volumes proved almost as useful to me as to their intended audience.

Index

A.F. Schnaufer, 32, 34, 44, 101
A.R. Clarke and Co., 25, 32
Aceff, George, 38
Albania, 3
Albert College, 64, 104
Alexandroff, Todor, 120
Allan Line, 42
Ambrose Kent and Son, 107
American Mission School: in Bitola, 103; in Salonica, 104
Andonoff, Christo, 78
Andreev, S., 50
Anglican church (Church of England in Canada). See Protestant churches
Ann Arbor (Michigan), 84
Archimandrite Theophilact. See Mallin, Dr Demetrius
Armensko, 3, 51, 54, 111
Asia Minor, 4
Atanasoff, Reverend, 61–2
Athens, 4, 7
Atlas Engineering and Machinery Co., 33

Balkan Cafe, xvii, 83, 84, 99
Balkanski Unak, 29, 49, 57, 115, 124–5

Balkan Wars of 1912–13, xv, 3, 14, 68
Banitsa, 3, 51, 54
Banitsa Benevolent Society Hope, 48, 49, 113
Bansko, 9
Baptist church. See Protestant churches
Barrymore Cloth Co., 16
Beaver Cloak Co., 102
Belcheff, Jordan, 23
Belgrade (Serbia/Yugoslavia), 42
Beneff, B., 134
benevolent organizations. See village societies
Berinkrantz, Moses, 21
Besvina, 3, 7, 54, 111
Bistreff and Dimitroff (book dealers), 98
Bitola, 7, 10, 49, 53, 103, 111
Bittoff (Bitove), Nicola, 95
Blagoi, Nicolas, 80, 115
Bloor-Danforth Viaduct, 35
boarding-houses: bachelor, 16–19; family-run, 81–4
Bobista, 3, 4, 7, 15, 78, 82, 88, 111, 174
Boston, 9

Brailsford, H.M., 4, 5, 7
brotherhoods. *See* village societies
Bucharest, 4
Buf, 3, 14, 44, 174
Buffalo (New York), 29
Buffalo Lunch, 84
Bulgaria, 3–5, 16, 31, 52, 76, 108, 147
Bulgarian exarchate, 3, 8, 50–1, 52, 112–13, 140–5
Bulgarian language, 68; school, 57–8, 121–4
Bulgarian Orthodox church. *See* Bulgarian exarchate
Bulgarians, 7, 8, 34, 38, 39, 40, 42, 60
Bull's Head Hotel, 38, 49, 71–2, 112
Bunda, M.T., 102
Burlington (Ontario), 72

Cabbagetown: as a heterogeneous settlement area, 111; growth and development of Macedonian settlement area, 13, 24; Macedonian exodus from, 92–3; subject of Hugh Garner's novel, xvi
California (state), 16
Canada, 4, 68, 75
Canada Packers, 33, 35, 36
Canadian Baptist Home Mission Board, 60–1
Canadian National Exhibition (CNE), 41, 56, 70
Canadian Northern Ontario Railway, 19, 21, 92
Canadian Pacific Railway (CPR), 24
Canadian Tumbler Co., 106
Cherbourg (France), 77
Cherry Beach, 37
Chinatown, 93
children: dating and marriage, 88; education and, 66–8, 104; neighbourhoods and, 86; work and, 87, 102–3
Chinese, 20, 32, 60, 117
Chriss, George, 37
Chriss, Tony, 38

Christ the Saviour (Russian) Orthodox Cathedral, 78
Christie Brothers Enterprise, 105
Christo, John, 19
Christova, Marie, 79
Christova, Vena, 78
City of Toronto, Department of Health, 16, 22
Clarke and Clarke Ltd, 25, 32, 36
Clarke, Harry Gladstone (MP), 116
'Coca Cola,' Nick, 83
Columbus (Ohio), 44
commerce: competitive spirit, 106; growth and development of, 95–7, 108–9; Macedonian-American experience, 107; movement out of settlement areas, 104–5; relations with other Canadian entrepreneurs, 99–100, 106–7; restaurant and food services industry, 105, 107; steamship agents and bankers, 108–9; use of non-Macedonian employees, 97, 105
Constantinople. *See* Istanbul
Consumers' Gas Co., 73, 87
Copper Cliff (Ontario), 34, 38, 115
CPR Barbershop, 97, 99
Croatian Home Defenders of the United States, 160
Croatian Peasant party, 160
Cunard Line, 42
Czechs, 125

Davenport Public School, 102
Day, Ralph C. (mayor), 143
Daylight Studio, 106
Debretz, 54
Demitroff, Andrew, 79
Detroit (Michigan), 39, 44
dictionaries. *See* guidebooks
Dimitroff, Andrew, 44
Dimitroff, Dr Toma, 125
Dimitroff, Luben, 158
Dimitroff, Norman, 106
Dimitroff, Pavel, 55

Dimitroff, Vasil, 71
Dimitry, George, 23
Dimoff, Trayon, 50
Dineff, Georgi, 55
Dixon, Rev. Hilliard Cameron, 62
Djidroff, Cosmja, 38
Dolno Kotori, 54
Dominion Bridge Co., 35
Dominion Hotel, 71
Dominion Line, 42
Dominion Silk Mills, 33
Donaldson Line, 42
Dryden (Ontario), 42
Dufferin Grill, 96, 105
Duke, Stoyan, 72
Dumbeny, 111
Dunlop, Helen Grand, 80, 115

East End settlement area. See Cab-
  bagetown
Eastern Construction Co., 42
Efendi, Husain, 7
Elieff, Nikola, 20
Elieff, Rev. Haralampi, 135–7, 141,
  144
Ellis Island (New York), 78
Embore, 4, 5, 111
enemy aliens: Macedonians as, 69
English-Bulgarian and Bulgarian-
  English Letters (1911). See guide-
  books
English-language instruction:
  industry and, 65; occupational
  mobility and, 98; Toronto Board of
  Education night school program,
  64–5; women and, 65–6
Evanoff, Mary, 56, 125
Evans, Dono, 44
Exarchists. See Bulgarian exarchate;
  see also Patriarchists
Exchange Hotel, 99

F.A. Hallman Co., 32
farming: Macedonians and, 98
Filkoff, Staso, 43–4, 55

First Bulgarian-English Pocket Dic-
  tionary (1913). See guidebooks;
  Mallin, Dr Demetrius
First World War, xv–xvi, 69–70, 75,
  100. See also enemy aliens
Florina, district of. See Lerin
  (Florina), district of
Foteff, Dimitar, 95
'From Baba's Hope Chest'
  (Macedonian textiles), 193n16

Gabresh, 3, 6–7, 18, 20, 52, 54, 75,
  111
Gabresh Benevolence Society, 48,
  113
Galt (Ontario), 105
Garner, Hugh, xvi, 85
Gecheff, Nako, 55
Geleff, Elena, 122
Geleff, Stoyan, 109
Gemandoff, Stavro, 77, 82, 96
George, Lambo, 79
George Petroff Grocery Market
  Lunch, 99, 100
Georgieff, Andrew D., 23
Georgieff, James, 44
Georgiev, Nikola, 121
Georgiev, Vasil, 121
Germans, 125
Gheroghieff, Vladimir, 160
Gigeroff, Alex K., xvii
Gooderham and Worts Ltd, 73
Gooderham, George, 61
Gorna Djumaya, 9
Gorno Kotory, 54, 111
Grand Trunk Railway, 24, 73
Granite City (Illinois), 148
Great Britain, 70
Greek islands, 7
Greek Orthodox. See Greek
  patriarchate
Greek patriarchate, 3, 7–8, 51, 52
Greeks, 60, 76, 96
Greenshields, J.H., 99
Greenwood Raceway, 96

Grozdanoff, Nako, 95, 104
Grudeff, John, 72, 103–4
Grueff, Damien, 8
Guelph (Ontario), 80, 115, 120
guidebooks, 17, 23, 28, 29, 45–6,
    97–8. *See also* Mallin, Dr Demetrius
Guleff, Hadji, 55
Gunns Ltd, 19, 25, 33, 37, 90, 95
Gurcomans. *See* Patriarchists
gypsies, 6, 79

Halifax (Nova Scotia), 77, 78
Hallman and Sable Ltd, 32
Hamilton (Ontario), 39, 105, 115, 120
Harney, Robert F., xv, xviii
Harris Abattoir Co., 25, 33, 37, 38
Hastings, Dr Charles (MOH), 22, 78
Hearst (Ontario), 34
Heighington, Wilfrid (MPP), 116,
    159
Hepburn, Mitchell F. (premier), 138,
    147
Herman, Rev. Frank, 80
Hieromonak Theophilact. *See*
    Mallin, Dr Demetrius
High Park, 118
hinterland settlements (northern
    Ontario and other regions), 27–8,
    80–1, 115–16
Hospital for Sick Children, 84
Hotel Balkan (New York City), 78
House of Industry, 41

Ideal Bedding Co., 26, 33, 49
Ilinden Picnic. *See* leisure activities
Ilinden Uprising, 9–10, 13–14, 68
*Immigrants: A Portrait of the Urban
    Experience, 1890–1930*, xv
immigration: to Australia, 15; to the
    United States, 15
industry: labour needs of, 15, 20–1,
    25; Macedonians in, 32–3, 34;
    working conditions, 34–5;
    work skills of migrants, 31–2
Intercity and Street Railways, 33–4

intergroup relations: Macedonians
    and, 73–4, 116–17
Internal Macedonian Revolutionary
    Organization (IMRO), 8–10
International Lunch, 84, 107
Islam, 6
Istanbul (Constantinople), 3–5, 51,
    69
Italians, 20, 32, 34, 60, 98, 102, 105,
    117
Ivanhoff, George, 42

J. Shifman and Son, 106
Jack Canuck, 25, 42–3, 73
Jaroshurski, Rev., 142
Jarvis Collegiate, 103
Jarvis Street Baptist Church, 61, 103
Jehovah's Witnesses, 134
Jerome Theophilact. *See* Mallin, Dr
    Demetrius
Jews, 20, 32, 88, 98, 102, 117
Jimmy's Meat Market, 98, 106
job opportunities: denial to
    Macedonians, 26–7
John Inglis Co., 70
Johnson, Charlie. *See* Evans, Dono

Kailary, 52
Kaiser Wilhelm II of Germany, 70
Kalavasoff, Apostol, 57
Karajoff, Rev. Velik, 142
Karsto Mladen Confectionery, 96
Katsunoff, Rev., 61–3
Kemp, A.E., 43
Kemp Manufacturing Co., 25, 33–7,
    43–4
Kemp's. *See* Kemp Manufacturing
    Co.
King Alexander I of Yugoslavia, 160
King George VI, 135
Kirigieva, Milko, 79
Kitchener (Ontario), 39, 105
Knox, Gladys, 80
Kolesnikoff, Rev. John, 60–2
Kone, Dedo, 51

Konomladi, 7, 10, 54, 111
Kostur (Kastoria), district of, 3, 5, 10
Kusitaseff, Nick, 115
Kuzoff, A., 95

labour agents, 23, 36, 43–4
Lambton Park, 119
Lamport, Allan (alderman), 159
landlords, 21
La Paloma Grille, 107
Lazaroff, Done P., 55
leisure activities: picnics, 119–20;
  women's, 118–19
Lenin, Mary, 80
Lerin, city of, 5, 15
Lerin (Florina), district of, 3, 5, 10,
  52, 53
Levack Co., 25
Lever Brothers Ltd, 25
Levi, Judah, 21
Lithuanians, 99
Little Italies, 93
Little Trinity Church, 62
Los Angeles (California), 148
Louis Meat Market, 95, 105

Macedonia, 6, 8, 9–11, 108, 112, 116;
  Republic of, 174. See also 176–82
Macedonia: Its Races and Their Future
  (1906), 4
Macedonian Brass Band, 61
Macedonian Political (later Patriotic)
  Organization (MPO), 48, 50, 80,
  84–5, 138–40; annual conventions,
  154–7; Macedonian Tribune
  (Makedonska tribuna), 153–4;
  members' rights and duties,
  149–51; organizations, 151–3;
  origins, 148–9; relations with
  others, 157–64; see also Pravda
  (MPO Toronto local)
Macedonian standard language, 17
MacMurchy, A. (chairman, House of
  Industry), 41
Makedonska Krvava Svadba, 126

Malincheff, D.G. See Mallin, Dr
  Demetrius
Mallin, Dr Demetrius (= D.G.
  Malincheff = J. Theophilact), 17,
  23, 28, 45, 51–2, 54–6, 62–3, 68,
  80, 140, 168–70, 173–4; see also
  guidebooks; SS Cyril and Methody
  Church
Manonis Italiano Cheese, 100
Mansfield (Ohio), 39, 44
Markoff, Blazo, 16
marriage and family life, 75–81,
  86–8. See also children
Martin, Alex, 104
Massey-Harris Co., 33, 35–7
Matova, Vera, 56
Matthews Blackwell Abattoir, 35, 37
Mecca Steak House and Tavern, 96,
  105
Metropolitan Lunch, 104
migration: bartering system and, 6;
  cash economy and, 5–6; decline of
  local migration, 3–5, 10; land
  shortage and, 5–7; local, 4–5;
  migrant philosophy, 16, 23–4;
  pioneer migrants to Toronto, 14;
  tradition of, 3–5, 7; village and
  family migration chains, 15–16;
  western (Vardar) Macedonia and,
  10
Mihailoff, Ivan, 138, 147, 160
Mihailoff, Rev. Vasil, 131, 141, 144
Milwaukee (Wisconsin), 79
Moler Barber College, 96
Monastir, 63
Montenegrins, 60
Municipal Abattoir, 24, 37, 72
Muskoka Lakes (Ontario), 72
Muslims, 3
mutual aid societies. See village
  societies

Nakeff, Dimitri, 98
Nakeff, Naum, 126
Nakoff, Rev. David, 121, 138, 140–1

Naroden Glas, 122, 124
National Council of Women, 101
National Iron Corp., 25
National Show Case Co., 107
Nedelkoff, C. *See* guidebooks
Nevoleni, 3, 6, 54
New York City (New York), 29, 79, 103
Niagara Falls (Ontario), 120
Niagara Street (settlement area): distance from the initial area of settlement, 88; growth and development of, 13–14, 24–5; Macedonian enterprise in, 98–9; site of struggles between Exarchists and Patriarchists, 114; Zhelevtsi and, 112
Niagara Street School. *See* English-language instruction; *see also* children
Nikoloff, Rev., 115
Nikolovsky, Andrea, 14
Nikolovsky, Lambro, 14
Novachoff, Pencho, 121

occupational fluidity and mobility, 36, 109–10
Ochrida archbishopric, 51–2
Odessa (Russia), 54
Office of the Parks Commissioner, 41
Office of the Registrar of Enemy Aliens, 69
Oliver, Frank (minister of the interior), 42
Ondaatje, Michael, xvi
oral testimony: importance and use, xvi
Osaka/Port Hope: Macedonians in, 72, 98
Oshchima, 3, 5, 54, 111
Oshchima Benefit Society St Nicholas, 47, 49
Ottoman Empire, 4, 9, 10, 68, 69; Macedonians and religion in, 3, 8; Macedonians and schools in, 8; relations with authorities, 7–8

Pacini, S., 108
padroni. *See* labour agents
Palmetto Beer Garden, 107
Palmolive Soap Co., 34–5, 45
Parkdale Dairies, 105
Park School, 114. *See also* children
Patriarchists, 8, 52, 54, 112–13
Paul's Lunch, 103
Pavel, Hadji, 8, 52, 54
Peroff, Hadji D., 13, 19, 23, 37, 49, 51, 108
Perrin–Turner Ltd, 107
Petroff, Anastas, 21
Petroff, Gina, xviii, 76, 77, 82, 83, 89, 174
Petroff, Noe, 16, 89, 96, 115
Phillips, Naum, 55, 57, 90, 108–9
Phillips Manufacturing Co., 37
Poles, 60, 85, 99, 117
police: Macedonians and the, 117
political left. *See* Progressives
Popovsky, Vasil Stoyanoff, 49, 70
Pozdivista, 54
Pravda (MPO Toronto local), 50, 122, 138–40, 147–66
Presbyterian church. *See* Protestant churches
Prilep, 50, 53
Progressives, 114, 137
property: factors affecting choice of residence and location, 91; renting v. buying, 88–92
Prospect Park Cemetery, 47
Prosveta, 57, 121–2
Protestant churches: Macedonians and, 59–64; Protestants (Macedonians), 63–4, 103–4
Psoderi, 7
Purdoff, Phillip, 79

Queen Portrait Studio, 106

Raycoff, A.G., 98
recession of 1907, 40–2, 47
Red Cross, 135
Regent Park, 92
religion, 50; celebrations (Christmas, Easter, and SS Cyril and Methody Day [24 May]), 120–1. *See also* Ottoman Empire; Protestant churches; SS Cyril and Methody Church
returnees, 15
Robertson, E. Blake (assistant superintendent of immigration), 42
Roebuck, Arthur W. (attorney general), 147
Romania, 4, 5, 31
Rose Marie Beverage Co., 106
Roula, 54
Royal Cafe, 109
Royal York Hotel, 155
Russian Metropolitan Platon, 121
Russian Orthodox church, 54
Russians, 7, 60
Ruthenians, 60

Sackville Street School. *See* English-language instruction; *see also* children
St Clement churches: in Detroit, 143; in Toronto, 181
St John's Ward (The Ward), 19–20
St Louis (Missouri), 20, 116
SS Cyril and Methody Church: Bulgarian exarchate and, 50–2; church governance, 129–30, 132–4; consecration, 54; financing, 130–1; Macedonian-American experience, 47–8; marriage and wedding ceremonies, 78–81; membership fees, 130; MPO and, 138–40; North American influences, 134–6; parish hall, 125–7; voluntary labour, 131–2
Salonica, 4, 63, 103
San Francisco (California), 148
Saraffoff, Boris, 9

Sault Ste Marie (Ontario), 39
Scarborough Heights, 119
Second World War, 174
Serbia, 3, 4, 7
Serbians, 60
settlers: Macedonians and the decision to stay, 68, 70–2
Shamanduroff, Stavro, 121
Sheet Metal Products Co., 43
Short History of Zhelevo Village, Macedonia, 14
Simoni, Matilda, 168
Skopje, 149
Skopje, district of, 10
Slave Petroff and Co., 44
Smerdesh, 3, 4, 54, 82, 111
Smiliakova, Gena, 115
Smilevo, 8
social gospel, 59–60
sojourners. *See* migration
Sokols, 125
Soren Brothers (Louis and Morris), 35
Sorovich, 111
Sotiroff, Lambro, 148
Spanish-American War, 9
Srebreno, 111
Stamenova, Parashka, 103, 168–9
Star Coal Co., 21
Statica, 54
statistical data, xvi, 13, 14, 52, 56–7
Stavroff (Stavro), A., 95
Steelton (Pennsylvania), 51
Stefoff, Trpo, 49
Step-In Lunch, 99
Stock Yard Lunch, 99
Stoicheff, Nikola, 121
Stone, Helen, 9
Stoyanoff, Dimitar, 55
Stoyanoff, E., 120
Stoyanoff, George, 23
Stoyanoff, Ivan, 42
Stoyanoff, Samuel T., 23
street vending, 98
Stringing Peppers on Niagara Street, xvii

Stronach and Sons, 106
Strumitsa, 103
Sudbury (Ontario), 39, 115
Sunnyside, 118
Swift Canadian Co. Ltd, 33, 83, 92

Tashoff, Nikolov, 8
Taylor, E.P., 96
Temelcoff, Nicholas, xvi, 35
Temelkoff, Kuzo, 122
Temiskaming Railway, 42
Temoff, Bojin C., 49
Temovski, Hristo, 35
Tenekoff, Lambro (Louis), 57, 85, 95, 120
Tersiani, 137
Tersie, 3–6, 111
The Eagle and Stork: An American Memoir (1976), 9, 20, 70
Theophilact, J. *See* Mallin, Dr Demetrius
'The Ward.' *See* St John's Ward
Thorold (Ontario), 120
Tipton, Chris, 44
Todoroff, Mite, 38
Tomev, Foto Spiro, xvii, 8, 14, 16, 17, 19, 26, 35, 126
Toronto: as a migratory stop, 14; as a source of cash, 4, 10; industrial take-off, 32
Toronto Board of Education. *See* English-language instruction; *see also* children
Toronto Daily News, 41
Toronto Department of Health, 16, 22
Toronto Dwellings Co., 21
Toronto General Hospital, 21
Toronto Iron Works Ltd, 33
Toronto Railway, 73
Toronto Star, 28, 102, 160
Toronto Transit Commission (TTC), 119

Treaty of Bucharest. *See* Balkan Wars of 1912–13
Trenton, Vasil, 78, 97
Trinity Anglican Church, 57
Troper, Harold, xi–xiii
Turkey, 7
Turks, 3, 6, 7, 60, 69
Turnverein, 125

Ukrainians, 85
unemployment, 20, 36, 47
Union Station, 26, 76
Union Stock Yards, 21, 92
United States, 4, 9, 50, 68, 79
University of Toronto, 103, 104
Uzunoff, George, 19

Vane, Tase, 115
Various Bulgarian-American Letters (1917). *See* guidebooks
Varna (Bulgaria), 13
Vasil, Anton, 37
Vassil, Tina, 76
Vecherinki, 127
Velcoff, Argie, 38
Velianoff, Mitre, 55
Velianoff, Simo, 57, 121
Velichki, Bishop Andrey, 142–4
Verbnik, 6, 51, 54, 95, 111
Victoria College (University of Toronto), 64
Victoria Fruit Market, 105
Victory (MPO Toronto local), 165–6
village societies, 47–50, 117–18
Voden, 120
Vumbul, 82, 111

W. Harris Co., 44
Welland Canal, 39
Western Cattle Market and Livestock Exchange, 26, 37–8
Weston Consumptive Hospital, 49
West Toronto Junction settlement

area: growth and development,
24–5; Macedonian enterprise in,
98–9
White Way Linen, 107
Wickett and Craig Ltd, 25, 32
Wilder, Chaim, 21
William Davies Co., 25, 33, 38, 102
Windsor (Ontario), 39, 105, 115
women: adaptation to urban life,
84–5; intergroup relations and,
85–6; role in religious and communal life, 48, 56; work and
economic role, 100–2
Wood, Angela (Annie), 193n16

xenophobia. See intergroup
relations

York Knitting Mills, 26, 33, 37–9, 49,
90, 102
Young Women's Christian
Association, 101
Yovcheff, A.C. See guidebooks
Yugoslavia (kingdom of), 148

Zabardeni, 111
Zagoricheni, 3, 82, 111
Zagoriskoto Benevolence Society
Peace, 48
Zeleniche, 82, 111
Zhelevo, 4, 6–8, 15, 53–4, 68–9, 76,
78, 111
Zhelevo Benevolence Brotherhood.
See Zhelevo Brotherhood
Zhelevo Brotherhood, 48–9, 72, 112
Zhelevtsi, 7, 14, 22, 48–9, 82, 112–13
Zlateff, Peter, 105
Zolumoff, Stavro, 20